Efficient Algorithms for Strong Local Consistencies and Adaptive Techniques in Constraint Satisfaction Problems

Anastasia Paparrizou
University of Western Macedonia

Published by

AI Access

AI Access is a not-for-profit publisher with a highly respected scientific board that publishes open access monographs and collected works. Our text are available electronically for free and in hard copy at close to cost. We welcome proposals for new texts.

ISBN 978-1-329-01009-3

AI Access
Managing editor: Toby Walsh
Monograph editor: Kristian Kersting
Collected works editor: Pascal Poupart
URL: aiaccess.org

Commitee members:

Kostas Stergiou (Principal advisor)
Manolis Koubarakis (Co-advisor)
Nikolaos Samaras (Co-advisor)
Christian Bessiere
Ioannis Refanidis
Nick Bassiliades
Minas Dasygenis

Date approved: 13 November 2013

This work first appeared as a dissertation submitted in partial fulfillment of the requirements for the Degree of Doctor of Philosophy in the Department of Informatics and Telecommunications Engineering at the University of Western Macedonia. The thesis received an Honourable Mention in the 2013 ECCAI Artificial Intelligence Dissertation Award.

This research has been co-financed by the European Union (European Social Fund - ESF) and Greek national funds through the Operational Program "Education and Lifelong Learning" of the National Strategic Reference Framework (NSRF) - Research Funding Program: Heracleitus II. Investing in knowledge society through the European Social Fund.

European Union
European Social Fund

Abstract

Constraint Programming (CP) is a successful technology for solving a wide range of problems in business and industry which require the satisfaction of a set of complex constraints. Examples include product configuration, resource allocation, transportation, and scheduling. As the simultaneous satisfaction of different constraints is intractable in general, problems can become very difficult to solve as their size increases. CP has thus developed various techniques to tackle this inherent problem. Enforcing a local consistency property is one of the most important such techniques.

Bounds Consistency (BC) and Generalised Arc Consistency (GAC) are the two most widely studied and used local consistencies in CP solvers. While there exist stronger local consistency (SLC) properties, their usage is limited due to their prohibitive cost. Examples are max Restricted Path Consistency (maxRPC) and max Restricted PairWise Consistency (maxRPWC).

In our research, we propose efficient filtering algorithms for enforcing SLCs. In particular, we propose new algorithms for maxRPC and maxRPWC that advance the existing algorithms (theoretically and practically). We also propose algorithms that achieve weaker consistencies with a lower cost. In addition, we have extended the recent algorithms from the family of Simple Tabular Reduction (STR) to achieve a higher-order local consistency property. Experiments demonstrate that these algorithms can significantly outperform various state-ot the-art (G)AC algorithms, even by orders of magnitude, and thus can become very useful additions to the propagation techniques that CP solvers currently apply. Additionally, we have introduced and defined a new strong Bounds Consistency, called PWBC, as well as a polynomial filtering algorithm based on this consistency for the important class of linear inequalities. Theoretical and experimental results demonstrate the potential of SLCs that reason on bounds.

Finally, since SLCs may still be too expensive to maintain during search in many problems, we have suggested ways to interleave them with weaker propagation methods such as GAC. We have proposed fully automated heuristics that can dynamically select the most appropriate filtering algorithm. All algorithms are incorporated in an adaptive filtering scheme to further tackle the inherent difficulty of constraint satisfaction, resulting in a more robust constraint solver. Overall, this research proposes filtering algorithms and adaptive techniques that exploit the filtering power offered by SLCs in an efficient way, in order to increase the efficacy of CP solvers.

Περίληψη

Ο Προγραμματισμός με Περιορισμούς (Constraint Programming - CP) είναι μια επιτυχημένη τεχνολογία για την επίλυση πολλών προβλημάτων από το χώρο των επιχειρήσεων και της βιομηχανίας, που απαιτούν την ικανοποίηση μιας σειράς πολύπλοκων περιορισμών. Παραδείγματα τέτοιων προβλημάτων είναι η διαμόρφωση προϊόντος, η κατανομή πόρων, τα προβλήματα μεταφοράς και χρονοπρογραμματισμού. Επειδή η ταυτόχρονη ικανοποίηση των διαφόρων περιορισμών είναι γενικά δυσεπίλυτη, τα προβλήματα μπορεί να γίνουν ακόμη δυσκολότερα καθώς αυξάνει το μέγεθός τους. Ο Προγραμματισμός με Περιορισμούς έχει αναπτύξει διάφορες τεχνικές για να αντιμετωπίσει αυτό το εγγενές πρόβλημα. Μια από τις πιο σημαντικές τέτοιες τεχνικές είναι η εφαρμογή τοπικής συνέπειας.

Οι τοπικές συνέπειες που έχουν ευρέως μελετηθεί και χρησιμοποιηθεί από συστήματα επίλυσης είναι η συνέπεια ορίων (Bounds Consistency - BC) και η συνέπεια τόξου (Arc Consistency - AC). Παρότι έχουν προταθεί και ισχυρότερες τοπικές συνέπειες, η χρήση τους είναι περιορισμένη λόγω του απαγορευτικού κόστους τους. Παραδείγματα αποτελούν οι συνέπειες max Restricted Path Consistency (maxRPC) και max Restricted PairWise Consistency (maxRPWC).

Στην παρούσα έρευνα προτείνουμε αποδοτικούς αλγόριθμους ελέγχου συνέπειας για την επιβολή ισχυρών τοπικών συνεπειών. Συγκεκριμένα, προτείνουμε νέους αλγόριθμους για τις συνέπειες maxRPC και maxRPWC που βελτιώνουν (θεωρητικά και πρακτικά) τους προηγούμενους. Επίσης, προτείνουμε αλγόριθμους που εφαρμόζουν ασθενέστερες συνέπειες με χαμηλότερο κόστος, έχουμε επεκτείνει τους πρόσφατους από την οικογένεια των STR (Simple Tabular Reduction) αλγόριθμων για την επίτευξη υψηλότερης τάξης (higher-order) τοπικής συνέπειας. Πειράματα δείχνουν ότι αυτοί οι αλγόριθμοι μπορούν να ξεπεράσουν state-ot-the-art AC αλγόριθμους με σημαντικές διαφορές, ακόμη και κατά τάξεις μεγέθους, και συνεπώς, μπορούν να αποτελέσουν χρήσιμες προσθήκες στις τεχνικές διάδοσης περιορισμών για τους σύγχρονους CP επιλυτές. Επιπρόσθετα, εισάγουμε και ορίζουμε μια νέα ισχυρή συνέπεια ορίων, που ονομάζεται PWBC, καθώς και έναν πολυωνυμικό αλγόριθμο ελέγχου συνέπειας που βασίζεται σε αυτήν για την σημαντική κατηγορία των γραμμικών ανισοτήτων. Τα θεωρητικά και πειραματικά αποτελέσματα αναδεικνύουν τις δυνατότητες των ισχυρών συνεπειών που επιβάλλονται στα όρια.

Τέλος, δεδομένου ότι οι ισχυρές συνέπειες μπορεί να εξακολουθούν να είναι ακριβές στην εφαρμογή τους κατά την αναζήτηση σε πολλά προβλήματα, προτείνουμε τρόπους ώστε να παρεμβάλλονται μαζί με ασθενέστερες συνέπειες, όπως η συνέπεια τόξου. Προτείνουμε πλήρως αυτοματοποιημένες ευρετικές μεθόδους, που μπορούν να επιλέξουν δυναμικά τον καταλληλότερο αλγόριθμο φιλτραρίσματος. Οι προτεινόμενοι αλγόριθμοι ενσωματώνονται σε ένα προσαρμοστικό σύστημα διάδοσης περιορισμών για να αντιμετωπίσει περαιτέρω την εγγενή δυσκολία ικανοποίησης περιορισμών, με αποτέλεσμα έναν ισχυρότερο επιλυτή. Συνολικά, η έρευνα προτείνει αλγόριθμους φιλτραρίσματος και προσαρμοστικές τεχνικές που εκμεταλλεύονται το μεγάλο φιλτράρισμα των ισχυρών συνεπειών με αποτελεσματικό τρόπο, προκειμένου να αυξηθεί η αποτελεσματικότητα των CP επιλυτών.

Acknowledgements

This dissertation records the results of an effort that lasted from 2009 to 2013, four years of research, experiences and emotions. For this beautiful trip I need to express my deepest acknowledgements towards people with whom I shared this route.

I consider myself extraordinarily fortunate for having the chance to be supervised by Kostas Stergiou. Kostas is the person who had the patience, the willing and the right way to introduce me to research. I owe to him almost everything I know about constraint programming, algorithmic proofs, writing and reviewing papers, expressing my ideas and undertaking initiatives. I always felt his strong encouragement, his sincere interest for my development and his silent comprehension. I am grateful for being mentored by a researcher of his personality and integrity.

I need to express my special thanks to Toby Walsh for his active participation to two of our papers and his wider support. I also need to thank Christophe Lecoutre for his collaboration and critical contribution to our paper, as well as Christian Bessiere for our fruitful discussions on adaptive techniques and bounds consistencies. All of them have been a great inspiration and influence to continue this research journey.

I also thank my committee members Manolis Koubarakis, Nikos Samaras, Christian Bessiere, Ioannis Refanidis, Minas Dasygenis and Nikolaos Vasiliadis for their insightful comments.

Furthermore, I owe a great thanks to Thanasis Balafoutis for his willingness to explain his implementations and everything I needed on the solver. I am indebted to Chariton Karamitas for offering his expert knowledge to help me debug my code and his priceless time to hear me practicing my presentations. It is my pleasure to have my precious friends Marina, Grigoris, Giannis, Vaso, Makis, Eleni, Chariton, by my side or backing me up.

My personal deep thanks go to my brother for being so concerned, carrying and supportive and to my mother for her endless love, patience and warm company.

Finally, I thank the Greek Ministry of Education for the Heraclitus fellowship, a generous support for all these years.

This work is dedicated to my father who influenced me to get involved into research and trusted my capabilities.

Declarations

Part of the material presented in this dissertation has been previously published in conference, journal and workshop papers. We list below the papers that correspond to each chapter.

Parts of **Chapter 4** are included in the following papers:

[1] T. Balafoutis, A. Paparrizou, K. Stergiou, T. Walsh. Improving the Performance of maxRPC. In *Proceedings of the 16th International Conference on Principles and Practice of Constraint Programming* (CP 2010), LNCS, Vo 6308, pp. 69-83, 2010.

[2] T. Balafoutis, A. Paparrizou, K. Stergiou, T. Walsh. New Algorithms for of max Restricted Path Consistency. Constraints, Volume 16, Number 4, Pages 372-406, Springer, October 2011.

Parts of **Chapter 5** are included in the following papers:

[3] A. Paparrizou, K. Stergiou. An Efficient Higher-Order Consistency Algorithm for Table Constraints. In *Proceedings of the 26th International Conference on Artificial Intelligence* (AAAI-12), pp. 535-541, 2012

[4] A. Paparrizou, K. Stergiou. Extending Generalized Arc Consistency. In *Proceedings of the 7th Hellenic Conference on Artificial Intelligence* (SETN 2012), LNCS (LNAI), Vo. 7297, pp. 174-181, 2012.

[5] A. Paparrizou, K. Stergiou. Strong Local Consistency Algorithms for Table Constraints. Constraints, (accepted with major revisions).

Parts of **Chapter 6** are included in the following papers:

[6] C. Lecoutre, A. Paparrizou, K. Stergiou. Extending STR to a Higher-Order Consistency. In *Proceedings of the 27th International Conference on Artificial Intelligence* (AAAI-13), pp. 576-582, 2013.

We need to mention that Christophe Lecoutre has made significant contributions to the research work presented in Chapter 5.7, mainly regarding the theoretical results and the presentation of the algorithms.

Parts of **Chapter 7** can be found in:

[7] A. Paparrizou, K. Stergiou. Evaluating Simple Fully Automated Heuristics for Adaptive Constraint Propagation. In *Proceedings the 24th IEEE International Conference on Tools with Artificial Intelligence* (ICTAI-12), pp. 880-885, 2012.

Other Publications

[8] A. Paparrizou. Efficient Algorithms for Strong Local Consistencies in Constraint Satisfaction Problems. In *Proceedings of AAAI-13, AAAI/SIGART Doctoral Consortium*, pp. 1674-1675, Bellevue, Washington, USA, 2013.

1. T. Balafoutis, A. Paparrizou, K. Stergiou. Experimental Evaluation of Branching Schemes for the CSP. In *Proceedings of TRICS 2010, 3rd Workshop on Techniques foR Implementing Constraint programming Systems* (in conjunction with CP 2010), LNCS, pp. 1-12, St Andrews, Scotland, 2010.

To my father...

Contents

List of Figures

List of Tables

Introduction

Constraint programming (CP) is a powerful programming paradigm for solving combinatorial satisfaction and optimization search problems that includes a wide range of techniques from artificial intelligence, computer science, operations research, databases etc. Applications of CP include scheduling, planning, timetabling, routing, product configuration, resource allocation, transportation, design, matchmaking in web services, verification etc. Following the CP approach, such problems are first modelled as Constraint Satisfaction (or Optimization) Problems (CSPs or COPs) by specifying variables, domains, constraints, and in the case of COPs, an optimization function. This is typically done using a high-level language offered by modern CP solvers. The formulated problem is then solved by the solver used through a combination of heuristically guided backtracking search and inference methods.

A Constraint Satisfaction Problem (CSP) involves finding solutions by assigning values to a given set of variables that satisfy a given set of constraints. Constraints are defined over subsets of variables and specify combinations of values that these variables are allowed to take. In this thesis, we are only concerned with CSPs where variables take their values in a finite domain.

CSPs can model a wide range of combinatorial problems and cover a variety of applications in the areas of Artificial Intelligence, Operations Research, Programming Languages, Databases and other areas of Computer Science.

As a simple example of constraint satisfaction, consider the real task of *course scheduling*, where we try to build the schedule of courses for a university department. Such a problem can be modeled with variables that represent the courses, where each variable has a domain that expresses the day, time, and room of the course. Then, various constraints naturally arise: i) All courses of the same year must be taught in different days and/or hours, ii) No more than one course can take place in the same day, time and room, iii) In one day, up to four courses of the same year can be taught. Constraints can become more complex if we consider the duration of each course and constraints regarding the availability of lecturers and rooms.

CSP solvers take a real-world problem like this, represented in terms of decision variables and constraints, and try to find a solution. A solution is an assignment of a single value to each variable, where the value is taken from the variable's domain, such than no constraint is violated. A problem may have one, many, or no solutions. A problem that has one or more solutions is *satisfiable* or *consistent*. If there is no possible assignment of values to variables that satisfies all the constraints, then the problem is *unsatisfiable* or *inconsistent*.

Inference methods are at the core of CP's practical success and they are usually referred to as constraint propagation methods. These encompass numerous filtering algorithms that can detect and prune infeasible values from the domains of the problem variables, exploiting the semantics of the constraints that are present in the problem. As a result, the size of the search space is significantly reduced, making the problem easier to solve. Constraint propagation algorithms typically enforce some local consistency property on the problem.

Local consistencies, such as Bounds Consistency (BC) and Generalised Arc Consistency (GAC), are widely studied and used in CP solvers. These local consistencies have proved their practical importance that justifies their wide spread use and acceptance. From another point of view, since they operate on one constraint at a time, there are cases where the pruning they achieve is limited. This is why stronger local consistency (SLC) properties have been proposed and have started to receive increasing interest lately. Examples are max Restricted Path Consistency (maxRPC) and max Restricted PairWise Consistency (maxRPWC) for binary and non-binary constraints respectively. Even though many SLCs have been proposed, the prohibitive cost of algorithms that apply them prevents them from being widely adopted. Therefore, BC and GAC are predominantly used in CSP solvers.

The aim of this research is to overcome the cost limitations that make SLCs impractical and thus to demonstate the advantages offered by strong propagation. Our research focuses on strong local consistencies for binary and table constraints; two of the most widely studied classes of constraints, but it also covers linear constraints as well as generic constraints with no particular semantics. Specifically, we propose new algorithms for maxRPC and maxRPWC that advance theoretically and practically existing state-of-the-art algorithms. We also extend recent algorithms for table constraints to achieve strong local consistency properties. Our experimental evaluation demonstrates that these algorithms can significantly outperform existing ones, even by orders of magnitude.

Additionally, we introduce and study a new local consistency that extends BC to achieve stronger domain shrinking by considering constraint intersections. Based on this new local consistency, we propose a polynomial filtering algorithm for linear inequality constraints that achieves stronger pruning than BC, the standard consistency used on such constraints.

Finally, since there are still many problems where SLCs are too expensive to maintain during search, we suggest ways to combine them with weaker local consistencies. More precisely, we propose adaptive heuristics that can dynamically select the most appropriate filtering algorithm in a fully automated way. All algorithms are incorporated in an adaptive filtering scheme to further tackle the inherent difficulty of constraint satisfaction, resulting in a more robust constraint solver.

1.1   Definition of the problem

Generalized Arc Consistency (GAC), and Bounds Consistency (BC) are the two local consistencies that are predominantly used for propagation by finite domain constraint solvers. Numerous local consistencies that are stronger (i.e. achieve more filtering) than GAC have been proposed. Some of these have shown promise (e.g. SAC, maxRPC, maxRPWC) but generally, they are all too expensive to apply throughout search. So despite the strong pruning that can be achieved, they are rarely used because existing algorithms for SLCs suffer from overheads and redundancies. Therefore, an important question is how CSP research to best exploit the filtering power of SLCs without paying a high cpu time penalty. This research tries to answer this question by proposing and evaluating techniques that can boost the performance of algorithms for SLCs by eliminating many of the overheads and redundancies.

Existing algorithms for SLCs are typically generic and do not take the semantics of constraints into account. We address this by proposing specialized algorithms for very common classes of constraints, such as table and linear constraints.

Binary constraints cover a big part of CSPs and, since the early days of CP, researchers were proposing algorithms to solve them efficiently. Arc Consistency (AC) is the most widely studied and used consistency for binary constraints. Despite the fact that stronger consistencies than AC have been proposed, that display promising results, like maxRPC, they are rarely used in practice due to their high computational cost.

Regarding the special case of table constrtains, which are constraints given in extension by listing the tuples of values allowed by a set of variables, research has mainly focused on the development of fast algorithms to enforce GAC. Such constraints are widely studied in constraint programming, since they appear in many real-world applications from areas such as design and configuration, databases, and preferences' modeling. GAC is a consistency that allows us to identify only inconsistent values, that are deleted from variable domains, and achieve the maximum level of filtering when constraints are treated independently. In this research, we propose specialized filtering algorithms for table constraints that achieve stronger consistency properties than GAC.

There are also cases where it is beneficial to achieve an approximation of a SLC, even if it cannot be formally characterized, than the full SLC because the filtering achieved is almost the same, but with much lower cost. Along this line, we investigate approximation of SLCs for binary and non-binary constraints.

Even though constraint propagation is at the core of CP's strength, the decision on which algorithm to select for the different constraints of the CP model is either predetermined or placed on the shoulders of the user/modeler. For instance, the modeler may select to propagate the *alldifferent* constraints in a problem using a GAC algorithm. However, during search it may turn out that this consistency achieves little extra pruning compared to BC. Unfortunately, standard CP solvers do not allow to change the decisions taken prior to search "on the fly". Hence, it will not be possible to automatically switch to a bounds consistency propagator during search.

The interleaved application of SLCs and standard local consistency methods can be very beneficial as the advances of both sets of techniques can be exploited. However, there are very few studies on this topic. We address this by proposing simple fully automated heuristics that can dynamically adapt propagation during search.

1.2   Contributions

The conducted research contributes to the field of Constraint Satisfaction Problems and Artificial Intelligence in general. It proposes new efficient constraint propagation algorithms for problems expressed both with binary and non-binary constraints. The new algorithms improve theoretically and practically existing relevant state-of-the-art algorithms. In more detail:

1. We propose efficient algorithms that achieve strong filtering on binary constraints. The proposed algorithms improve the performance of existing maxRPC algorithms by eliminating many redundancies through the combined use of two sophisticated data structures. Based on these, we propose a number of algorithms that acheive either maxRPC or approximate this property. We also propose heuristics that can boost algorithms' performance during search. The experimental evaluation shows that our algorithms are more efficient than existing maxRPC algorithms and constitute a viable alternative of Arc Consistency in many binary CSPs

2. We propose efficient algorithms for non-binary table constraints that extend existing ones to apply stronger pruning. Specifically, the new algorithms, based on maxRPWC, enforce stronger consistency properties than GAC by exploiting intersections between constraints.

The first algorithm, called maxRPWC+, extends the GAC algorithm of [72], while the second one extends the state-of-the-art STR-based GAC algorithms to stronger relation filtering consistencies, i.e., consistencies that can remove tuples from constraints' relations. Both algorithms handle efficiently table constraints that have more than one variable in common, resulting in more value deletions and thus, reducing the search space considerably. These algorithms constantly outperform the algorithms of [19] and are more robust than state-of-the-art GAC algorithms on many problems with intersecting table constraints.

3. We propose a new algorithm for table constraints that achieves both pairwise consistency and GAC through the use of counters. Importantly, the basic filtering procedure at the heart of this algorithm has a worst-case time complexity very close to that of the state-of-the-art STR algorithms [63] that it extends. Experiments on problems with table constraints show that our algorithm is significantly faster than STR algorithm in many cases where constraint intersections exist.

4. Regarding adaptive propagation, we propose heuristic techniques for the automated selection between weak and strong propagation methods. The heuristics, being generic, can be applied in either binary or non-binary CSPs. The advantages offered by strong propagation algorithms are exploited by our methods in a fully automated way and significantly, do not require the users' involvement (i.e., by setting parameters). Our evaluation demonstrates that these methods display a stable performance and thus, can be preferable to a predefined propagator.

5. Finally, we define a new local consistency that extends Bounds Consistency (BC) in order to achieve stronger filtering on domain bounds. Apart from the theoretical advantages, we also show the practical importance of such consistencies by proposing a polynomial filtering algorithm that achieves stronger pruning than BC. This algorithm handles constraints of linear inequalities, an important subclass of linear constraints. Experiments demonstrate that the proposed algorithm can in many cases replace the standard weak propagation of BC that CP solvers currently apply on linear constraints.

Overall, the presented results demonstrate the potential of strong local consistencies that, until now, are rarely used due to their prohibitive cost. The new algorithms for SLCs along with the adaptive techinques that control their application, exploit the strong filtering they offer by avoiding overheads, resulting thus in increasing the efficacy of CP solvers.

1.3   Structure and content

The thesis consists of nine chapters (including this one). The rest of the chapters are structured as follows

- The second chapter provides the necessary background information. In detail, we define the Constraint Satisfaction Problem and informally discuss constraint propagation techniques. We also refer to search algorithms (i.e., backtracking search algorithms), branching methods and variable/value ordering heuristics. Finally, we describe systems that solve such problems (CSP solvers) and give the notation in order to describe consistency properties and algorithms in the rest of the thesis.

- The third chapter includes a review of the literature on local consistencies, for binanry and non-binary CSPs. We describe some propagation algorithms for binary and non-binary constraints as well as a review on algorithms specialized for table constraints. Then we survey existing adaptive techniques for selecting the appropriate propagation method for solving CSPs.

- In the fourth chapter we propose a new set of algorithms that apply the strong local consistency called max Restricted Path Consistency (maxRPC) for binary constraints. Moreover, we present algorithms that approximate this property, which are shown to be more efficient in practice. The proposed methods outperform existing maxRPC algorithms while being competitive or better than the most efficient Arc Consistency (AC) algorithm in many problem classes.

- In the fifth chapter we propose new algorithms for non-binary table constraints that are based on and expand the strong local consistency max Restricted PairWise Consistency (maxR-PWC). We present theoretical results, time and space complexities and compare them to other local consistencies. Experimental results show that the best among our new algorithms is more stable than the state-of-the-art Generalized Arc Consistency (GAC) algorithms, while in many problem classes it can be orders of magnitude faster.

- The sixth chapter also describes new strong local consistency algorithms for non-binary table constraints. These algorithms belong to the category of higher-order consistencies, which remove both values from variables' domains and tuples (combinations of values) from constraints' relations. We give some theoretical results, analyze time and space complexities and compare to other strong local consistencies. The process at the core of our algorithm, called eSTR, has slightly higher complexity than the state-of-the-art GAC algorithm for table constraints (STR) and is orders of magnitude faster in many problem classes.

- In the seventh chapter, we present and study fully automated heuristics that are applicable to non-binary constraints. The heuristics are based on the inspection of the propagation impact of constraints during search. The experimental evaluation shows that the proposed heuristics can outperform a standard approach that applies a default propagation algorithm on each constraint, resulting in a stable and efficient solver.

- In the eighth chapter, we study theoretically and practically a new strong local consistency that is based on Bounds Consistenciy (BC). Also, we propose a specialized algorithm for linear constraints with polynomial complexity. This algorithm is stronger that BC, reduces significantly the search space and thus the time required for solving certain problems of linear inequalities.

- The last chapter summarizes the conclusions and the overall contribution of the doctoral reaserch, and suggests some future research directions.

Background

In this chapter we describe Constraint Satisfaction Problems and some of the basic techniques for solving them. These techniques include constraint propagation methods along with backtracking search algorithms and branching heuristics. We also give the formal notation that we will follow throughout the thesis. Finally, we give some details on how CP solvers work and present the components and architecture of our own solver.

2.1   Constraint Satisfaction Problems

An instance of a Constraint Satisfaction Problem (CSP) is defined by a finite set of variables, a finite domain (i.e., set of values) for each variable, and by constraints that restrict the combinations of values that the variables can be assigned to. The CSP is the problem of seeking an assignment to each variable from a value of its domain in such a way that all the constraints are satisfied.

Constraints are defined on subsets of variables and can be exploited to reduce domains by pruning values that cannot participate in any solution. This process is called *constraint propagation* and constitutes the core mechanism of most CSP solvers.

A classical example of a simple CSP is the *map coloring* problem. For instance, coloring the map of the principal states of Australia, can be viewed as a constraint satisfaction problem. The goal is to assign a color to each region of the map, from a given set of colors, so that no adjacent regions have the same color. Figure 2.1 visualizes the map coloring problem of Australia. The map has seven regions that are to be colored with red, green, or blue.

More formally, the map coloring example can be defined by a tuple $(\mathcal{X}, \mathcal{D}, \mathcal{C})$, where:

- $\mathcal{X}$: WA, NT, Q, SA, NSW, V, and T are the variables that represent different regions in the map.

- $\mathcal{D}$: $\{red, green, blue\}$ is the domain for each variable.

- $\mathcal{C}$: $WA \neq NT$, $WA \neq SA$, $NT \neq SA$, $NT \neq Q$, $SA \neq Q$, $SA \neq NSW$, $SA \neq V$, $Q \neq NSW$, $NSW \neq V$ are the constraints between any two adjacent regions.

An indicative solutions is the assignment: $\{WA = red, NT = green, SA = blue, Q = red, NSW = green, V = red, T = red\}$.

A unary constraint is a constraint that involves only one variable (e.g. $x > 5$), a binary (resp. ternary) constraint involves two (resp. three) variables. Generally, non-binary constraints include n variables and are also called n-ary constraints (e.g. $x_1 + x_2 + x_3 + x_4 > 0$). A unary CSP includes only unary constraints, a binary CSP is a CSP of only unary and binary constraints. In the general

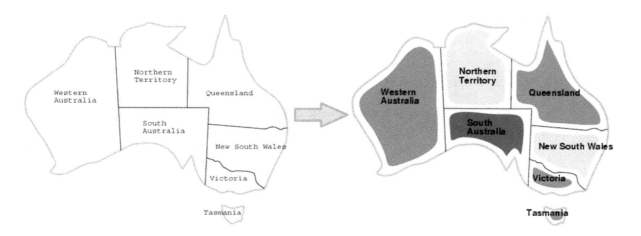

Figure 2.1: Visualization of the map coloring problem.

case, a non-binary or n-ary CSP includes constraints that are defined over at most n variables. Map coloring problems are binary CSPs.

Binary CSPs are usually represented by a constraint network (CN) (referred also as constraint graph), in which each node represents a variable, and each edge represents a constraint between variables represented by the end points of the edje. The visualization of the CN of the map coloring problem is shown in Figure 2.2.

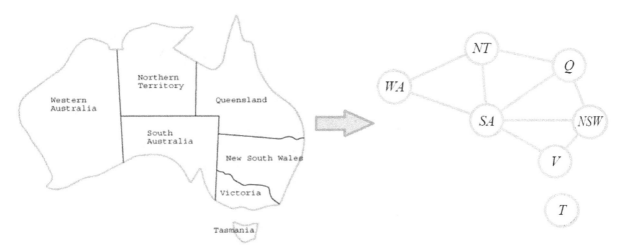

Figure 2.2: Visualization of the map coloring problem as a constraint graph.

A solution to a CSP is a complete assignment of values to variables such that no constraint is violated. It has been shown that the CSP, in its general form, is NP-hard [78]. This means that it is unlikely that an efficient general-purpose algorithm for finding a solution in polynomial time exists. Its worst-case time complexity is exponential in the size of the problem.

2.2 Formal Definitions

A *Constraint Satisfaction Problem* (CSP) is defined as a tuple $(\mathcal{X}, \mathcal{D}, \mathcal{C})$ where:

- $\mathcal{X} = \{x_1, \ldots, x_n\}$ is a set of n variables.

- $\mathcal{D} = \{D(x_1), \ldots, D(x_n)\}$ is a set of finite domains, one for each variable, with maximum cardinality d.

- $\mathcal{C} = \{c_1, \ldots, c_e\}$ is a set of e constraints.

We assume that domains are composed of integers. Given a variable x_i and its domain $D(x_i)$, $min_D(x_i)$ will denote the smallest value in $D(x_i)$ and $max_D(x_i)$ the greatest one. These two values are called the *bounds* of $D(x_i)$. For example, given a domain $D(x_1) = \{0, 2, 4, 7\}$, $min_D(x_1) = 0$ and $max_D(x_1) = 7$.

The *arity* of a constraint is the number of variables in the scope of the constraint; k denotes the maximum *arity* of the constraints. The *degree* of a variable x_i, is the number of constraints in which x_i participates. For instance, given a CSP that includes $c_1 : x_1 + x_2 = 5$ and $c_2 : x_1 + x_3 > 3$, then the degree of x_1 is 2, since it appears in two constraints, while the degrees of both x_2 and x_3 are equal to 1.

Each constraint c_i is a pair $(scp(c_i), rel(c_i))$, where $scp(c_i) = \{x_1, \ldots, x_r\}$ is an ordered subset of $\mathcal{X}$ referred to as the *constraint scope*, and $rel(c_i)$ is a subset of the *Cartesian* product $D(x_1) \times \ldots \times D(x_r)$ that specifies the allowed combinations of values (known also as c_i's relation) for the variables in $scp(c_i)$. Each tuple $\tau \in rel(c_i)$ is an ordered list of values of the form $< (x_1, a_1), \ldots, (x_r, a_r) >$, s.t. $a_j \in D(x_j), j = 1, \ldots, m$.

Constraints can be defined either extensionally by listing the allowed (or disallowed) combinations of values or intensionally through a predicate or arithmetic function. A *positive table constraint* is a constraint given in extension (i.e., by explicitly giving $rel(c_i)$) and defined by a set of allowed tuples. For each table constraint c_i, the size of $rel(c_i)$ is denoted by t_{c_i}. The maximum size of any constraint's relation in the problem is denoted by t.

Given a (table) constraint c_i, and a tuple $\tau \in rel(c_i)$, we denote by $\tau[x]$ the projection of τ on a variable $x \in scp(c_i)$ and by $\tau[X]$ the projection of τ on any subset $X \subseteq scp(c_i)$ of variables; $\tau[X]$ is called a *subtuple* of τ. For any constraint c_i we denote by $\top$ (resp. $\bot$) a dummy tuple s.t. $\tau < \top$ (resp. $\tau > \bot$) for any tuple $\tau \in rel(c_i)$. We assume that for any table constraint its tuples are stored in lexicographical order.

A tuple τ *satisfies* constraint c_i iff $\tau \in rel(c_i)$. Tuple $\tau = (a_1, \ldots, a_m)$ is *valid* iff $a_j \in D(x_j)$, for $j = 1, \ldots, m$. In words, a valid tuple is an assignment of values to the variables involved in the constraint such that none of these values has been removed from the domain of the corresponding variable. The process which verifies whether a given tuple is allowed by (i.e. satisfies) a constraint c_i is called a *constraint check*. In case a domain becomes empty, namely all values are deleted, we call it domain wipe-out (DWO).

Given two constraints c_i and c_j, if $|scp(c_i) \cap scp(c_j)| > 1$ we say that the constraints *intersect* non trivially. We denote by f_{min} the minimum number of variables that are common to any two constraints that intersect on more than one variable. Therefore, f_{min} is at least two. We will denote by g the maximum number of intersections between any constraint c_i and other constraints. For instance, given a CSP that includes $c_1 : x_1 + x_2 + x_3 + x_4 = 5$ and $c_2 : x_1 + x_2 + x_3 + x_5 > 3$, we see that $f_{min} = 3$ and $g = 1$.

2.3 Constraint Propagation

Solving Constraint Satisfaction Problems becomes more complex as their size increase. However, constraint solving involves various techniques to tackle this inherent problem. *Constraint Propagation* is one such technique.

Propagating the information contained in one constraint to the neighboring constraints, is called constraint propagation since it can reduce the parts of the search space that need to be visited. Constraint propagation is one of the core mechanisms for solving CSP problems and constitutes one of the basic reasons for CP's success. For instance, in a problem that contains two variables x_1 and x_2 with $D(x_1) = D(x_2) = [1 : 10]$, and a constraint specifying that $x_1 + x_2 \leq 5$, by propagating this constraint we can delete values 6,7,8,9 and 10 from the domains of both x_1 and x_2. Removing these 'nogoods' is a way to reduce the space of combinations that will be explored by a search mechanism.

Local consistencies are properties that are enforced on the constraints of a problem so that infeasible values are located and pruned. Algorithms that apply local consistencies can be even used as complete methods to find a solution to a problem, but this is never done in practice due their high cost. Typically, local consistency techniques are usually combined with a search algorithm and can be used to remove some, but usually not all, inconsistent values from variables' domains, resulting in a reduced problem size and search space. The process of propagation is aimed at transforming a CSP into an equivalent problem that is hopefully easier to solve, while no solutions are excluded.

The simplest consistency that can be enforced on a CSP is called *Node Consistency* (NC) and concerns only unary constraints. A CSP is node consistent iff for all variables all values in its domain satisfy the unary constraints on that variable. If the variable is not node consistent, then it means that the instantiation of the variable in question to an inconsistent value always results in an immediate failure. In other words, this value cannot be included in any solution. Hence, it can be removed. For example, if a CSP that includes the constraint $c : x > 5$ and the domain of x is $D(x) = [1..10]$, then x is not NC with respect to c. The propagation of c will remove values $[1..5]$ from $D(x)$.

The most commonly used local consistency is *Arc Consistency* (AC). This is a very simple concept that guarantees every value in a domain to be consistent with respect to every constraint. It considers binary constraints which correspond to arcs (i.e. directed edges) in the constraint graph. The arc (x_i, x_j) is arc consistent if for every value a_i in the domain of x_i, there is some value a_j in the domain of x_j such that $x_i = a_i$ and $x_j = a_j$ are permitted by the binary constraint between x_i and x_j. A CSP is arc consistent if all the constraints in the problem are arc consistent. Usually, the constraint is made AC by propagating the domain changes from one variable to the other variable and vice versa.

For example the map coloring problem shown in Figure 2.1 is arc consistent, because for any value of any variable there is a value to be assigned to the neighboring variables such that all constraints are satisfied. Consider now the case where the domain of variable SA is restricted to *blue*. It is easy to see that if we enforce AC on this CN, then *blue* will be inconsistent for WA, NT, Q, NSW, V that SA shares a constraint of inequality. As a consequence, this value will be removed from the respective domains. Interestingly, as soon as a local consistency is applied, the effects it causes may trigger new revisions, since variables are typically connected with several constraints. Therefore, the mechanism of constraint propagation is essential for the efficient solving of CSPs since it reduces notable the search space. AC as well as othe local consistencies are further discussed in Chapter 2.5.1 where algorithms for AC are also presented.

2.4 Backtracking search algorithms

Once a CSP is identified and modeled there is a variety of techniques that can be used to solve it [104]. In general, a CSP can be solved either systematically, as with backtracking (BT) search, or using local search methods that are typically incomplete. A backtracking search algorithm performs a depth-first traversal of a search tree, where each level of the tree corresponds to a decision (e.g., variable assignment). The search tree is generated progressively; as soon as a node is visited, branches are built. Branches represent alternative choices that may be examined in order to find a solution. A node in the search tree is a dead-end if it provably does not lead to a solution. The method of extending a node in the search tree is called *branching strategy*, and several alternatives have been proposed and examined in the literature (see Section 2.4.3).

More analytically, basic backtrack search builds up a partial solution by choosing values for variables until it reaches a dead-end, where the partial solution cannot be consistently extended. When it reaches a dead-end it cancels the last decision and tries another. This is done in a systematic manner that guarantees that all possible branches will be tried. It improves on simply enumerating and testing of all candidate solutions step by step, meaning that it checks if the respective constraints are satisfied each time it makes a new choice, rather than checking after a complete assignment is generated for all variables.

The backtrack search process is often represented as a search tree, where each node (below the root) represents an assignment of a value to a variable, and each branch represents a candidate partial solution. The branches consist of all possible ways of extending the node of a particular decision on a variable. Discovering that a partial solution cannot be extended results in pruning the subtree from consideration. Backtracking search algorithms are typically complete. That is, they guarantee that a solution will be found if one exists, or show that a CSP does not have a solution. They are also useful in optimizations problems to find the optimal solution, a task that requires the whole exploration of the tree.

When a node is visited during chronological BT search, only constraints with instantiated variables (i.e., constraints between the current variable and the past variables) are checked at a node. If a constraint is violated, the next value of the current variable is tried. If there are no more values left, BT backtracks to the most recently instantiated variable. A solution is found if all constraint checks succeed after the last variable has been instantiated. It should be mentioned that backtracking search algorithms require a polynomial amount of space.

An example of a search tree built by the backtracking algorithm is shown in Figure 2.3, using the map coloring problem. Recall that this problem requires coloring n regions to d colors in such a way that no adjacent regions have the same color. In our example of Figure 2.1 this problem has 7 variables, one for each region, and each variable has domain $\{reg, green, blue\}$ representing the 3 different colors. The root node at level 0 is the empty set of assignments and a node at level i is a set of assignments $x_1 = a_1, \ldots, x_i = a_i$. For the assignments that do not satisfy the constraints (i.e., the left branch at level 2) the subtrees are pruned, and the next value of the current variable is tried. For simplicity, in Figure 2.3, we have assumed a static order of instantiation, namely variable x_i is always chosen at level i in the search tree and values are assigned to variables in the order $\{reg, green, blue\}$.

Since backtracking search is not guaranteed to terminate within polynomial time - in general there is no polynomial algorithm for CSPs - the research community has spent a considerable amount of effort on maximizing the practical efficiency of backtracking search. Usually this is done by combining backtracking search with constraint propagation techniques to filter inconsistent values, and by making use of effective heuristics to guide search. The techniques are not

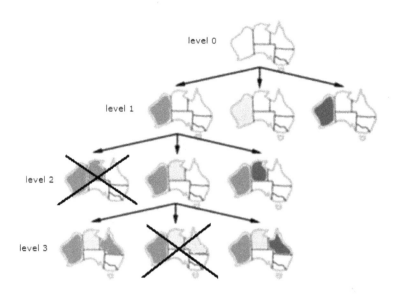

Figure 2.3: Search tree for the map coloring problem using backtracking search.

always orthogonal and sometimes combining two or more techniques into one algorithm can boost the search significantly. The best combinations of these techniques result in robust backtracking algorithms that can solve large, hard instances that demonstrate their of practical importance. Backtracking algorithms are typically guided by variable and value ordering heuristics and make use of a branching scheme to divide the search tree while the algorithm traverses it.

2.4.1   Maintaining a local consistency during search

A fundamental insight in improving the performance of backtracking search algorithms on CSPs is that filtering techniques, embedded in search, can lead to a solution with less effort. Backtracking search that incorporates constraint propagation has many significant benefits. First, inference methods remove inconsistencies during search which can dramatically prune the search tree by avoiding earlier many dead-ends and by simplifying the remaining subproblem. If constraint propagation causes an empty domain to a variable, then backtracking can be initiated as there is no solution along this branch of the search tree. In other cases, the variables will have their domains reduced, resulting in less branches to be explored in the future. Therefore, it can be much easier to find a solution to a CSP after constraint propagation or to show that the CSP does not have a solution. Second, some of the most important variable ordering heuristics exploit the information gathered by constraint propagation to make effective variable ordering decisions. As a result of these benefits, it is now standard for a backtracking algorithm to incorporate some form of constraint propagation.

The most widely used local consistency during backtracking is Arc Consistency (AC). However, many local consistencies can be embedded in BT search, that are either stronger or weaker than AC. There are also cases where the level of local consistency that is maintained in the nodes of the search tree is not uniform. This is the case of adaptive propagation that we examine in Chapter 6.5. For simplicity reasons, we describe MAC [91], which is the backtrack search algorithm that maintains AC during search. MAC is currently considered as the most efficient complete general-purpose approach to solving CSP instances. In Section 2.5 we describe how modern CP solvers operate having abandoned the standard MAC algorithm towards the application of different filtering algorithms on different constraints.

Within MAC the solution process proceeds by iteratively interleaving search phases and propagation phases. The description in this section and the in the next one is based on a standard d-way branching scheme that we describe in Section 2.4.3. During search, a node is visited when a variable is instantiated to a value of its domain. At each node visit of the search tree, an algorithm for enforcing arc consistency is applied to the CSP. Since AC is enforced on the parent of a node, initial constraint propagation needs only be enforced on the constraint that was followed by the branching strategy (e.g., the constraint $x = a$, after an instantiation). In turn, this may lead to other constraints becoming arc inconsistent and constraint propagation continues until no more changes are made to the domains. If, as a result of constraint propagation, a domain becomes empty, the branch is a dead-end and is rejected. If no domain is empty, the branch is accepted and the search continues to the next level.

In short, constraint propagation removes values from the variables' domains that are inconsistent with respect to the partial assignment built so far. Every time a constraint reduces a variable domain, other constraints that include that variable have to propagate again until a fixed point is reached. If a domain wipe out (DWO) occurs for a variable, then the search fails and backtracks to reconsider the branching decision. After achieving the fixed point, a new search step is performed. The solution process finishes when a solution is found, that is, a value is assigned to each variable and all constraints are satisfied, or when one of the following conditions is achieved: the tree has been fully explored without finding a solution, a time or a backtrack limit has been reached.

2.4.2 Variable/Value ordering heuristics

When solving a CSP using backtracking search, a sequence of decisions must be made on which variable to branch on or instantiate next and which value to give to the variable. These decisions are referred to as the variable and the value ordering. It has been shown that for many problems, the choice of variable and value ordering can drastically affect the efficiency of solving a CSP instance.

A variable or value ordering can be either *static*, where the ordering is fixed and determined prior to search, and is not altered thereafter, or *dynamic*, where the ordering depends on the current state of the search and is determined as the search progresses. Given a CSP and a backtracking search algorithm, a variable or value ordering is said to be *optimal* if the ordering results in a search that visits the fewest number of nodes over all possible orderings when finding one solution or showing that there does not exist a solution.

Many variable ordering heuristics have been proposed and evaluated in the literature. These heuristics can, with some omissions, be classified into two categories: heuristics that are based on the domain sizes of the variables and heuristics that are based on the structure of the CSP.

Static, or fixed, variable ordering heuristics (SVOs) keep the same ordering throughout the search, using only structural information about the initial state of search. The simplest such heuristic is the *lex* heuristic, which orders variables lexicographically. When variables are indexed by integers, *lex* is usually implemented so as to order the variables according to the value of their index. If $vars(P) = \{x_1, x_2, ..., x_n\}$, then *lex* will select first x_1, then $x_2,...$ and finally x_n.

In the example of Figure 2.4, where the search tree of the map coloring problem is depicted, the variable ordering heuristic select variables in lexicographic order[1]. The same lexicographic

---

[1]Assume that $x_1 = WA$, $x_2 = NT$, $x_3 = Q$, $x_4 = SA$, $x_5 = NSW$, $x_6 = V$, and $x_7 = T$

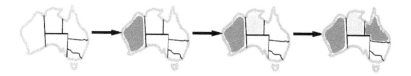

Figure 2.4: Variable assignments using the *lex* variable ordering heuristic.

ordering is also used for ordering the values. That is, initially assign to the first region the first color, then to the second region the first color available in its domain and so on. After a variable assignment, always the *red* color is tried for the next region. If a constraint is violated, the second color (i.e., *green*) is tried next e.t.c. Using a different variable ordering heuristic, simply means that at the top of the search tree the first color may paint a region different than the first. Respectively, using a different value ordering heuristic, a color different than the first (i.e.*red*) will be selected.

The heuristic *deg*, which is also known as *max degree*, orders variables in sequence of decreasing degree [32]. So variables with the highest initial size of their neighborhood are selected first. In the map coloring problem, SA is the variable with the highest degree and thus is firstly instantiated as shown in Figure 2.5.

Figure 2.5: Variable assignments using the *deg* variable ordering heuristic.

Other known static variable ordering heuristics are the *min width* heuristic which chooses an ordering that minimizes the width of the constraint network [39] and the *min bandwidth* heuristic which minimizes the bandwidth of the constraint graph [110]. Static variable ordering heuristics are considered weak heuristics, that miss valuable information and significant changes that occur during search, and nowadays they rarely used.

The basic idea for specifying *dynamic* variable ordering heuristics (DVOs), is based on the "fail-first" principle [48], which is explained as "To succeed, try first where you are most likely to fail". Many DVOs take into account the size of the domains in order to choose the next variable to be instantiated. When we apply filtering algorithms within the search procedure, the domain sizes are decreased from one branch to another. As a result, heuristics based on the size of the domains will change the order of variables that will be considered from one branch to the other. The heuristic introduced by Haralick and Elliott in [48] is called *dom* or *minimum domain* heuristic, and selects as the next variable the one with the smallest remaining domain. Figure 2.6 shows the search tree of map coloring example when *dom* is used.

A drawback of the simple *dom* heuristic is that in many case it remains inactive, namely it makes few changes to the order of variables. This is because variables often have the same size of domains and especially at the beginning of search, the heuristic *dom/deg* overcomes this difficulty by preferring the variable with the highest initial ratio of domain size over degree [40]. A similar approach called *dom/ddeg* prefers the variable with highest ratio of domain size over dynamic

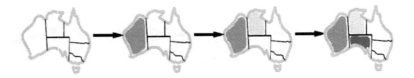

Figure 2.6: Variable assignments using the *dom* variable ordering heuristic.

(or future) degree, namely the variable that is constrained with the largest number of unassigned variables [98].

One of the most efficient modern heuristics for CSPs is the *dom/wdeg* variable ordering heuristic [23]. This heuristic assigns a weight to each constraint, initially set to one. Each variable is associated with a *weighted degree* (wdeg), which is the sum of the weights over all constraints involving the variable and at least another (unassigned) variable. Each time a constraint causes a domain wipeout (DWO) its weight is incremented by one. The *dom/wdeg* heuristic chooses the variable with minimum ratio of current domain size to weighted degree. It is a generic state-of-the-art variable ordering heuristic and the interesting is that it is adaptive, with the expectation to focus on the hard part(s) of the problem. Some variants of *dom/wdeg*, proposed in [5], are less amenable to changes in the revision ordering than *dom/wdeg* and therefore can be more robust. Refalo introduced an impact measure with the aim of detecting choices which result in the strongest search space reduction [89].

Once a variable has been selected, the algorithm must decide on the order in which to examine its values. Heuristics in [40] select the value that maximizes the summation of the remaining domain sizes after propagation. Geelen [41] proposes to choose a value that is most likely to participate in a solution. Early work on learning about values focused on nogoods that can guide search away from the re-exploration of fruitless subtrees [71]. In general, the "best-first" principle advocates the selection of a value most likely to be part of a solution. An approach called *survivors-first*, gave rise to the family of adaptive value ordering [113].

Value ordering heuristics are trying to leave the maximum flexibility for subsequent variable assignments. Of course, if we are trying to find all the solutions to a problem, not just the first one, then the ordering does not matter because we have to consider every value anyway. The same holds if there are no solutions to the problem. Although, a variety of value ordering heuristics existis, the *lex* heuristic is the one most commonly used because, the proposed heuristics are either costly when used dynamically or have not demonstrated significant gains over a wide variety of problems.

2.4.3 Branching schemes

The search tree is generated as the search progresses and represents alternative choices that may have to be examined in order to find a solution. The method of extending a node in the search tree is called *branching scheme*. Search is typically guided by variable and value ordering heuristics and makes use of a specific branching scheme like 2-way or *d*-way. These are the two most widely used branching schemes.

In *d*-way branching, after variable x with domain $D(x) = \{a_1, a_2, \ldots, a_d\}$ is selected, d branches are built, each one corresponding to one of the d possible value assignments of x. In the first branch, value a_1 is assigned to x and constraint propagation is triggered. If the branch corresponding to assignment $x = a_i$ fails, the assignment of a_2 to x is tried (second branch), and so on. If all d branches fail then the algorithm backtracks. The branching scheme we used in the map coloring problem depicted in Figure 2.3 is the d-way branching scheme. A general example of a search tree explored with d-way branching is shown in Figure 2.7.

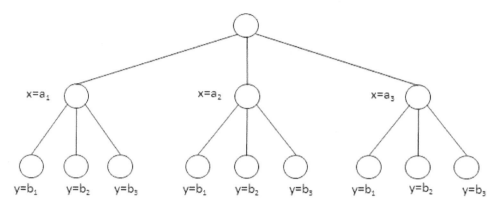

Figure 2.7: Example of search tree under a d-way branching schemes, using the lex variable and value ordering heuristic.

In 2-way branching, after a variable x is chosen and a value $a_i \in D(x)$ is selected, two branches are created [92]. In the left branch a_i is assigned to x, namely the constraint $x = a_i$ is added to the problem and is propagated. In the right branch, the constraint $x \neq a_i$ is added to the problem and is propagated. If the left branch fails and the propagation of $x \neq a_i$ succeeds then any variable can be selected next (not necessarily x). If both branches fail then the algorithm backtracks. Figure 2.8 shows a search tree explored with 2-way branching.

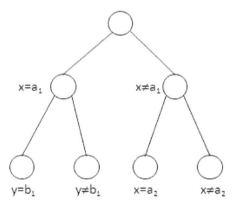

Figure 2.8: Example of search tree under a 2-way branching schemes, using the lex variable and value ordering heuristic.

There are two significant differences between these branching strategies. In 2-way branching, if the branch assigning a value a_i to a variable x fails, then the removal of a_i from $D(x)$ is propagated. Instead, in d-way the next available value a_j of $D(x)$ is tried. Note that the propagation of a_j subsumes the propagation of a_i's removal. In 2-way, after a failed branch corresponding to an assignment $x = a_i$, and assuming the removal of a_i from $D(x)$ is propagated successfully, the algorithm can choose to branch on any variable (not necessarily x), according to the variable ordering heuristic. In d-way branching the algorithm has to branch again on x after $x = a_i$ fails.

Another technique that is not oftenly used is dichotomic domain splitting [33]. This method proceeds by splitting the current domain of the selected variable into two sets, usually based on the lexicographical ordering of the values. Domain splitting is mainly used when the domains of the variables are very large. Although domain splitting drastically reduces the branching factor to two, it can result in a much deeper search tree. Recently, approaches that investigate adaptive search strategies have been proposed [3], in order to increase the practical efficiency of backtracking search. These heuristics can be applied at successful right branches (i.e of 2-way) to branch on another variable rather than trying the next value of the current (left) one.

Generally, an adaptive strategy uses the results of its own search experience to modify its subsequent behavior. In other words, a search-guiding strategy is said to be adaptive when it makes choices that depend on the current state of the problem instance an well as previous states. Thus, an adaptive strategy learns, in the sense that it takes account of information concerning the subtrees already been explored. Such an example of adaptive search is when interleaving 2-way and d-way in the same tree to solve an instance.

2.5 Constraint Solvers

Most of the CSP solvers are composed of three main components: i) a modeling language, ii) a set of filtering algorithms for specialized (global) constraints and iii) search strategies (algorithms and heuristics). Modeling languages are used by the CSP solvers in order to provide a representation of CP problems. That is, defining problem variables and their values, expressing the constraints, handling symmetries, defining viewpoints, e.t.c. Filtering algorithms are based on properties of constraint networks. The idea is to exploit such properties in order to identify some nogoods, where a nogood corresponds to a partial assignment (i.e. a set of variable assignments) that can not lead to any solution. Search is used to traverse the search space of a CSP in order to find a solution. For most of the complete CSP solvers, it respectively corresponds to constraint propagation and depth-first search with backtracking guided by some heuristics. Our thesis is concerned with the second component of CSP solvers, namely constraint propagation and especially strong local consistencies.

Modern complete CSP solvers like IBM ILog [52], Gecode [94], Minion [43] and Choco [62] offer a high-level modeling language and rich libraries of filtering algorithms for specialized global constraints, local search, search heuristics, symmetry breaking methods, etc. They are general-purpose constraint solvers, very fast and scale well as problem size increases. They use an expressive input language and a highly-optimized implementation. They also offer a clear separation between the model and the solving machinery (providing both modeling tools and innovative solving tools).

Despite the wealth of research on strong consistencies, they have not been widely adopted by CP solvers. The above CP solvers predominantly apply GAC, and lesser forms of consistency such as Bounds Consistency (BC), when propagating constraints. Algorithms for GAC can filter values from anywhere in the domain of a variable while algorithms for BC can only shrink the bounds of a variableŠs domain. They mainly use the 2-way branching and do not aplly GAC to all constraints (i.e., on global constraints they use specialized algorithms).

Even though, general-purpose constraint programming solvers can be efficiently used to solve a wide range of problems in AI and other areas of computer science, the mainstream solvers (like Ilog, Gecode, Minion, Choco, e.t.c.) do not include adaptive components in their search mechanisms and make no use of strong local consistencies. The notion of adaptiveness, in these solvers, is restricted only to the usage of certain variable ordering heuristics (like *dom/wdeg*).

2.5.1   Our CSP solver

The solver we use for the experimental evaluation has been developed from scratch by our research team. This solver includes a variety of branching methods, variable and value ordering heuristics, propagators for various constraints, many strong local consistency algorithms for binary and non-binary constraints, and heuristics for the adaptive control of propagation.

The decision to implement our CSP solving system instead of adapting or extending an existing one, was taken due to various reasons. Existing solvers do not offer algorithms for strong local consistencies, so we would have to implement them all (existing and new) from scratch anyway. The propagation mechanisms of available solvers are difficult to modify in order to obtain SLCs. Additionally, there is no publicly available solver that includes the latest algorithms that we use as base methods to compare against (i.e., STR2, GAC-va and maxRPWC1). In the experimental part we are interested in directly comparing our techniques against these base methods under the same implementation. On top of that, implementing strong local consistencies that consider intersections of constraints within a standard solver is not a straightforward task (for most solvers at least). Working out efficient ways of doing this is certainly interesting, but outside the scope of this research work.

The architecture

Our solver is implemented as an object-oriented system, with classes representing the core entities and concepts. Only the indispensable or required methods for direct interaction with the user are exposed, everything else is kept private to the class. Where possible, interfaces are implemented to abstract concepts from particular instantiations of them. The complexity of performing a particular task is hidden in the implementation of the class performing it.

Our CSP solver, written in the Java programming language, is a generic solver in the sense that it can handle constraints of any arity. This solver essentially implements various algorithms that enforce BC, AC, maxRPC, GAC, maxRPWC and other local consistencies or approximations of them. It also includes search algorithms that maintain the local consistences mentioned and supports a wide range of branching schemes, variable and value ordering heuristics, as well as heuristics for adaptive propagation.

Important to note that the aim of our study is to fairly compare the various algorithms and heuristics within the same solver's environment rather than building a state-of-the-art constraint solver. Although our implementation is reasonably optimized for its purposes, it lacks important aspects of state-of-the-art constraint solvers such as specialized propagators for global constraints.

Related work

Local consistencies constitute an important concept in CSPs, since they play a vital role in the solving process. They are defined over "local" parts of the CSP, e.g., properties defined over subsets of the variables and constraints of the CSP. A consistency technique can remove many inconsistent values from the variables' domains and, thus, simplify the problem and reduce the search space.

This chapter includes a review of the literature on local consistencies, for binanry and non-binary CSPs, and algorithms to enforce them. We also review the special case of table constraints where specialized algorithms have been proposed to handle them efficiently. Finally, we survey techniques that are used for adaptive propagation, namely techniques that can be used to select the appropriate propagation methods for solving a CSP instance.

3.1 Binary Constraints

Many local consistency properties on CSPs have been defined over decades of research (see [10] for a thorough review). In this section we enumerate the basic local consisties for binary CSPs and the relations among them, regarding their inference power and complexity. We also refer to algorithms for enforcing such consistencies.

3.1.1 Arc Consistency

We say that a value a_i of a variable x_i is arc consistent (AC) if for any constraint where x_i participates, there exists a value for the other variable in the constraint such that this value together with a_i satisfy the constraint.

Definition 1 *(Arc Consistency [78]) In a binary CSP, a value $a_i \in D(x_i)$ is arc consistent (AC) iff for every constraint $c_{i,j}$ there exists a value $a_j \in D(x_j)$ s.t. the pair of values (a_i, a_j) satisfies $c_{i,j}$. In this case a_j is called an* AC-support *of a_i. A variable is AC iff all its values are AC. A problem is AC iff there is no empty domain in D and all the variables in X are AC.*

Usually, a constraint is made AC by propagating the effects from a domain reduction of one variable to the other variable and vice versa (both directions). This is called revision of the (directed) arc in the graph, where the arc is denoted as (x_i, c_{i_j}). In general, the *revision* of a constraint c using a local consistency A is the process of checking whether the values of each $x \in scp(c)$ verify the property of A. For example, the revision of $c_{i,j}$ using AC verifies if all values in $D(x_i)$ have *AC-supports* in $D(x_j)$. We say that a revision is *fruitful* if it deletes at least one value, while it is *redundant* if it achieves no pruning. The REVISE function presented below does precisely

---

REVISE $(x_i, c_{i,j})$

   DELETE $\leftarrow$ false;
   for each $a_i \in D(x_i)$ **do**
     if $\nexists\, a_j \in D(x_j)$ s.t. (a_i, a_j) satisfies c_{i_j} **then**
       delete a_i from $D(x_i)$;
       DELETE $\leftarrow$ true;
   return DELETE;

---

that. A CSP is made AC by repeated revisions of the arcs. Note that the deletion of arc inconsistent values does not eliminate any solution of the original CSP.

The simplest/naive algorithm for achieving arc consistency repeats the revisions until all domains remain unchanged at their last revision. If at least one domain is changed, all arcs are revised. This is the AC1 algorithm that suffers from unnecessary repetition of revisions [78].

AC1

   $Q \leftarrow (x_i, c_{i,j})$, $c_{i,j} \in C$, $x_i \in \text{scp}(c_{i,j})$;
   repeat
     CHANGE $\leftarrow$ false;
     for each (x_i, x_j) in Q **do**
       CHANGE $\leftarrow$ REVISE$(x_i, c_{i,j})$ or CHANGE;
   until !CHANGE

The AC1 algorithm is not efficient because the succesfull revision of even one arc in some iteration forces all the arcs to be revised again in the next iteration, even though only a small number of them are really affected by this revision. In practice, the only arcs affected by the reduction of the domain of x_i are the arcs (x_k, x_i). The following arc consistency algorithm, called AC3 [78], removes this drawback of AC1 and performs re-revision only for those arcs that are possibly affected by a previous revision.

AC3

   $Q \leftarrow (x_i, c_{i,j})$, $c_{i,j} \in C$, $x_i \in \text{scp}(c_{i,j})$;
   while $Q \neq \emptyset$ **do**
     select and delete $(x_i, c_{i,j})$ from Q;
     if REVISE$(x_i, c_{i,j})$ **then**
       if $D(x_i) = \emptyset$ **then return** false;
       $Q \leftarrow Q \cup (x_k, c_{k,i})$, $c_{k,i} \in C$, $x_k \in \text{scp}(c_{k,i}, k \neq j)$

The AC3 algorithm uses a queue to keep track of the arcs that need to be checked for inconsistency. Each arc $(x_i, c_{i,j})$ is in turn removed from the queue and checked. If any values need to be deleted from the domain of x_i, then every arc $(x_k, c_{k,i})$ pointing to x_i must be reinserted in the queue. The complexity of AC3 can be analyzed as follows: a binary CSP has at most $O(n^2)$ arcs; each arc can be inserted in the queue only d times, because x_i has at most d values in its domain. Checking consistency of an arc can be done in $O(d^2)$ time; so the total worst-case time complexity is $O(n^2 d^3)$.

Since the AC3 algorithm may revise an edge many times it re-tests many pairs of values which are already known (from the previous iteration) to be consistent or inconsistent respectively and which are not affected by the reduction of the domain. As this is a source of potential inefficiency, algorithm AC4 [84] was introduced to refine the handling of edges (constraints), by maintaining a support set for each value. In particular, for each value of a variable there is a counter indicating how many supports this value has in the domain of the other variable that shares the costraint. It also stores a structure for the pairs (variable, value) which are supported by the current value. By maintaining these structures, some constraint checks can be fully avoided. AC4 algorithm has an optimal time complexity of $O(ed^2)$ and requires $O(ed^2)$ space for its structures. Despite being optimal, it is very expensive during the initialization phase, which can be prohibitive in terms of time.

AC4 is the first *'fine-grained'* algorithm, because it performs propagation (via a queue) at the level of values. *'Coarse-grained'* algorithms, such as AC3, propagate at the level of constraints (or arcs), which is less precise and can include redundancies. On the other hand, coarse-grained algorithms are simpler to implement and do not require expensive data structures. A compromise between AC3 and AC4 is the AC6 algorithm ([9]), which remains optimal having the worst-case time complexity of AC4 and stops searching for support for a value on a constraint as soon as the first support is verified, like AC3 does. In addition, AC6 maintains a data structure lighter than AC4, which instead of counting all supports of value on a constraint, it just ensures that it has at least one. Hence, AC6 has an $O(ed)$ space complexity.

Coarse-grained algorithms do not propagate the consequences of value removals to other values. Instead, they propagate pairs $(x_i, c_{i.j})$ for which $D(x_j)$ has changed. Although coarse-grained algorithms are more abstract in the way they propagate, they have two advantages. First, CP solvers usually support arc-oriented propagation instead of value-oriented. Second, all fine-grained algorithms require data structures for supported values, which is more complex to implement and maintain. AC2001/3.1 [17, 111, 18], is the first (and only) optimal coarse-grained algorithm. It adopts the AC3 framework, but achieves optimality by storing the smallest support for each value on each constraint, like AC6.

Specifically, when a support of a value has to be detected, AC3 starts the search for a new support from scratch whereas AC2001/3.1 starts the search from a resumption point which corresponds to the last support found for this value. This requires the introduction of a data structure, denoted $Last$, to store the last support of any triplet (x_i, a, x_j) belonging to the arc $(c_{i,j}, x_i)$ and a value $a \in D(x_i)$. Initially, $Last$ must be initialized to $\perp$ (i.e., the lexicographically smallest tuple; $\tau > \perp$ for any tuple $\tau \in rel(c_{i,j})$). The revision involves testing for any value the validity of the last support and in case it is not valid, looking for a new support. The pointer $Last(x_i, a, x_j)$ is updated to the most recently found AC-support of (x_i, a) in $D(x_j)$. Importantly, optimality is obtained because values in $D(x_j)$ that are smaller than $Last(x_i, a, x_j)$ are not checked again because they were already unsuccessfully checked in previous revisions. AC2001/3.1 achieves arc consistency on binary problems in $O(ed^2)$ time and $O(ed)$ space.

Constraints are said to be multidirectional because when a tuple τ is found to support (x_i, a) on a constraint c, it is also a support for any (x_j, b) that belongs to τ [64, 76]. The binary version of multidirectionality is called bidirectionality and it is exploited by the AC3^{rm} algorithm (*rm* stands for multi-directional residues) [68]. In more detail, when $Last(x_i, a, x_j)$ is updated to b, which is the AC-support of (x_i, a) in $D(x_j)$, then $Last(x_j, b, x_i)$ is also set to a (bidirectionality). Additionally, AC3^{rm} does not maintain $Last$ during seach, namely upon backtracking the supports of $Last$ are not updated. $Last$ is treated as a *residual support*, or *residue*, which is a support that has been stored during a previous execution of the procedure which determines if a value is supported by a constraint. In contrast tothe use of $Last$ by AC2001/3.1 ,in the AC3^{rm} algorithm a residue is not guaranteed to represent a lower bound of the smallest current support of a value. Obviousy,

$\text{AC}3^{rm}$ is not optimal in the worst case, having $O(ed^3)$ time complexity, but in practice it behaves very efficiently. The $\text{AC}7$ [12, 13] algorithm, which is an extension of $\text{AC}6$, is also exploiting bidirectionality of supports. Its time and space complexity is $O(ed^2)$.

Arc consistency checking can be applied either as a preprocessing step before the beginning of the search process, or as a propagation step (during backtracking) after every assignment or value removal made during search. This algorithm that does this is called MAC [91], for Maintaining Arc Consistency. In either case, the process must be applied repeatedly until no more inconsistencies remain. This is because, whenever a value is deleted from some variable's domain to remove an inconsistency, a new arc inconsistency could arise in arcs pointing to that variable.

3.1.2 Strong local consistencies

Arc consistency is a *domain filtering* (or first-order) consistency, meaning that it can only identify inconsistent values, thereby filtering variable domains. As a result, domain filtering consistencies do not alter either the constraint graph by adding new constraints, or the constraints' relations by removing inconsistent tuples [31]. *Relation filtering* (or higher-order) consistencies allow us to identify inconsistent tuples of values from constraints' relations.

Several local consistencies stronger than AC, that are either domain or relation filtering, have been proposed in the literature. Examples of domain filtering consistencies for binary constraints include Restricted Path Consistency [8], Path Inverse Consistency (PIC) [37], max Restricted Path Consistency [29], and Singleton Arc Consistency (SAC) [31]. The most famous local consistency that is not cast as domain filtering is Path Consistency [29]. When enforced, path consistency can remove inconsistent 2-tuples from binary relations and/or introduce new binary constraints. Another recent example of such a local consistency is dual consistency [66]. We give the formal definitions of these consistencies.

Definition 2 *(**Path Consistency** [29]) A pair of values $((x_i, a_i), (x_j, a_j))$ is path consistent (PC) if for all $x_k \in X$ s.t. $x_j \neq x_k \neq x_i \neq x_j$, this pair of values can be extended to a consistent instantiation of $\{x_i, x_j, x_k\}$. (x_j, a_j) is a path consistent support (PC-support) for (x_i, a_i) if $(a_i, a_j) \in rel(c_{i,j})$ and $((x_i, a_i), (x_j, a_j))$ is path consistent. In every third variable, the pair (x_k, a_k) is a PC-witness for (a_i, a_j) in x_k.*

Definition 3 *(**Restricted Path Consistency** [8]) A value $a_i \in D(x_i)$ is restricted path consistent (RPC) iff (x_j, a_j) is the only AC-support of a_i in x_j and $((x_i, a_i), (x_j, a_j))$ is path consistent. A binary CSP is RPC iff it is AC and for each constraint $c_{i,j}$ and each value $a_i \in D(x_i), a_i$ is RPC.*

Definition 4 *(**Path Inverse Consistency** [37]) A value $a_i \in D(x_i)$ is path inverse consistent (PIC) iff for all $x_j, x_k \in X$, s.t. $x_i \neq x_j \neq x_k \neq x_i$, there exist $b_j \in D(x_j)$ and $d_k \in D(x_k)$, s.t. the assignments (x_i, a_i), (x_j, b_j) and (x_k, d_k) satisfy the constraints between the three variables.*

max Restricted Path Consistency

Since part of the thesis is about algorithms for max Restricted Path Consistency (maxRPC) and approximations of maxRPC, we will devote more space to explain past works on maxRPC. maxRPC is a strong domain filtering consistency for binary constraints introduced in 1997 by Debruyne and Bessiere [29], as an extension to *Restricted Path Consistency* (RPC). The basic idea of maxRPC is to delete any value a of a variable x that has no arc consistency (AC) or path consistency (PC) support in a variable y that is constrained with x. A value b is an AC support for a if the two values are compatible, and it is also a PC support for a if this pair of values is path consistent. We give the formal definition of maxRPC.

Definition 5 (**max Restricted Path Consistency** [29]) *A value $a_i \in D(x_i)$ is maxRPC iff it is AC and for each constraint $c_{i,j}$ there exists a value $a_j \in D(x_j)$ that is an AC-support of a_i s.t. the pair of values (a_i, a_j) is path consistent. A variable is maxRPC iff all its values are maxRPC. A problem is maxRPC iff there is no empty domain in D and all variables in X are maxRPC.*

maxRPC achieves a stronger level of local consistency than arc consistency (AC), and in [31] it was identified, along with singleton AC (SAC), as a promising alternative to AC. The first algorithm for maxRPC was proposed in [29], and two more algorithms have been proposed since then [47, 106]. The first maxRPC algorithm, called `maxRPC1` [29], is a fine-grained algorithm based on AC6 ([9]) and has optimal $O(end^3)$ time complexity and $O(end)$ space complexity. The second algorithm, called `maxRPC2` [47], is a coarse-grained algorithm that uses ideas similar to those used by `AC2001/3.1` to achieve $O(end^3)$ time and $O(ed)$ space complexity at the cost of some redundant checks compared to `maxRPC1`. The third algorithm, `maxRPC`^{rm} [106], is a coarse-grained algorithm based on AC3^{rm} [68]. The time and space complexities of `maxRPC`^{rm} are $O(en^2d^4)$ and $O(end)$. Note that in [106] the complexities are given as $O(eg + ed^3 + csd^4)$ and $O(ed + cd)$, where c is the number of 3-cliques, g is the maximum degree of a variable and s is the maximum number of 3-cliques that share the same single constraint in the constraint graph. Considering that c is $O(en)$ and s is $O(n)$, we can derive the complexities for `maxRPC`^{rm} given here. This algorithm has a higher time complexity than the other two, but it has some advantages compared to them because of its lighter use of data structures during search (this is explained below and in section 3.2). Finally, `maxRPCEn1` is a fine-grained algorithm closely related to `maxRPC1` [28]. This algorithm is based on AC7 ([12]) and achieves maxRPCEn, a local consistency stronger than maxRPC.

Among the three algorithms `maxRPC2` seems to be the most promising for stand-alone use as it has a better time and space complexity than `maxRPC`^{rm} without requiring heavy data structures or complex implementation as `maxRPC1` does. On the other hand, `maxRPC`^{rm} can be better suited for use during search as it avoids the costly maintainance of data structures as explained below.

Central to `maxRPC2` is the *LastPC* data structure, as we call it here. For each constraint $c_{i,j}$ and each value $a_i \in D(x_i)$, $LastPC_{x_i,a_i,x_j}$ gives the most recently discovered PC-support of a_i in $D(x_j)$. `maxRPC2` maintains this data structure incrementally. This means that a copy of *LastPC* is made when moving forward during search (i.e. after a successfully propagated variable assignment) and *LastPC* is restored to its previous state after a failed variable assignment (or value removal in the case of 2-way branching). Data structures with such a property are often referred to as *backtrackable*. Their use implies an increased space complexity as copies need to be made while search progresses down a branch. On a brighter note, since *LastPC* is backtrackable, `maxRPC2` displays the following behavior: When looking for a PC-support for a_i in $D(x_j)$, it first checks if $LastPC_{x_i,a_i,x_j}$ is valid. If it is not, it searches for a new PC-support starting from the value *immediately after* $LastPC_{x_i,a_i,x_j}$ in $D(x_j)$. In this way a good time complexity bound is achieved.

On the other hand, `maxRPC`^{rm} uses a data structure similar to *LastPC* to store *residual supports* or simply *residues* and thus, does not maintain this structure incrementally (it only needs one copy). Therefore, no additional actions need to be taken (copying or restoration) when moving forward or after a fail. Such data structures are often referred to as *backtrack-stable*. When looking for a PC-support for a_i in $D(x_j)$, if the residue $LastPC_{x_i,a_i,x_j}$ is not valid then `maxRPC`^{rm} searches for a new PC-support from scratch in $D(x_j)$. This results in higher time complexity, but crucially does not require costly maintainance of $LastPC$ during search. The algorithm also makes use of residues for the PC-witnesses found in every third variable for each pair (a_i, a_j). These are stored in a data structure with an O(end) space complexity. The initialization of this structure causes an extra overhead which can be significant on very large problems.

A major overhead of both maxRPC2 and maxRPC^{rm} is the following. When searching for a PC-witness for a pair of values (a_i, a_j) in a third variable x_k, they always start the search from scratch, i.e. from the first available value in $D(x_k)$. As these searches can be repeated many times during search, there can be many redundant constraint checks. In contrast, maxRPC1 manages to avoid searching from scratch through the use of an additional data structure. This saves many constraint checks, albeit resulting in O(end) space complexity and requiring costly maintainance of this data structure during search. The algorithms we describe in Chapter 3.4 largely eliminate these redundant constraint checks with lower space complexity, and in the case of maxRPC3^{rm} with only light use of data structures.

A theoretical analysis and experimental results presented in [31] demonstrated that maxRPC is more efficient compared to RPC and PIC. Hence it was identified as a promising alternative to AC. This is why we focus on this local consistency.

Singleton Arc Consistency

Singleton arc consistency (SAC) enhances arc consistency by ensuring that the network cannot become arc inconsistent after the assignment of a value to a variable. Ensuring that a given local consistency does not lead to a failure when we enforce it after having assigned a variable to a value, is a common idea in constraint propagation. The general idea is trying in turn different assignments of a value to a variable, and performing constraint propagation on the subproblem obtained by this assignment. If the problem is found to be inconsistent, this means that this value does not belong to any solution and thus can be pruned. This kind of technique has been applied in constraint problems with numerical domains by limiting the assignments to bounds in the domains and ensuring that bounds consistency does not fail (3B-consistency in [73]). This idea was formalized as a class of local consistencies in discrete CSPs under the name *singleton consistencies* [88, 31]. We give the definition in the case where arc consistency is applied to each subproblem is arc consistency. Any other local consistency can be used in a similar way. In the following, the subnetwork obtained from a network N by reducing the domain of a variable x_i to the singleton $\{a\}$ is denoted by $N|x_i = a$.

Definition 6 (*Singleton Arc Consistency* [30]) *A value $a \in D(x_i)$ is singleton arc consistent (SAC) iff the problem derived from assigning a to x_i (i.e., $N|x_i = \{a\}$) is AC [31]. A problem is SAC iff every value of every variable is SAC.*

SAC is strictly stronger than maxRPC and obviously, strictly stronger than AC. SAC1 [30] is a brute-force algorithm that checks SAC of each value by performing AC on each subproblem $N|x_i = \{a\}$. After each change in a domain, it rechecks SAC of every remaining value, meaning that it performs AC nd times on each subproblem. Because there are nd subproblems, it runs in $O(en^2d^4)$. SAC2 [7], avoids unnecessary work in a similar way of AC4, by storing lists of supports. Unfortunately, its worst-case time complexity is the same as that of SAC1. A more recent advancement of SAC, called SAC-Opt [11], has a $O(end3)$ time complexity, but requires $O(end^2)$ space to store its large data structures. SAC-SDS (Sharing Data Structures) uses lighter structures, has lower complexity ($O(end^4)$) than former SAC algorithms, whereas its space complexity is the same as SAC2, namely $O(n^2d^2)$. Lecoutre and Cardon proposed SAC3 [65], which incrementally assigns values to variables in the network until arc consistency wipes out a domain. Despite the fact that SAC3 is not optimal, it works well in practice.

Finally, the implementation of SAC can be simply done on top of any AC algorithm. Many other singleton consistencies can be constructed because any local consistency can be used to detect the possible inconsistency of the network $N|x_i = \{a\}$.

The following definition characterizes the relationship between two consistencies in terms of their pruning power (strengthness).

Definition 7 *Following [31], a local consistency ϕ is stronger than ψ iff in any CN in which ϕ holds then ψ holds, and strictly stronger iff it is stronger and there is one CN for which ψ holds but ϕ does not. Accordingly, ϕ is incomparable to ψ iff neither is stronger than the other.*

In Figure 3.9 we summarize the relationships between the mentioned local consistencies.

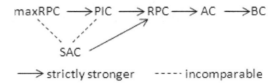

Figure 3.9: Relationships between consistencies for binary CSPs.

3.2   Non-Binary Constraints

Constraints including more than two variables, belong to the category of non-binary constraints, and naturally arise in many real-life problems. Many local consistencies are applicable on both binary and non-binary constraints after small modifications, whereas there are others that are only defined for binary constraints. For instance, AC belongs to the former case while maxRPC to the latter. However, many local consistencies for binary CSPs have been either extended to or have inspired consistencies for non-binary CSPs.

3.2.1   Generalized Arc Consistency

The notion of arc consistency was the first to be extended to non-binary constraints, resulting in the definition of Generalized Arc Consistency (GAC), which is also known as Domain Consistency [84, 79]. In few words, a constraint c is GAC if for any value a of any variable x in the constraint's scope there exist values for the other variables in the constraint such that, together with a, they satisfy the constraint. More formally:

Definition 8 *(Generalized Arc Consistency) A value $a_i \in D(x_i)$ is GAC iff for every constraint c s.t. $x_i \in scp(c)$ there exists a valid tuple $\tau \in rel(c)$ that includes the assignment of a_i to x_i. In this case τ is called a GAC-support of a_i on c. A variable is GAC iff all its values are GAC. A problem is GAC iff there is no empty domain in $\mathcal{D}$ and all the variables in $\mathcal{X}$ are GAC.*

The AC3 algorithm can be naturally extended to make the constraint network generalized arc consistent resulting in algorithm GAC3 [79, 78]. Instead of revising the binary arc, this algorithm revises the hyper-arcs, where each hyper-arc corresponds to a constraint and linking nodes in the network corresponding to the variables that are subject to the constraint. GAC3 is the baseline algorithm on which a variety of algorithms (not necessarily for GAC) are built on, while it is commonly used during backtracking search. GAC3 utilizes a queue of variables; variables are inserted to queue when their domains are pruned. Hence, the effects of this reduction need to be propagated. GAC3 is a *variable oriented* algorithm. Correspondingly, algorithms that trace arcs (resp. constraints) are arc (resp. constraint) oriented.

Now we describe one iteration of GAC3. Once a variable x_i is extracted from Q, each constraint c that involves x_i is examined and all the variables that appear in c, except x_i, are revised. For each value $a_j \in D(x_j)$, such that $x_j \in scp(c)$, a GAC-support is sought. This is done by iterating through the valid tuples of c. In case a tuple τ that is valid and satisfies c is located, then a support for a_j has been established and GAC3 moves to the next value of $D(x_j)$. Values that have become inconsistent with respect to c, are deleted. If a revision is fruitful (at least one value has been removed), the queue has to be updated, by adding x_j to queue. The algorithm stops when a domain wipe-out occurs or the queue becomes empty.

GAC3 achieves generalized arc consistency in $O(er^3d^{r+1})$ time and $O(er)$ space, where r is the greatest arity among all constraints. As with AC3, various AC algorithms are modified to handle n-ary CSPs. The extensions of AC4 and AC2001/3.1 resulted in GAC4 and GAC2001/3.1 respectively. The time complexity of GAC2001/3.1 is $O(er^2d^r)$, while the fine-grained GAC-Schema [16], taking advantage of multidirectionality, has an optimal time complexity of $O(erd^r)$. Because of multidirectionality GAC-Schema avoids checking a tuple r times for each value composing it. The non-binary version GAC4 [86] also has optimal $O(erd^r)$ time complexity, because it computes the dr possible constraint checks on a constraint once and for all during initialization, storing the information in lists of supported values.

Finally, the GAC3^{rm} [68] algorithm originates from the AC3^{rm} [68] algorithm. Residual supports of the *Last* structure are used during revisions in order to speed up the search. As opposed to GAC2001/3.1, if a residue is no longer valid, the search for a valid tuple starts from scratch, which allows keeping residues from one call to another, even after a backtrack. Although GAC3^{rm} is not optimal ($O(er^3d^{r+1})$), experiments have shown that maintaining GAC3^{rm} during search is more efficient than maintaining GAC2001/3.1.

3.2.2   Bounds consistency

Local consistencies weaker than GAC have been proposed in order to overcome the prohibitive cost of GAC on some non-binary constraints. The idea behind these consistencies is to use the fact that domains are usually composed of integers. Integer domains inherit the total ordering of the integers and hence they also inherit the bounds of $D(x_i)$.

As recognized in [10, 27] there is a number of different definitions of bounds (sometimes called interval) consistency in the literature. The most commonly used defintion is based on the notion of a bound support.

A tuple $\tau = (a_1, \ldots, a_m)$ is a *Bound-support* on a constraint c, with $scp(c) = \{x_1, \ldots, x_m\}$, iff τ satisfies c and for each $x_i \in scp(c)$, $min_D(x_i) \leq a_i \leq max_D(x_i)$. Note that in case each a_i belongs to $D(x_i)$, τ is also a GAC-support.

Definition 9 *(Bounds(Z) Consistency) A constraint c is* bounds(Z) *consistent (BC(Z)) iff for all* $x_i \in scp(c)$, *there exist Bound-supports* τ_{min} *and* τ_{max} *on c s.t.* $\tau_{min}[x_i] = min_D(x_i)$ *and* $\tau_{max}[x_i] = max_D(x_i)$ *(i.e. both bounds belong to a Bound-support on c).*

Definition 10 (*Bounds(D) Consistency*) *A constraint c is bounds(D) consistent (BC(D)) iff for all* $x_i \in scp(c)$, $min_D(x_i)$ *and* $max_D(x_i)$ *belong to a GAC-support on c. Applying BC(D) ensures GAC-support on a constraint c only for the bounds of the domain of each variable in* $scp(c)$.

Another definition, called BC(R) in [10], is similar to BC(Z) but instead of looking for a Bound-support consisting of integers, it looks for one consisting of reals. Finally, another relevant local consistency is range consistency. A constraint c is *range consistent* (RC) iff for all $x_i \in scp(c)$, each $v_i \in D(x_i)$ belongs to a Bound-support on c.

Although many strong local consistencies based on GAC have been proposed (see below), similar consistencies that are based on BC have been overlooked. One exception is Singleton Bounds Consistency [70], which can be seen an extension of BC(D). This local consistency is an adaptation of 3B Consistency [73] from numerical to finite domain CSPs.

3.2.3 Strong Local Consistencies

Examples of domain filtering consistencies for non-binary constraints include Singleton Generalized Arc Consistency (SGAC) [31], Restricted Pairwise Consistency (RPWC) and max Restricted PairWise Consistency (maxRPWC) [19], and relational Path Inverse Consistency (rPIC) [101]. Some of the consistencies, are directly defined on both binary and non-binary constraints (i.e., SAC for binary and SGAC for non-binary constraints). Others, like maxRPWC and rPIC, are defined on non-binary constraints but are inspired by relevant consistencies for binary constraints (i.e., maxRPC and PIC). We give the formal definitions of these consistencies.

Definition 11 (*Singleton Generalized Arc Consistency* [31]) *A non-binary CSP is singleton arc consistent (SGAC) iff* $\forall x_i \in \mathcal{X}$ *and* $\forall a_i \in D(x_i)$ *the problem derived from assigning a to* x_i *(i.e.,* $N|x_i = \{a\}$) *is GAC.*

Definition 12 (*Restricted Pairwise Consistency* [19]) *A non-binary CSP is restricted pairwise consistent (RPWC) iff* $\forall x_i \in \mathcal{X}$, *all values in* $D(x_i)$ *are GAC and,* $\forall a_i \in D(x_i)$, $\forall c_j \in C$, *s.t. there exists a unique valid* $\tau \in rel(c_j)$ *with* $\tau[x_i] = a_i$, $\forall c_k \in C$ ($c_k \neq c_j$), *s.t.* $scp(c_j) \cap scp(c_k) \neq \emptyset$, *and exists a valid* τ' *on* c_k *s. t.* $\tau[scp(c_j) \cap scp(c_k)] = \tau'[scp(c_j) \cap scp(c_k)]$.

Definition 13 (*relational Path Inverse Consistency* [101]) *A non-binary CSP is relational rath inverse consistenct (rPIC) iff* $\forall x_i \in \mathcal{X}$ *and* $\forall a_i \in D(x_i)$, $\forall c_j \in C$, *where* $x_i \in scp(c_j)$, *and* $\forall c_k \in C$, *s.t.* $scp(c_j) \cap scp(c_k) \neq \emptyset$, *there exists a GAC-support* τ *on* c_j *s. t.* $\tau[x_i] = a_i$, *and there exists a GAC-support* τ' *on* c_k *s. t.* $\tau[scp(c_j) \cap scp(c_k)] = \tau'[scp(c_j) \cap scp(c_k)]$. *In this case we say that* τ' *is a PW-support of* τ.

max Restricted PairWise Consistency

When GAC or its weaker variants, such as Bounds Consistency, are applied, they process one constraint at a time. In contrast, some strong local consistencies exploit the fact that very often constraints have two or more variables in common, to achieve stronger pruning. One of the most promising consistencies of this type is max Restricted PairWise Consistency (maxRPWC) [19]. A theoretical and experimental evaluation presented in [19] demonstrated that maxRPWC is a promising alternative to GAC.

Definition 14 (*max Restricted PairWise Consistency* [19]) *A value* $a_i \in D(x_i)$ *is max restricted pairwise consistenct (maxRPWC) iff* $\forall c_j \in C$, *where* $x_i \in scp(c_j)$, a_i *has a GAC-support* $\tau \in$

$rel(c_j)$ s.t. $\forall c_k \in C$ $(c_k \neq c_j)$, s.t. $scp(c_j) \cap scp(c_k) \neq \emptyset, \exists \tau' \in rel(c_k)$, s.t. $\tau[scp(c_j) \cap scp(c_k)] = \tau'[scp(c_j) \cap scp(c_k)]$ and τ' is valid. In this case we say that τ' is a PW-support of τ and τ is a maxRPWC-support of a_i. A variable is maxRPWC iff all values in its domain are maxRPWC. A problem is maxRPWC iff there is no empty domain in $\mathcal{D}$ and all variables are maxRPWC.

From the definition of maxRPWC we can see that the value deletions from some $D(x_i)$ may trigger the deletion of a value $b \in D(x_j)$ in two cases:

1. b may no longer be maxRPWC because its current maxRPWC-support in some constraint c is no longer valid and it was the last such support in c. We call this case *maxRPWC-support loss*.

2. The last maxRPWC-support of b in some constraint c may have lost its last PW-support in another constraint c' intersecting with c. We call this case *PW-support loss*.

The definition of maxRPWC, and its name, resembles that of the binary local consistency maxRPC from which it was inspired. However, as proved in [19] the two are not equivalent when maxRPWC is applied on binary constraints.

Three algorithms for achieving maxRPWC were proposed in [19]. The first one, maxRPWC1, has $O(e^2 r^2 d^p)$ worst-case time complexity and $O(erd)$ space complexity, where p is the maximum number of variables involved in two constraints that share at least two variables. The second one has $O(e^2 rd^r)$ time complexity but its space complexity is exponential in p, and this can be prohibitive. The third one has the same time complexity as maxRPWC1 but $O(e^2 rd)$ space complexity. Although maxRPWC1 is less sophisticated than the other two, its performance when maintained during search is on average better than theirs because it uses lighter data structures. All these algorithms are generic in the sense that they do not consider any specific semantics that the constraints may have.

Despite the wealth of research on strong consistencies, they have not been widely adopted by CP solvers. State-of-the art solvers such as Gecode, ILOG, Choco, Minion, etc. predominantly apply GAC, and lesser forms of consistency such as bounds consistency, when propagating constraints.

3.2.4 Relation Filtering Consistencies

Pairwise Consistency is a relational (or higher-order) consistency, namely it prunes tuples from a constraint's relation instead of values from a variable's domain.

Definition 15 (*Pairwise Consistency* [19]) *A non-binary CSP is (PWC) iff $\forall c_j \in C$, all $\tau_j \in rel(c_j)$ are valid and $\forall c_k \in C$ $(c_k \neq c_j)$, s.t. $scp(c_j) \cap scp(c_k) \neq \emptyset$, exists a valid τ' on c_k s.t. $\tau[scp(c_j) \cap scp(c_k)] = \tau'[scp(c_j) \cap scp(c_k)]$. A tuple τ_j in the table of a constraint c_j is pairwise consistent (PWC) $\forall c_k \in C$, $\exists \tau_k$ in $rel(c_k)$ which is a PW-support of τ_j.*

We use the name *Full Pairwise Consistency* (FPWC) for the consistency that achieves both PWC and GAC (PWC+GAC).

Definition 16 (*Full PairWise Consistency*) *A non-binary CSP is full pairwise consistent (FPWC) iff $\forall c_j \in C$, all $\tau_j \in rel(c_j)$ are PWC and $\forall x_i \in \mathcal{D}$, all $a_i \in D(x_i)$ are GAC.*

Many algorithms that achieve higher-order consistencies exist in the literature, e.g., see [87, 53, 54, 67] that identify inconsistent tuples of values (nogoods of size 2 or more). In contrast to GAC algorithms, which consider constraints one by one when trying to filter values of variable domains, the proposed algorithms to enforce higher-order consistencies are able to reason from several constraints simultaneously, as, for example, constraint intersections with pairwise consistency (PWC) [53].

Relation filtering algorithms take advantage of the intersections between constraints in order to identify and remove inconsistent tuples or to add new constraints to the problem (e.g., [105, 54]). Moreover, efficient ways to apply relational consistencies were recently proposed and new consistencies of this type were introduced for binary [66, 55] and non-binary constraints [57, 108]. Specifically, the algorithms of [57, 108] concern the application of various relational consistencies on (mainly) table constraints through the exploitation of a problem's dual encoding.

In the following, when referring to constraint intersections we will mean non trivial intersections (containing more than one variable) since higher-order consistencies based on PWC do not offer any extra pruning compared to GAC on constraints intersecting on one variable [19].

In Figure 3.10 we summarize the relationships between the mentioned local consistencies for non-binary CSPs.

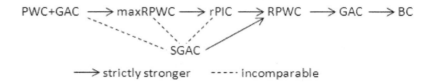

Figure 3.10: Relationships between consistencies for non-binary CSPs.

3.3   Table Constraints

Table constraints, i.e., constraints given in extension, are ubiquitous in constraint programming (CP). First, they naturally arise in many real applications from areas such as configuration and databases. And second, they are a useful modeling tool that can be called upon to, for instance, easily capture preferences [56]. Given their importance in CP, it is not surprising that table constraints are among the most widely studied constraints and as a result numerous specialized algorithms that achieve GAC on them have been proposed. Since GAC is a property defined on individual constraints, algorithms for GAC operate on one constraint at a time trying to filter infeasible values from the variables of the constraint.

Table constraints can be *positive* (resp. *negative*), when constraints are defined by sets of allowed (resp. disallowed) tuples, namely tuples that satisfy (resp. do not satisfy) the constraints. GAC algorithms for positive table constraints have received the bulk of the attention. Such algorithms utilize a number of different techniques to speed-up the check for generalized arc consistency. For example, the generic GAC-Schema of [16] can be instantiated to either a method that searches the lists of allowed tuples for suppports, or to one that searches the valid tuples. Other approaches build upon GAC-schema by interleaving the exploration of allowed and valid tuples using either intricate data structures [75] or binary search [72]. Algorithms in [72], based on GAC3 (or GAC3.1/2001 [18]), utilize a data structure for each constraint variable value triplet (c, x, a), such that x is in the scope of c. GAC3-valid+allowed, which is the most efficient in [72], improves upon GAC-schema by interleaving the exploration of allowed and valid tuples using binary search. Such an approach is also found in [75]. However, in this case it is implemented through the use of an elaborate data structure (*Hologram*) introduced in [74].

Other methods compile the tables into efficient data structures that allow for faster support search (e.g., [44] and [25]). These methods are based on the compression of the allowed tuples in order to perform a fast traversal. One such compression-based method uses, an alternative data structure, called *trie*, for each variable [44]. Also, authors in [58] used a compact representation for allowed and disallowed tuples which can be constructed from a decision tree that represents the original tuples. Another approach of compression-based techniques uses a Multi Valued Decision Diagram (MDD) to store and process table constraints more efficiently [25]. Simple Tabular Reduction (STR) [103] and its refinements, STR2 [63] and STR3 [69], maintain dynamically the support tables by removing invalid tuples from them during search. The recent algorithms of [80] are partly based on similar ideas as the Hologram method. That is, they hold information about removed values in the propagation queue and utilize it to speed up support search.

Experimental results show that the most competitive approaches are the ones based on STR and the MDD approach. The algorithm of [72], is very competitive with the Trie approach, outperforms the Hologram method and has the advantage of easier implementation and lack of complex data strucures over all other methods. Albeit, it is clearly slower than the best methods on most problems.

A different line of research has investigated stronger consistencies and algorithms to enforce them. Some of them are domain filtering, meaning that they only prune values from the domains of variables, e.g. see [31, 19], whereas a few other ones are higher-order (or relation filtering), e.g. see [53, 54, 105, 57, 67], indicating that inconsistent tuples of values can be identified. In contrast to GAC algorithms, the proposed algorithms to enforce these stronger consistencies are able to consider several constraints simultaneously. For example, pairwise consistency (PWC) [53] considers intersections between pairs of constraints.

Typically, such local consistencies take advantage of the intersections between constraints in order to identify and remove inconsistent tuples or to add new constraints to the problem (e.g., [105, 54]). Quite recently, strong domain filtering consistencies have received attention [19, 99]. Moreover, efficient ways to apply relational consistencies were proposed and new consistencies of this type were introduced for binary [66, 55] and non-binary constraints [57, 108].

The works of [57, 108] concern the application of various relational consistencies on (mainly) table constraints through the exploitation of a problem's dual encoding. Experimental results show that very high local consistencies (higher than FPWC) can pay off when they are applied through efficient algorithms. However, the proposed algorithms were not compared to state-of-the-art GAC methods such as STR2. Interestingly, the authors of [57] propose the so called index-tree data structure to locate all tuples in a constraint's relation that are consistent with a tuple of another intersecting constraint.

3.4 Adaptive Propagation

Selecting the appropriate propagator for a constraint is a problem that is essential to CP and therefore has attracted a lot of interest. Standard solvers do not use adaptive methods to tackle this problem. They either preselect the propagator or use costs and other measures to order the various propagators. Regarding the second approach, Schulte and Stuckey describe some state-of-the-art methods which are used to order propagators by many well known solvers (e.g. Gecode, Choco) [97]. The fundamental approaches for selecting a propagator are based on tracking fixpoints using idempotence reasoning of variables' domains, on tracking domain changes, called *events*, and on a priority-based queues for choosing the next propagator for a single constraint based on costs.

Automatic CP solver tuning has attracted a lot of interest recently. Several researchers have approached this problem through the use of ML methods (e.g. [83, 36]). In this case, the goal of the learning process is to automatically select or adapt the search strategy, so that the performance of the system is improved. There are two main approaches that have been studied. In the first case, a specific strategy (e.g. a search algorithm or a specific solver) is selected automatically among an array of available strategies, either for a whole class of problems or for a specific instance. Such methods have mainly been proposed for SAT and to a lesser extent for CSPs. In the second case, using ML, a new strategy can be synthesized (e.g. a combination of search algorithm and heuristics) [36]. Such attempts have mainly focused on learning strategies for combining heuristics, resulting for example in new, hybrid variable ordering heuristics. These strategies are learned before solving particular problems and are applied unchanged throughout the search. Again the bulk of the existing methods come from the SAT community. For example, in the SATenstein system [59] learning allows the synthesis of novel local search algorithms for specific problems through the composition of entire solver sub-modules.

[109] proposed the use of reinforcement learning for the dynamic selection of a variable ordering heuristic at each point of search for CSPs. Another recent work uses ML to decide prior to search whether lazy learning will be switched on or off [42]. There has been little research on learning strategies for constraint propagation. [35] uses ML methods for the automatic selection of constraint propagation techniques. In particular, a static method for the pre-selection between Forward Checking and Arc Consistency is proposed. [60] evaluates ensemble classification for selecting an appropriate propagator for the alldifferent constraint. Again this is done in a static way prior to search.

An alternative approach proposes heuristic methods for the automatic tuning of constraint propagation in [100]. Their advantage is twofold: they are inexpensive to apply, and they are perfectly suited to a dynamic application because they exploit information concerning the actual effects of propagation during search. These heuristics are based on the continuous monitoring of propagation events, such as domain wipeouts (DWOs) and value deletions, caused by individual constraints during search. When certain conditions regarding these events are met, the propagation method applied on any constraint may switch from a weaker and cheaper to a stronger and more expensive one (and vice versa). Although this approach displayed quite promising results, it suffered by important limitations. First, the description as well as the evaluation of the heuristics was limited to binary constraints. And second, their successful application depended on user interference for careful parameter tuning. The former limits the applicability of the heuristics while the latter severely compromises their autonomicity and puts burden on the shoulders of the users.

Following a different line of work, but with a similar goal, there are some works proposing heuristic methods to automatically adapt contraint propagation. Apart from [100], we can mention the following: El Sakkout et al. proposed a scheme called *adaptive arc propagation* for dynamically deciding whether to process individual constraints using AC or forward checking [34]. Freuder and Wallace proposed a technique, called *selective relaxation* which can be used to restrict AC propagation based on two local criteria; the distance in the constraint graph of any variable from the currently instantiated one, and the proportion of values deleted [38]. *Probabilistic arc consistency* is a scheme that can dynamically adapt the level of local consistency applied avoids some constraint checks and revisions that are unlikely to cause pruning [82]. Chmeiss and Sais presented a back-track search algorithm, MAC (dist k), that also uses a distance parameter k as a bound to maintain a partial form of AC [26].

Quite recently, the authors of [6] proposed the *parameterized local consistency* approach to adjust the level of consistency depending on a stability parameter over values. Parameterized local consistencies choose to enforce either arc consistency or a stronger local consistency on a value depending on whether the stability of the value is above or below a given threshold. Interestingly, they propose ways to dynamically adapt the parameter, and thus the level of local consistency, during search. The adaptiveness criterion is based on DWOs (like [100]) to locate the difficult parts of the instance. Both the approaches of [6] and [100] approach are only defined and tested on binary CSP's.

New efficient maxRPC algorithms for Binary CSPs

In this chapter we study strong local consistencies for binary constraints that widely and intensely studied. As discussed in Section 3.1, many strong local consistencies have been proposed for binary constraints, with maxRPC being one of the most promising. Therefore, we develop new efficient algorithms for this local consistency.

We propose and evaluate techniques that can boost the performance of maxRPC algorithms by eliminating many of these overheads and redundancies. These include the combined use of two data structures to avoid many redundant constraint checks, and the exploitation of residues to quickly verify the existence of supports. Based on these, we propose a number of closely related maxRPC algorithms. The first one, maxRPC3, has optimal $O(end^3)$ time complexity, displays good performance when used stand-alone, but is expensive to apply during search. The second one, maxRPC3^{rm}, has $O(en^2d^4)$ time complexity, but a restricted version with $O(end^4)$ complexity can be very efficient when used during search. The other algorithms are simple modifications of maxRPC3^{rm}. All algorithms have $O(ed)$ space complexity when used stand-alone. However, maxRPC3 has $O(end)$ space complexity when used during search, while the others retain the $O(ed)$ complexity. Experimental results demonstrate that the resulting methods constantly outperform previous algorithms for maxRPC, often by large margins, and constitute a viable alternative to arc consistency on some problem classes.

4.1 Introduction

Max Restricted Path Consistency (maxRPC) is a strong domain filtering consistency for binary constraints introduced in 1997 by Debruyne and Bessiere [29]. maxRPC achieves a stronger level of local consistency than arc consistency (AC), and in [31] it was identified, along with singleton AC (SAC), as a promising alternative to AC. Although SAC has received considerable attention since, maxRPC has been comparatively overlooked. Fewer new algorithms have been proposed and their experimental evaluation has been very limited. In this chapter we propose new algorithms for maxRPC and evaluate them empirically on a wide range of problems.

The basic idea of maxRPC is to delete any value a of a variable x that has no arc consistency (AC) or path consistency (PC) support in a variable y that is constrained with x. A value b is an AC support for a if the two values are compatible, and it is also a PC support for a if this pair of values is path consistent. A pair of values (a, b) is path consistent iff for every third variable there exists at least one value, called a PC witness, that is compatible with both a and b.

In Section 3.1 we have discribed various maxRPC algorithms, focusing on their operations and structures. Briefly, the first algorithm for maxRPC was proposed in [29] while two more algorithms have been proposed since then [47, 106]. The algorithms of [29] and [106] have been evaluated on random problems only, while the algorithm of [47] has not been experimentally evaluated at all. Despite achieving stronger pruning than AC, existing maxRPC algorithms suffer from overhead and redundancies as they can repeatedly perform many constraint checks without triggering any value deletions. These constraint checks occur when a maxRPC algorithm searches for an AC support for a value and when, having located one, it checks if it is also a PC support by looking for PC witnesses in other variables. As a result, the use of maxRPC during search often slows down the search process considerably compared to AC, despite the savings in search tree size.

In this chapter we propose techniques to improve the applicability of maxRPC by eliminating some of these redundancies while keeping a low space complexity. We also investigate approximations of maxRPC that only make slightly fewer value deletions in practice, while being significantly faster. We first demonstrate that we can avoid many redundant constraint checks and speed up the search for AC and PC supports through the careful and combined application of two data structures already used by maxRPC and AC algorithms [47, 106, 18, 68, 77]. Based on this, we propose a coarse-grained maxRPC algorithm called maxRPC3 with optimal $O(end^3)$ time complexity. This algorithm displays good performance when used stand-alone (e.g. for preprocessing), but is expensive to apply during search. We then propose another maxRPC algorithm, called maxRPC3^{rm}. This algorithm has $O(en^2d^4)$ time complexity, but a restricted version with $O(end^4)$ complexity can be very efficient when used during search through the use of *residues*. Both algorithms have $O(ed)$ space complexity when used stand-alone. However, maxRPC3 has $O(end)$ space complexity when used during search, while maxRPC3^{rm} retains the $O(ed)$ complexity.

We further investigate the use of residues to improve the performance of maxRPC filtering during search. To be precise, we adapt ideas from [77] to obtain two variants of the maxRPC3^{rm} algorithm. The first one achieves a better time complexity but is inferior to maxRPC3^{rm} in practice, while the second one exploits in a simple way information obtained in the initialization phase of maxRPC3^{rm} to achieve competitive performance.

Similar algorithmic improvements can be applied to *light maxRPC* (lmaxRPC), an approximation of maxRPC [106]. This achieves a lesser level of consistency compared to maxRPC, but still stronger than AC, and is more cost-effective when used during search. Experiments confirm that lmaxRPC is indeed a considerably better option than maxRPC when used throughout search. We also propose a number of heuristics that can be used to order the searches for PC supports and witnesses during the execution of a coarse-grained maxRPC algorithm, and in this way potentially save constraint checks.

Finally, we make a detailed experimental evaluation of new and existing algorithms on various problem classes. This is the first wide experimental study of algorithms for maxRPC and its approximations on benchmark non-random problems. We ran experiments with maxRPC algorithms under both a 2-way and a d-branching scheme. Results show that our methods constantly outperform existing algorithms, often by large margins, especially when 2-way branching is used. When applied during search our best method offers up to one order of magnitude reduction in constraint checks, while cpu times are improved up to three times compared to the best existing algorithm. In addition, these speed-ups enable a search algorithm that applies lmaxRPC to compete with or outperform MAC on some problems. Finally, we explore a simple hybrid propagation scheme where AC and maxRPC are interleaved under 2-way branching. Results demonstrate that instantiations of this scheme offer an efficient alternative to the application of a fixed propagation method (either AC or maxRPC) throughout search.

The remainder of this chapter is structured as follows. Section 2 reviews background information on CSPs and related work on maxRPC algorithms. Section 3 presents two new algorithms, maxRPC3, maxRPC3^{rm} and their corresponding approximations, and analyzes their complexities. Section 4 discusses the further exploitation of residues on two variations of the maxRPC3^{rm} algorithm. Section 5 discusses heuristics for (l)maxRPC algorithms, and Section 6 presents our experimental results on benchmark problems. Finally, Section 7 concludes and discusses possible directions for future work.

4.2   New Algorithms for maxRPC

We first recall the basic ideas of algorithms maxRPC2 and maxRPC^{rm} as described in [47] and [106]. Both algorithms use a propagation list Q where variables whose domain is pruned are added. Once a variable x_j is removed from Q all neighboring variables are revised to delete any values that are no longer maxRPC. For any value a_i of such a variable x_i there are three possible reasons for deletion:

- The first is when a_i no longer has an AC-support in $D(x_j)$.

- The second, which we call *PC-support loss* hereafter, is when the unique PC-support $a_j \in D(x_j)$ for a_i has been deleted.

- The third, which we call *PC-witness loss* hereafter, is when the unique PC-witness $a_j \in D(x_j)$ for the pair (a_i, a_k), where a_k is the unique PC-support for a_i on some variable x_k, has been deleted.

If any of the above cases occurs then value a_i is no longer maxRPC.

We now present the pseudocodes for the new maxRPC algorithms, maxRPC3 and maxRPC3^{rm}. Both algorithms utilize data structures *LastPC* and *LastAC* which have the following functionalities: For each constraint $c_{i,j}$ and each value $a_i \in D(x_i)$, $LastPC_{x_i,a_i,x_j}$ and $LastAC_{x_i,a_i,x_j}$ point to the most recently discovered PC and AC supports of a_i in $D(x_j)$ respectively. Initially, all *LastPC* and *LastAC* pointers are set to a special value $\perp$, considered to precede all values in any domain. As will be explained, algorithm maxRPC3 updates the *LastPC* and *LastAC* structures incrementally like maxRPC2 and AC2001/3.1 respectively do. In contrast, algorithm maxRPC3^{rm} uses these structures as residues like maxRPC^{rm} and AC3^{rm} do.

4.2.1   maxRPC3

The main part of maxRPC3 is described in Algorithm 1. Since maxRPC3 is coarse-grained, it uses a propagation list Q (typically implemented as a queue) where variables that have their domain filtered are inserted. This may happen during initialization (explained below) or when PC-support or PC-witness loss is detected. When a variable x_j is removed from Q, at line 4, each variable x_i constrained with x_j must be checked for possible AC-support, PC-support or PC-witness loss. We now discuss the overall function of the algorithm before moving on to explain it in detail.

For each value $a_i \in D(x_i)$, Algorithm 1 first checks whether a_i has suffered AC-support or PC-support loss in $D(x_j)$ by calling function *checkPCsupLoss*, provided that $LastPC_{x_i,a_i,x_j}$ is not valid anymore (line 7). This function, which will be explained in detail below, returns *false* if no new PC-support exists for a_i in $D(x_j)$ and as a result a_i is deleted (line 8). If a_i is not deleted, either because $LastPC_{x_i,a_i,x_j}$ is still valid or because a new PC-support for a_i has been found in $D(x_j)$, then possible PC-witness loss is examined by calling function *checkPCwitLoss* (line 11). If this function returns *false*, then a_i is deleted (line 12). If a value is deleted from $D(x_i)$ then x_i is inserted to Q (lines 9 and 13). After deleting values from the domain of a variable, the algorithm checks whether the domain is empty (line 14). If so, the algorithm returns FAILURE.

An important remark about Algorithm 1 is the following. Assuming a value a_i has been examined in lines 6-13 and has not been deleted, then this does not necessarily mean that a_i is maxRPC. Indeed there is the possibility that $LastPC_{x_i,a_i,x_j}$ is valid but the last PC-witness of the pair $(a_i, LastPC_{x_i,a_i,x_j})$ in some variable x_k has been deleted. Hence, if $LastPC_{x_i,a_i,x_j}$ is the last PC-support of a_i in $D(x_j)$ then a_i is not maxRPC. Such a situation will be identified at some point during the execution of the algorithm once x_k is removed from Q and its neighboring variables are examined. This guarantees the algorithm's completeness as will be further explained in Section 3.4.

Algorithm 1 maxRPC3

1: **if** ¬ initialization(Q, LastPC, LastAC) **then**
2:    return FAILURE;
3: **while** Q ≠ ∅ **do**
4:    Q ← Q−$\{x_j\}$;
5:    **for each** $x_i \in X$ s.t. $c_{i,j} \in C$ **do**
6:      **for each** $a_i \in D(x_i)$ **do**
7:        **if** LastPC$_{x_i,a_i,x_j} \notin D(x_j)$ AND ¬ checkPCsupLoss(x_i, a_i, x_j) **then**
8:          remove a_i;
9:          Q ← Q ∪ $\{x_i\}$;
10:        **else**
11:          **if** ¬ checkPCwitLoss(x_i, a_i, x_j) **then**
12:            remove a_i;
13:            Q ← Q ∪ $\{x_i\}$;
14:      **if** D(x_i) = ∅ **then**
15:        return FAILURE;
16: **return** SUCCESS;

The initialization step of `maxRPC3` (Fun. 2) is a brute-force function, where each value a_i of each variable x_i is checed for being maxRPC. This is done by iterating through the variables constrained with x_i and looking for a PC-support for a_i in their domains. For each such variable x_j and value $a_j \in D(x_j)$, we first check if the pair (a_i, a_j) is arc consistent by calling function *isConsistent* at line 6. *isConsistent* returns *true* if (a_i, a_j) satisfies the constraint, meaning that a_j AC-supports a_i. In this case $LastAC_{x_i,a_i,x_j}$ is set to a_j (line 7). If a_j is verified as an AC-support of a_i, we examine if it is also a PC-support by calling function *searchPCwit*. If *searchPCwit* returns *true* (detailed analysis follows below), then $LastPC_{x_i,a_i,x_j}$ is set to a_j (line 10), since a_j is the most recently found PC-support for a_i. Line 11 will be explained below when algorithm `maxRPC3`^{rm} is presented. Then, the next variable constrained with x_i will be considered, and so on.

If there is no AC-support in $D(x_j)$ for a_i or none of the AC-supports is a PC-support, then a_i will be removed at line 14 and x_i will be added to queue Q. Eventually, a_i is established to be maxRPC when a PC-support is found in each $D(x_j)$, where x_j has a constraint with x_i. Finally, if function *initialization* causes an empty domain (line 17), then `maxRPC3` returs FAILURE in line 2 of Algorithm 1. Note that *initilization* is called only when `maxRPC3` is used stand-alone (e.g. for preprocessing) and not during search, as in this case Q is initialized with the variable of the latest

---

Function 2 initialization(Q, $LastPC$, $LastAC$):**boolean**

1: **for each** $x_i \in X$ **do**
2:   **for each** $a_i \in D(x_i)$ **do**
3:     **for each** $x_j \in X$ s.t. $c_{i,j} \in C$ **do**
4:       maxRPCsupport $\leftarrow$ FALSE;
5:       **for each** $a_j \in D(x_j)$ **do**
6:         **if** isConsistent(a_i, a_j) **then**
7:           $LastAC_{x_i,a_i,x_j} \leftarrow a_j$;
8:           **if** searchPCwit(x_i, a_i, x_j, a_j) **then**
9:             maxRPCsupport $\leftarrow$ TRUE;
10:             $LastPC_{x_i,a_i,x_j} \leftarrow a_j$;
11:             **if** (rm) **then** $LastPC_{x_j,a_j,x_i} \leftarrow a_i$;
12:             **break**;
13:       **if** $\neg$ maxRPCsupport **then**
14:         remove a_i;
15:         Q $\leftarrow$ Q $\cup$ $\{x_i\}$;
16:         **break**;
17:   **if** $D(x_i) = \emptyset$ **then**
18:     return FALSE;
19: return TRUE;

---

decision.

    Assuming the initialization phase succeeded, the propagation list Q will include those variables that have their domain filtered. The main part of `maxRPC3` (Alg. 1) starts when a variable x_j is extracted from Q (line 4) in order to determine whether a neighbouring variable (x_i) has suffered PC-support or PC-witness loss due to the filtering of the extracted variable's domain. These checks are implemented by calling functions *checkPCsupLoss* and *checkPCwitLoss*, at lines 7 and 11 of Algorithm 1, for each value $a_i \in D(x_i)$. If value $LastPC_{x_i,a_i,x_j}$ is still in $D(x_j)$ line 7, then a *possible* PC-support has been immediately located (the PC-support will be established later as explained in the remark about the algorithm given above) and *checkPCsupLoss* is not called. In the opposite case where $LastPC_{x_i,a_i,x_j}$ is not valid, *checkPCsupLoss* is called to search for a new PC-support in $D(x_j)$.

Checking for PC-support loss

Function *checkPCsupLoss* (Fun. 3) takes advantage of the $LastPC$ and $LastAC$ pointers to avoid starting the search for PC-support from scratch. Specifically, we know that no PC-support can exist before $LastPC_{x_i,a_i,x_j}$, and also none can exist before $LastAC_{x_i,a_i,x_j}$, since all values before $LastAC_{x_i,a_i,x_j}$ are not AC-supports of a_i. Lines 1-4 in *checkPCsupLoss* take advantage of these to locate the appropriate starting value b_j. Note that `maxRPC2` always starts the search for a PC-support from the value after $LastPC_{x_i,a_i,x_j}$ and thus may perform redundant constraint checks.

    For every value $a_j \in D(x_j)$, starting with b_j, we first check if it is an AC-support of a_i by calling function *isConsistent* (line 6). If it is, then we can update $LastAC_{x_i,a_i,x_j}$ under a certain condition (lines 7-8). Specifically, if $LastAC_{x_i,a_i,x_j}$ was deleted from $D(x_j)$, then we can set $LastAC_{x_i,a_i,x_j}$ to a_j in case $LastAC_{x_i,a_i,x_j} > LastPC_{x_i,a_i,x_j}$. If $LastAC_{x_i,a_i,x_j} \leq LastPC_{x_i,a_i,x_j}$ then we cannot do this update, as there may be AC-supports for a_i between

---

Function 3 checkPCsupLoss(x_i, a_i, x_j):**boolean**

1: **if** $LastAC_{x_i,a_i,x_j} \in D(x_j)$ **then**
2:     $b_j \leftarrow \max(LastPC_{x_i,a_i,x_j}+1, LastAC_{x_i,a_i,x_j})$;
3: **else**
4:     $b_j \leftarrow \max(LastPC_{x_i,a_i,x_j}+1, LastAC_{x_i,a_i,x_j} + 1)$;
5: **for each** $a_j \in D(x_j), a_j \geq b_j$ **do**
6:     **if** isConsistent(a_i, a_j) **then**
7:         **if** $LastAC_{x_i,a_i,x_j} \notin D(x_j)$ AND $LastAC_{x_i,a_i,x_j} > LastPC_{x_i,a_i,x_j}$ **then**
8:             $LastAC_{x_i,a_i,x_j} \leftarrow a_j$;
9:         **if** searchPCwit(x_i, a_i, x_j, a_j) **then**
10:             $LastPC_{x_i,a_i,x_j} \leftarrow a_j$;
11:             return TRUE;
12: return FALSE;

$LastAC_{x_i,a_i,x_j}$ and $LastPC_{x_i,a_i,x_j}$ in the lexicographical ordering. We then move on to verify the path consistency of (a_i, a_j) through function *searchPCwit* (line 9). If no PC-support for a_i is found in $D(x_j)$, *checkPCsupLoss* will return *false*, a_i will be deleted and x_i will be added to Q in Algorithm 1. Otherwise, $LastPC_{x_i,a_i,x_j}$ is set to the discovered PC-support a_j (line 10).

Function 4 searchPCwit(x_i, a_i, x_j, a_j):**boolean**

1: **for each** $x_k \in X$ s.t. $c_{i,k}$ and $c_{j,k} \in C$ **do**
2:     maxRPCsupport $\leftarrow$ FALSE;
3:     **if** $((LastAC_{x_i,a_i,x_k} \in D(x_k))$ AND $(LastAC_{x_i,a_i,x_k}=LastAC_{x_j,a_j,x_k}))$ OR $((LastAC_{x_i,a_i,x_k} \in D(x_k))$ AND $(isConsistent(LastAC_{x_i,a_i,x_k}, a_j)))$ OR $((LastAC_{x_j,a_j,x_k} \in D(x_k))$ AND $(isConsistent(LastAC_{x_j,a_j,x_k}, a_i)))$ **then**
4:         **continue**;
5:     **if** $\neg$searchACsup(x_i, a_i, x_k) OR $\neg$searchACsup(x_j, a_j, x_k) **then**
6:         return FALSE;
7:     **for each** $a_k \in D(x_k), a_k \geq \max(LastAC_{x_i,a_i,x_k}, LastAC_{x_j,a_j,x_k})$ **do**
8:         **if** isConsistent(a_i, a_k) AND isConsistent(a_j, a_k) **then**
9:             maxRPCsupport $\leftarrow$ TRUE;
10:             **break**;
11:     **if** $\neg$ maxRPCsupport **then**
12:         return FALSE;
13: return TRUE;

Function *searchPCwit* (Fun. 4) checks if a pair of values (a_i, a_j) is PC by doing the following for each variable x_k constrained with x_i and x_j[2]. First, taking advantage of the $LastAC$ pointers, it makes a quick check in constant time which, if successful, can save searching in the domain of x_k. To be precise, it checks if $LastAC_{x_i,a_i,x_k}$ is valid and $LastAC_{x_i,a_i,x_k}$ equals $LastAC_{x_j,a_j,x_k}$, or if $LastAC_{x_i,a_i,x_k}$ is valid and consistent with a_j or if $LastAC_{x_j,a_j,x_k}$ is valid and consistent with a_i (line 3). The first part of the disjunction is of practical importance only, since if it is true, then the second part will necessarily also be true and the condition will be verified. However, including the

---

[2]Since AC is enforced by the maxRPC algorithm, we only need to consider variables that form a 3-clique with x_i and x_j [37].

first part of the condition saves constraint checks, and this reflects on run times in certain problems.

If one of these conditions holds then we have found a PC-witness for (a_i, a_j) without searching in $D(x_k)$ and we move on to the next variable constrained with x_i and x_j. Note that neither `maxRPC2` nor `maxRPC`^{rm} can do this check as they do not have the $LastAC$ structure. In contrast, algorithm `maxRPCEn1` is able to do such reasoning. Experimental results in Section 4.5 demonstrate that these simple conditions of line 3 can eliminate a very large number of redundant constraint checks.

Function 5 searchACsup(x_i, a_i, x_j):**boolean**

1:   **if** $LastAC_{x_i,a_i,x_j} \in D(x_j)$ **then**
2:     return TRUE;
3:   **else**
4:     **for each** $a_j \in D(x_j), a_j > LastAC_{x_i,a_i,x_j}$ **do**
5:       **if** isConsistent(a_i, a_j) **then**
6:         $LastAC_{x_i,a_i,x_j} \leftarrow a_j$;
7:         return TRUE;
8: return FALSE;

If none of the conditions in line 3 of Fun. 4 holds, searching for a new PC-witness in $D(x_k)$ is necessary. This is done by first calling function *searchACsup* (Fun. 5), first with (a_i, x_k) and then with (a_j, x_k) as parameters. This function locates the lexicographically smallest AC-supports for a_i and a_j in $D(x_k)$. More precisely, *searchACsup* checks if the current $LastAC$ value exists in the corresponding domain (line 1 of Fun. 5), and if not it searches for a new AC-support after that (line 4). If it finds one, it updates $LastAC$ accordingly (line 6). Then, going back to *searchPCwit*, the search for a PC-witness starts from $b_k = max\{LastAC_{x_i,a_i,x_k}, LastAC_{x_j,a_j,x_k}\}$ (line 7), exploiting the $LastAC$ structure to save redundant checks (a similar operation is performed by `maxRPCEn1`). This search looks for a value of x_k that is compatible with both a_i and a_j (line 8). If no AC-support is found for either a_i or a_j (in which cases *searchACsup* returns *false*) or no PC-witness is located, then subsequently *searchPCwit* will also return *false*.

Checking for PC-witness loss

In `maxRPC3`, if value a_i is not removed after checking for possible PC-support loss using *checkPCsupLoss*, function *checkPCwitLoss* (Fun. 6) is called to check for PC-witness loss. This is done by iterating over the variables that are constrained with both x_i and x_j. For each such variable x_k, we first check if $a_k = LastPC_{x_i,a_i,x_k}$ is still in $D(x_k)$ (line 3). If so then we verify if there is still a PC-witness in $D(x_j)$. As in function *searchPCwit*, taking advantage of the $LastAC$ pointers, we first make a quick check in constant time which, if successful, can save searching in the domain of x_j. That is, we check if $LastAC_{x_i,a_i,x_j}$ is valid and $LastAC_{x_i,a_i,x_j}$ equals $LastAC_{x_k,a_k,x_j}$ or if $LastAC_{x_i,a_i,x_j}$ is valid and consistent with a_k or if $LastAC_{x_k,a_k,x_j}$ is valid and consistent with a_i (line 4). If none of these conditions holds then we search for a PC-witness starting from $b_j = max\{LastAC_{x_i,a_i,x_j}, LastAC_{x_k,a_k,x_j}\}$ (line 8), after checking the existence of AC-supports for a_i and a_k in $D(x_j)$, by calling *searchACsup* (line 7). Right here the procedure is quite similar to *searchPCwit*. If there is no AC-support in $D(x_j)$ for either a_i or a_k we avoid searching for a PC-witness in $D(x_j)$ and move on to seek a new PC-support for a_i in $D(x_k)$. Note that `maxRPC2` does not do the check of line 4 and always starts the search for a PC-witness from the first value in $D(x_j)$.

Function 6 checkPCwitLoss(x_i, a_i, x_j):**boolean**

1: **for each** $x_k \in X$ s.t. $c_{i,k}$ and $c_{k,j} \in C$ **do**
2:     witness $\leftarrow$ FALSE;
3:     **if** $a_k \leftarrow LastPC_{x_i,a_i,x_k} \in D(x_k)$ **then**
4:         **if** $((LastAC_{x_i,a_i,x_j} \in D(x_j))$ AND $(LastAC_{x_i,a_i,x_j}{=}LastAC_{x_k,a_k,x_j}))$ OR
        $((LastAC_{x_i,a_i,x_j} \in D(x_j))$ AND $(isConsistent\ (LastAC_{x_i,a_i,x_j}, a_k)))$ OR
        $((LastAC_{x_k,a_k,x_j} \in D(x_j))$ AND $(isConsistent(LastAC_{x_k,a_k,x_j}, a_i)))$ **then**
5:           witness $\leftarrow$ TRUE;
6:         **else**
7:           **if** searchACsup(x_i, a_i, x_j) AND searchACsup(x_k, a_k, x_j) **then**
8:             **for each** $a_j \in D(x_j), a_j \geq \max(LastAC_{x_i,a_i,x_j}, LastAC_{x_k,a_k,x_j})$ **do**
9:               **if** isConsistent(a_i, a_j) AND isConsistent(a_k, a_j) **then**
10:               witness $\leftarrow$ TRUE;
11:               **break**;
12:     **if** $\neg$ witness AND $\neg$ checkPCsupLoss(x_i, a_i, x_k) **then**
13:         return FALSE;
14: return TRUE;

If $LastPC_{x_i,a_i,x_k}$ has been removed or the pair (a_i, a_k) has no PC-witness in $D(x_j)$, we search for a new PC-support for a_i in $D(x_k)$ in line 12 by calling function *checkPCsupLoss*. Search starts at an appropriate value calculated taking advantage of $LastPC_{x_i,a_i,x_k}$ and $LastAC_{x_i,a_i,x_k}$ (lines 1-4 in Fun. 3). The procedure was explained above when describing *checkPCsupLoss*. If the search for a PC-support fails for any third variable x_k then *false* will be returned, and in the main algorithm a_i will be deleted and x_i will be added to Q.

maxRPC3 terminates when Q becomes empty, meaning that all values are maxRPC, or, when a domain of some variable becomes empty, meaning that the problem is not consistent.

As observed above, when maxRPC3 is applied during search, the propagation list Q is initialized with the variable at the current decision (assignment or value removal). If propagating a decision results in an empty domain, then both the $LastAC$ and $LastPC$ data structures must be restored to their state prior to the decision.

4.2.2 maxRPC3^{rm}

maxRPC3^{rm} is a coarse-grained maxRPC algorithm that exploits backtrack-stable data structures inspired from AC3^{rm} (rm stands for multidirectional residues). $LastAC$ and $LastPC$ are not maintained incrementally as in maxRPC3, but are only used to store residues. As explained, a residue is a support which has been located and stored during the execution of the procedure that proves that a given value is AC or PC. The algorithm stores the most recently discovered AC (resp. PC) supports, but does not guarantee that any lexicographically smaller value is not an AC (resp. PC) support. Consequently, when we search for a new AC or PC support in a domain, we always start from scratch. $LastAC$ and $LastPC$ need not be restored after a failure; they can remain unchanged, hence a minimal overhead on the management of data.

Another difference with maxRPC3 is that since maxRPC3^{rm} handles $LastPC$ only as a residue, it can exploit the bidirectionality of support. This means that when a PC-support $a_j \in D(x_j)$ is located for a value $a_i \in D(x_i)$ then a_i is a PC-support for a_j. As a result, we can assign $LastPC_{x_i,a_i,x_j}$ and $LastPC_{x_j,a_j,x_i}$ to a_j and to a_i respectively. Although the property of bidirectionality obviously also holds for AC-supports, we do not exploit this since experiments demonstrated that it does not offer any benefits in most cases. Moreover, $LastAC$ is updated when a PC-support is found, since it is also the most recent AC-support found. This assignment may speed up subsequent searches for PC-witness as the conditions in line 3 of $searchPCwit^{rm}$ and line 4 of $checkPCwitLoss^{rm}$ are more likely to be *true*.

Function 7 checkPCsupLoss$^{rm}(x_i, a_i, x_j)$:**boolean**

1: **for each** $a_j \in D(x_j)$ **do**
2:     **if** isConsistent(a_i, a_j) **then**
3:         **if** searchPCwit$^{rm}(x_i, a_i, x_j, a_j)$ **then**
4:             $LastPC_{x_i,a_i,x_j} \leftarrow LastAC_{x_i,a_i,x_j} \leftarrow a_j$;
5:             $LastPC_{x_j,a_j,x_i} \leftarrow a_i$;
6:             return TRUE;
7: return FALSE;

We omit presenting the main algorithm for maxRPC3^{rm} as it is the same as Algorithm 1 with the only difference being that we call $checkPCsupLoss^{rm}$ and $checkPCwitLoss^{rm}$ instead of $checkPCsupLoss$ and $checkPCwitLoss$ respectively. When maxRPC3^{rm} is used for preprocessing, the *initialization* function (Fun.2) is called to initialize Q and structures $LastAC$ and $LastPC$. The difference with maxRPC3 concerns the bidirectionality of PC-supports. If the auxilary boolean variable rm is *true*, denoting the use of maxRPC3^{rm} instead of maxRPC3, we initialize the $LastPC$ residue exploiting bidirectionality. To be precise, when a PC-support is found for a_i in $D(x_j)$ we set $LastPC_{x_i,a_i,x_j}$ to a_j and additionally $LastPC_{x_j,a_j,x_i}$ to a_i (line 11 of Fun. 2).

When a variable is extracted from Q, we first explore the case of PC-support loss by calling function $checkPCsupLoss^{rm}$, after verifying that value $LastPC_{x_i,a_i,x_j}$ is not in $D(x_j)$ anymore. $checkPCsupLoss^{rm}$ (Fun. 7) searches for a new PC-support starting from scratch (line 1). In contrast, maxRPC3 would start from $b_j = max(LastPC(x_i, a_i, x_j), LastAC(x_i, a_i, x_j))$ and maxRPC2 from the value after $LastPC_{x_i,a_i,x_j}$. When an AC-support a_j is confirmed from *isConsistent* in line 2, function $searchPCwit^{rm}$ is called to determine if a_j is also a PC-support for a_i. If $searchPCwit^{rm}$ returns *true*, we assign $LastPC_{x_i,a_i,x_j}$ and $LastPC_{x_j,a_j,x_i}$ to a_j and to a_i respectively to exploit bidirectionality, and $LastAC_{x_i,a_i,x_j}$ is set to a_j (lines 4-5), since the discovered PC-support is also an AC-support.

Function $searchPCwit^{rm}$ (Fun. 8) checks if a pair of values (a_i, a_j) is PC by iterating over the variables x_k constrained with x_i and x_j. First, it checks the same conditions in line 3 as *searchPCwit* to locate, if possible, a PC-witness without searching. If none of these conditions holds, it searches for a new PC-support starting from the first value in $D(x_k)$ (line 5). If a PC-witness a_k is found (line 7) then both residues, $LastAC_{x_i,a_i,x_k}$ and $LastAC_{x_j,a_j,x_k}$, are set to a_k as they are the most recently discovered AC-supports (line 8). If no PC-witness is found we have determined that the pair (a_i, a_j) is not PC and as a result *false* will be returned and $checkPCsupLoss^{rm}$ will move to check if the next available value in $D(x_j)$ is a PC-support for a_i.

In maxRPC3^{rm}, if value a_i is not removed after checking for possible PC-support loss using $checkPCsupLoss^{rm}$, function $checkPCwitLoss^{rm}$ (Fun. 9) is called to check for PC-witness loss. This is done by iterating again, over the variables that are constrained with both x_i and x_j. For each such variable x_k, we first check if $a_k = LastPC_{x_i,a_i,x_k}$ remains in $D(x_k)$ (line 3) and if so, if any of the three conditions in line 4 is satisfied in order to avoid searching. In case each of these conditions fails, we search for a new PC-witness in $D(x_j)$ starting from the first value (line 7). For

---

Function 8 searchPCwit$^{rm}(x_i, a_i, x_j, a_j)$:**boolean**

1: **for each** $x_k \in X$ s.t. $c_{i,k}$ and $c_{j,k} \in C$ **do**
2:   maxRPCsupport $\leftarrow$ FALSE;
3:   **if** $((LastAC_{x_i,a_i,x_k} \in D(x_k))$ AND $(LastAC_{x_i,a_i,x_k} = LastAC_{x_j,a_j,x_k}))$ OR $((LastAC_{x_i,a_i,x_k} \in D(x_k))$ AND $(isConsistent(LastAC_{x_i,a_i,x_k}, a_j)))$ OR $((LastAC_{x_j,a_j,x_k} \in D(x_k))$ AND $(isConsistent(LastAC_{x_j,a_j,x_k}, a_i)))$ **then**
4:     **continue**;
5:   **for each** $a_k \in D(x_k)$ **do**
6:     **if** isConsistent(a_i, a_k) AND isConsistent(a_j, a_k) **then**
7:       maxRPCsupport $\leftarrow$ TRUE;
8:       $LastAC_{x_i,a_i,x_k} \leftarrow LastAC_{x_j,a_j,x_k} \leftarrow a_k$;
9:       **break**;
10:   **if** $\neg$ maxRPCsupport **then**
11:     return FALSE;
12: return TRUE;

Function 9 checkPCwitLoss$^{rm}(x_i, a_i, x_j)$:**boolean**

1: **for each** $x_k \in X$ s.t. $c_{i,k}$ and $c_{k,j} \in C$ **do**
2:   witness $\leftarrow$ FALSE;
3:   **if** $a_k \leftarrow LastPC_{x_i,a_i,x_k} \in D(x_k)$ **then**
4:     **if** $((LastAC_{x_i,a_i,x_j} \in D(x_j))$ AND $(LastAC_{x_i,a_i,x_j} = LastAC_{x_k,a_k,x_j}))$ OR $((LastAC_{x_i,a_i,x_j} \in D(x_j))$ AND $(isConsistent(LastAC_{x_i,a_i,x_j}, a_k)))$ OR $((LastAC_{x_k,a_k,x_j} \in D(x_j))$ AND $(isConsistent(LastAC_{x_k,a_k,x_j}, a_i)))$ **then**
5:       witness $\leftarrow$ TRUE;
6:     **else**
7:       **for each** $a_j \in D(x_j)$ **do**
8:         **if** isConsistent(a_i, a_j) AND isConsistent(a_k, a_j) **then**
9:           $LastAC(x_i, a_i, x_j) \leftarrow LastAC(x_k, a_k, x_j) \leftarrow a_j$;
10:           witness $\leftarrow$ TRUE;
11:           **break**;
12:   **if** $\neg$ witness AND $\neg$ checkPCsupLoss$^{rm}(x_i, a_i, x_k)$ **then**
13:     return FALSE;
14: return TRUE;

---

each value $a_j \in D(x_j)$, *checkPCwitLoss^{rm}* checks if it is compatible with a_i and a_k and moves the *LastAC* pointers accordingly (line 9), exploiting the bidirectionality of residues.

If $LastPC_{x_i,a_i,x_k}$ is not valid or the pair (a_i, a_k) fails to find a PC-witness in $D(x_j)$, we search for a new PC-support for a_i in $D(x_k)$ in line 12, by calling *checkPCsupLoss^{rm}*. If the search for a PC-support fails then *false* will be returned (line 13), a_i will be deleted, and x_i will be added to Q in the main algorithm.

4.2.3　Light maxRPC

Light maxRPC (lmaxRPC) is an approximation of maxRPC that only propagates the loss of AC-supports and not the loss of PC-witnesses [106]. That is, when removing a variable x_j from Q, for each $a_i \in D(x_i)$, where x_i is constrained with x_j, lmaxRPC only checks if there is a PC-support of a_i in $D(x_j)$. This ensures that the obtained algorithm enforces a consistency property that is at least as strong as AC.

lmaxRPC is a procedurally defined local consistency, meaning that its description is tied to a specific maxRPC algorithm. Hence when applying this consistency a fixed point is dependent on the particularities of the specific algorithm used, like the order in which the algorithm processes revisions of variables/constraints, and the order in which values are processed and supports as seeked. Light versions of algorithms maxRPC3 and maxRPC3^{rm}, simply noted lmaxRPC3 and lmaxRPC3^{rm} respectively, can be obtained by omitting the call to the *checkPCwitLoss* (resp. *checkPCwitLoss^{rm}*) function (lines 10-13 of Algorithm 1). In a similar way, we can obtain light versions of algorithms maxRPC2 and maxRPC^{rm}.

As already noted in [106], the light versions of different maxRPC algorithms may not be equivalent in terms of the pruning they achieve. To give an example, a brute-force algorithm for lmaxRPC that does not use any of the data structures described here can achieve more pruning than algorithms lmaxRPC2, lmaxRPC3, lmaxRPC^{rm}, and lmaxRPC3^{rm}, albeit being much slower in practice. This is because when looking for a PC-support for a value $a_i \in D(x_i)$ in a variable x_j, the brute-force algorithm will always search in $D(x_j)$ from scratch. In contrast, consider that any of the four more sophisticated algorithms will return *true* in case $LastPC_{x_i,a_i,x_j}$ is valid. However, although $a_j = LastPC_{x_i,a_i,x_j}$ is valid, it may no longer be a PC-support because the PC-witness for the pair (a_i, a_j) in some third variable may have been deleted, and it may be the last one. In a case where a_j was the last PC-support in x_j for value a_i, the four advanced algorithms will not delete a_i while the brute-force one will. This is because it will exhaustively check all values of x_j for PC-support, concluding that there is none.

The worst-case time and space complexities of algorithm lmaxRPC2 are the same as maxRPC2 . Algorithm lmaxRPC^{rm} has $O(end^4)$ time and $O(ed)$ space complexities, which are lower than those of maxRPC^{rm}. Experiments with random problems using algorithms lmaxRPC^{rm} and maxRPC^{rm} showed that the pruning power of lmaxRPC is only slightly weaker than that of maxRPC [106]. At the same time, it can offer significant gains in run times when used during search. These results were also verified by us through a series of experiments on various problem classes.

4.2.4　Correctness and Complexities

We now prove the correctness of algorithms maxRPC3 and maxRPC3^{rm} and analyze their worst-case time and space complexities.

Proposition 1 Algorithm `maxRPC3` is sound and complete.

Proof: *Soundness.* To prove the soundness of `maxRPC3` we must prove that any value that is deleted by `maxRPC3` is not maxRPC. Let $a_i \in D(x_i)$ be a value that is deleted by `maxRPC3`. It is either removed from $D(x_i)$ during the initialization phase (line 14 Fun. 2) or in line 8 of Algorithm 1, after *checkPCsupLoss* has returned *false*, or in line 12, after *checkPCsupLoss* has returned *true* and *checkPCwitLoss* has returned *false*.

In the first case, since function *initilization* checks all values in a brute-force manner, it is clear that any deleted value a_i either has no AC-support or none of its AC-supports is a PC-support in some variable x_j. The non-existence of a PC-support is determined using function *searchPCwit* whose correctness is discussed below.

In the second case, since *checkPCsupLoss* returns *false*, as long as $LastPC_{x_i,a_i,x_j}$ is not valid in Alg. 1, a new PC-support in $D(x_j)$ is sought (lines 5-11 in Fun. 3). This search starts with the value at $\max(LastPC_{x_i,a_i,x_j}+1, LastAC_{x_i,a_i,x_j})$ or at $\max(LastPC_{x_i,a_i,x_j}+1, LastAC_{x_i,a_i,x_j}+1)$, depending on whether $LastAC_{x_i,a_i,x_j}$ is valid or not. This is correct since any value before $LastPC_{x_i,a_i,x_j}+1$ and any value before $LastAC_{x_i,a_i,x_j}$ is definitely not an AC-support for a_i (similarly for the other case). *checkPCsupLoss* will return false either because no AC-support for a_i can be found in $D(x_j)$, or because for any AC-support found, *searchPCwit* returned false. In the former case there is no PC-support for a_i in $D(x_j)$ since there is no AC-support. In the latter case, for any AC-support a_j found there must be some third variable x_k for which no PC-witness for the pair (a_i, a_j) exists. For each third variable x_k *searchPCwit* correctly identifies a PC-witness if one of the conditions in line 3 holds. In none holds then *searchPCwit* searches for a PC-witness starting from $\max(LastAC_{x_i,a_i,x_k}, LastAC_{x_j,a_j,x_k})$. This is correct since $LastAC_{x_i,a_i,x_k}$ and $LastAC_{x_j,a_j,x_k}$ are updated with the lexicographically smallest support of a_i (resp. a_j) in $D(x_k)$ by calling function *searchACsup*, meaning that any value smaller than $\max(LastAC_{x_i,a_i,x_k}, LastAC_{x_j,a_j,x_k})$ is incompatible with either a_i or a_j. Therefore, if *searchPCwit* returns *false* then there is no PC-witness for some third variable x_k. Hence, if *checkPCsupLoss* returns *false*, it means no PC-support for a_i can be found in $D(x_j)$ and it is thus correctly deleted.

Now assume that $LastPC_{x_i,a_i,x_j}$ is valid in Algorithm 1 and a_i was removed after *checkPCwitLoss* returned *false*. This means that for some variable x_k, constrained with both x_i and x_j, both the first part (lines 3-11) and the second part (line 12) in Fun. 6 of *checkPCwitLoss* failed to set the boolean *witness* to *true*. Regarding the first part, the failure means that the pair of values (a_i, a_k), where a_k is the last PC-support of a_i in $D(x_k)$ found, has no PC-witness in $D(x_j)$. In more detail, the search for a PC-witness correctly starts from $\max(LastAC_{x_i,a_i,x_j}, LastAC_{x_j,a_j,x_j})$, after both $LastAC$ pointers have been updated by *searchACsup*. The condition in line 4 is similar to the corresponding condition in *searchPCwit* and thus, if it is true, the search for PC-witness is correctly overridden. Regarding the second part, the failure means that no alternative PC-support for a_i in $D(x_k)$ was found. In more detail when calling *checkPCsupLoss*(x_i, a_i, x_k), the search for a PC-support starts from $\max(LastPC_{x_i,a_i,x_k}+1, LastAC_{x_i,a_i,x_k})$ or $\max(LastPC_{x_i,a_i,x_k}+1, LastAC_{x_i,a_i,x_k}+1)$, depending on the existence of $LastAC_{x_i,a_i,x_k}$. This is correct since no earlier value can be a PC-support. If there is no consistent (a_i, a_k) pair or *searchPCwit* returns *false* for all consistent pairs found, then a_i has no PC-support in $D(x_k)$ and is thus correctly deleted.

Completeness. To prove the completeness of `maxRPC3` we need to show that if a value is not maxRPC then the algorithm will delete it. The initialization function checks all values of all variables one by one in a brute-force manner and removes any value that is not maxRPC. Values that are maxRPC have their $LastPC$ pointers set to the discovered PC-supports. Thereafter, the effects of such removals are propagated by calling Algorithm 1 and as a result new value deletions may occur. Now consider a value $a_i \in D(x_i)$ that was not removed by the initialization function but after propagation is no longer maxRPC. This is either because of PC-support or PC-witness loss.

In the first case assume that x_j is the variable in which a_i no longer has a PC-support. Since the previously found PC-support of a_i has been deleted, x_j must have been added to Q at some point. When x_j is removed from Q all neighboring variables, including x_i will be checked. Since $LastPC_{x_i,a_i,x_j}$ is no longer valid function *checkPCsupLoss* will be called to search for a new PC-support concluding that there is none. Therefore, it will return *false* and a_i will be deleted.

In the second case assume that the pair of values (a_i, a_j), where a_j is the last PC-support of a_i in $D(x_j)$, has lost its last PC-witness a_k in variable x_k. If $LastPC_{x_i,a_i,x_j}$ is not valid, which means that x_j was added to Q, then we have the same case as above. Therefore, after x_j is removed from Q, *checkPCsupLoss* will find out that there is no PC-support for a_i in $D(x_j)$ and will delete it. If $LastPC_{x_i,a_i,x_j}$ is valid then *checkPCsupLoss* will be omitted (line 7 of Alg. 1). Since a_k was deleted, x_k was added to Q at some point. When x_k is removed from Q all neighboring variables, including x_i will be checked. If a_i has no longer a PC-support in $D(x_k)$, this will be detected by *checkPCsupLoss* and a_i will be deleted. Otherwise, function *checkPCwitLoss* will be called. The for loop in line 1 will go through every variable constrained with both x_i and x_k, including x_j. Since $LastPC_{x_i,a_i,x_j}$ is valid, a new PC-witness for (a_i, a_j) in $D(x_k)$ will be sought (lines 3-11). Since a_k was the last PC-witness, none will be found and as a result a new PC-support for a_i in $D(x_j)$ will be sought (line 12). Since a_j was the last PC-support for a_i in $D(x_j)$, none will be found, *checkPCwitLoss* will return *false*, and a_i will be deleted. ∎

Proposition 2 Algorithm maxRPC3^{rm} is sound and complete.

Proof: The proof is very similar to the corresponding proof for maxRPC3. As explained, the main difference between the two algorithms concerns the use of the *LastAC* and *LastPC* structures. As maxRPC3^{rm} does not maintain these structures incrementally, the searches for PC-supports in *checkPCsupLoss^{rm}* and *checkPCwitLoss^{rm}* and the searches for PC-witnesses in *searchPCwit^{rm}* and *checkPCwitLoss^{rm}* start from scratch. Clearly, this has no effect on the soundness or completeness of the algorithm since it guarantees that all potential PC-supports and PC-witnesses are checked. Furthermore, the conditions for avoiding redundant searches using residues are the same as in maxRPC3. Finally, another difference between the two algorithms is the exploitation of bidirectionality by maxRPC3^{rm}. By the definition of path and arc consistency, bidirectionality holds. That is, when a PC-support (AC-support) $a_j \in D(x_j)$ is located for a value $a_i \in D(x_i)$ then a_i is a PC-support (AC-support) for a_j. Since the property of bidirectionality is exploited only to update residues, it does not affect the correctness of the algorithm. ∎

We now discuss the complexities of algorithms maxRPC3 and maxRPC3^{rm} and their light versions. To directly compare with existing algorithms for (l)maxRPC, the time complexities give the asymptotic number of constraint checks[3]. Folllowing [77], the *node* time (resp. space) complexity of a (l)maxRPC algorithm is the worst-case time (resp. space) complexity of invoking the algorithm after a decision has been made (e.g. a variable assignment or a value removal). The corresponding *branch* complexities of an (l)maxRPC algorithm are the worst-case complexities of any incremental sequence of $k \leq n$ invocations of the algorithm. That is, the complexities of incrementally running the algorithm down a branch of the search tree until a fail occurs.

Proposition 3 The node and branch time complexity of (l) maxRPC3 is O(end^3).

---

[3]However, constraint checks do not always reflect run times as other operations may have an equal or even greater effect.

Proof: The complexity is determined by the total number of calls to function *isConsistent* in *checkPCsupLoss*, *checkPCwitLoss*, and mainly *searchPCwit* where most checks are executed.

Each variable can be inserted and extracted from Q every time a value is deleted from its domain, giving $O(d)$ times in the worst case. Each time a variable x_j is extracted from Q, *check-PCsupLoss* will look for a PC-support in $D(x_j)$ for all values $a_i \in D(x_i)$, s.t. $c_{i,j} \in C$. For each variable x_i, $O(d)$ values are checked. Checking if a value $a_j \in D(x_j)$ is a PC-support involves first checking in $O(1)$ if it is an AC-support (line 6 in *checkPCsupLoss*) and then calling *search-PCwit* (line 9). The cost of *searchPCwit* is $O(n + nd)$ since there are $O(n)$ variables constrained with both x_i and x_j and, after making the checks in line 3, their domains must be searched for a PC-witness, each time from scratch with cost $O(nd)$. Through the use of $LastPC$ no value of x_j will be checked more than once over all the $O(d)$ times x_j is extracted from Q, meaning that for any value $a_i \in D(x_i)$ and any variable x_j, the overall cost of *searchPCwit* will be $O(dn + nd^2) = O(nd^2)$. Hence, *checkPCsupLoss* will cost $O(nd^2)$ for one value of x_i, giving $O(nd^3)$ for d values. Since, in the worst case, this process will be repeated for every pair of variables x_i and x_j that are constrained, the total cost of *checkPCsupLoss* will be $O(end^3)$. This is the node complexity of `lmaxRPC3`.

In *checkPCwitLoss* the algorithm iterates over the variables in a triangle with x_j and x_i. In the worst case, for each such variable x_k, $D(x_j)$ will be searched from scratch for a PC-witness of a_i and its current PC-support in x_k. As x_j can be extracted from Q $O(d)$ times and each search from scratch costs $O(d)$, the total cost of checking for a PC-witness in $D(x_j)$, including the checks of line 4 in *checkPCwitLoss*, will be $O(d + d^2)$. For d values of x_i this will be $O(d^3)$. As this process will be repeated for all triangles of variables, whose number is bounded by en, its total cost will be $O(end^3)$. If no PC-witness is found then a new PC-support for a_i in $D(x_k)$ is sought through *searchPCwit*. This costs $O(nd^2)$ as explained above but it is amortized with the cost incurred by the calls to *searchPCwit* from *checkPCsupLoss*. Therefore, the cost of *checkPCwitLoss* is $O(end^3)$. This is also the node complexity of `maxRPC3`.

The branch complexity of (1)`maxRPC3` is also $O(end^3)$. This is because the use of $LastPC$ ensures that for any constraint $c_{i,j}$ and a value $a_i \in D(x_i)$, each value of x_j will be checked at most once for PC-support while going down the branch. Therefore, the cost of *searchPCwit* is amortized. ■

Proposition 4 The node and branch time complexities of `lmaxRPC3`^{rm} and `maxRPC3`^{rm} are $O(end^4)$ and $O(en^2d^4)$ respectively.

Proof: The proof is similar to that of Proposition 3. The main difference with `lmaxRPC3` is that since $lastPC$ is not updated incrementally, each time we seek a PC-support for a value $a_i \in D(x_i)$ in x_j, $D(x_j)$ will be searched from scratch in the worst case. This incurs an extra $O(d)$ cost to *checkPCsupLoss*^{rm} and *searchPCwit*^{rm}. Hence, the node complexity of `lmaxRPC3`^{rm} is $O(end^4)$. Also, the total cost of *searchPCwit*^{rm} in one node cannot be amortized. This means that the cost of *searchPCwit*^{rm} when called within *checkPCwitLoss*^{rm} is $O(nd^2)$. Hence, the node complexity of `maxRPC3`^{rm} is $O(en^2d^4)$. The branch complexities are the same because the calls to *searchPCwit*^{rm} are amortized. ■

The space complexities of the algorithms are determined by the space required for data structures $LastPC$ and $LastAC$. Since both require $O(ed)$ space, this is the node space complexity of (1)`maxRPC3` and (1)`maxRPC3`^{rm}. (1)`maxRPC3` has $O(end)$ branch space complexity because of the extra space required for the incremental update and restoration of the data structures. As (1)`maxRPC3`^{rm} avoids this, its branch space complexity is $O(ed)$.

4.3   Further exploitation of residues in maxRPC algorithms

As detailed above, the use of the *LastPC* and *LastAC* data structures by algorithms such as `maxRPC2`, `maxRPC3`, and `AC2001/3.1` can give optimal time complexity bounds. However, the overhead for maintaining the required data structures during search can outweigh the benefit of the optimal theoretical results. On the other hand, the use the *LastPC* and *LastAC* structures as residues by algorithms such as `maxRPC`^{rm}, `maxRPC3`^{rm}, and `AC3`^{rm} sacrifices the optimal time complexity to achieve better average performance in practice[4].

In this section we investigate variants of `maxRPC3`^{rm} that are a compromise between `maxRPC3` and `maxRPC3`^{rm} by exploring ideas presented in [77] regarding the use of residues in AC algorithms. The first variant of `maxRPC3`^{rm}, called `maxRPC3-resOpt`, uses an extra data structure to record the current PC-supports before the invocation of the maxRPC algorithm at each node of the search tree. As explained below, by exploiting this data structure we can achieve an improved node time complexity. The second variant, called `maxRPC3-start`, also introduces an additional data structure, but only makes use of information obtained during the initialization phase of the maxRPC algorithm. This does not improve the asymptotic time complexity, but results in better average performance in practice.

4.3.1   maxRPC3-resOpt

Algorithm `maxRPC3-resOpt` is inspired from the `ACS-resOpt` algorithm of [77]. Adapting the main idea of `ACS-resOpt` to maxRPC, we use a data structure, called *Stop*, to copy and remember the residues in *LastPC* each time a node is visited right before the maxRPC algorithm is invoked. Also, we view each domain as being "circular". That is, the last value in the initial domain of a variable is followed by the first value. Once a branching decision is made (e.g. variable assignment), `maxRPC3-resOpt` copies all the *LastPC* residues to the *Stop* data structure. Then, as `maxRPC3-resOpt` is executed at this specific node, the search for a new PC-support for $a_i \in D(x_i)$ in $D(x_j)$ starts from the value immediately after $LastPC_{x_i,a_i,x_j}$, continues through the end of the domain, if no PC-support is found, and back to the start of the domain until it encounters $Stop_{x_i,a_i,x_j}$. This may save many checks since, unlike `maxRPC3`^{rm}, each value in $D(x_j)$ can be checked for PC-support at most once.

Function 10 checkPCsupLoss-resOpt(x_i, a_i, x_j):**boolean**

1:    $a_j \leftarrow LastPC_{x_i,a_i,x_j}+1$;
2: **while** $a_j \neq Stop_{x_i,a_i,x_j}$ **do**
3:      **if** isConsistent(a_i, a_j) **then**
4:        **if** searchPCwit$^{rm}(x_i, a_i, x_j, a_j)$ **then**
5:          $LastPC_{x_i,a_i,x_j} \leftarrow a_j$;
6:          $LastAC_{x_i,a_i,x_j} \leftarrow a_j$;
7:          return TRUE;
8:      $a_j \leftarrow$ next value in $D(x_j)$;
9: return FALSE;

We now explain in detail functions *checkPCsupLoss-resOpt* and *checkPCwitLoss-resOpt*, that replace functions *checkPCsupLoss*^{rm} and *checkPCwitLoss*^{rm}. In function

---

[4]This is verified by experimental results given in [68, 77, 106] and also in Section 4.5 here.

checkPCsupLoss-resOpt (Fun. 10), we set a_j to the next value after $LastPC_{x_i,a_i,x_j}$, which is the first value to be checked for being a PC-support in line 1. When the search for PC-support encounters $Stop_{x_i,a_i,x_j}$ (line 2), all possible PC-supports will have been examined. Note that since we consider the domains to be circular, once the last available value in $D(x_j)$ has been unsuccessfuly checked, the search for PC-support will continue from the start of $D(x_j)$. That is, in line 8 a_j will be set to the first available value in $D(x_j)$.

A significant difference from maxRPC3^{rm} is that maxRPC3-resOpt cannot exploit the bidirectionality of *LastPC*. When a PC-support $a_j \in D(x_j)$ is found for $a_i \in D(x_i)$ then only $LastPC_{x_i,a_i,x_j}$ is set to a_j. We do not set $LastPC_{x_j,a_j,x_i}$ to a_i, as done in maxRPC3^{rm}, because bidirectionality no longer holds. To demonstrate this, assume that during the application of maxRPC3-resOpt at some node, we discover the PC-support $a_j \in D(x_j)$ for $a_i \in D(x_i)$ and through bidirectionality $LastPC_{x_j,a_j,x_i}$ is set to a_i. Now a later point in search when maxRPC3^{rm} is invoked we set $Stop_{x_j,a_j,x_i}$ to a_i and continue propagation. If during the search for PC-support for value $a_i' \in D(x_i)$, $a_i' \neq a_i$, in $D(x_j)$ we discover a_j then $LastPC_{x_j,a_j,x_i}$ will be set to a_i'. Now assume that later we seek a PC-support for a_j in $D(x_i)$ and a_i' is no longer valid. Then all values located between a_i and a_i' will be skipped because the search will start at a_i'+1 and will terminate when $a_i = Stop_{x_j,a_j,x_i}$ is reached. Consequently, bidirectionality cannot be exploited. To this end, the auxilary variable *rm*, used in *initialization* function is set to *false* to skip line 11.

On the other hand, *LastAC* is used as in maxRPC3^{rm} and thus it is updated when a PC-support is found, since this is also an AC-support. Furthermore, the search for a PC-witness for a pair of values is conducted by *searchPCwit^{rm}*, as the changes concern *LastPC* and do not affect *LastAC*.

Function *checkPCwitLoss-resOpt* is called when a_j is not removed by *checkPCsupLoss-resOpt*. The pseudocode is simply described in text form, since it is the same as *checkPCwitLoss^{rm}* (Fun. 9) until line 11. The second part of the function (line 12) is executed when $LastPC_{x_i,a_i,x_k}$ is not valid (line 3), or because there is no PC-witness for the pair (a_i, a_k) in $D(x_j)$. In these cases a new PC-support for a_i is sought in $D(x_k)$, and this is done essentially in the same way as in function *checkPCsupLoss-resOpt* (Fun. 10).

Comparing with previous algorithms, maxRPC3-resOpt is sound and complete, as no supports nor witnesses can be overlooked and thus the proof of correctness is very similar to the one given for maxRPC3^{rm}. The node time complexity of (1) maxRPC3-resOpt is O(end^3), the same as maxRPC3, since the search for a new PC-support starts from *LastPC*+1 and not from scratch as in maxRPC3^{rm}. Before maxRPC3-resOpt is invoked, we set*Stop=LastPC* and thus for any constraint $c_{i,j}$ and a value $a_i \in D(x_i)$, each value of x_j will be checked at most *nd* times for PC-support while going down the branch. As a result the branch complexity is O(en^2d^4). The node space complexity is determined by the space required for storing the *LastAC*, *LastPC*, and *Stop* structures, which is O(ed). The branch space complexity is also O(ed), because the data structures are not copied/restored.

Although maxRPC3-resOpt achieves a better node complexity than maxRPC3^{rm}, it carries the additional overhead of having to initialize the *Stop* data structure at each node of the search tree. Experiments in section 4.5 show that this is indeed an important drawback. The copying of *LastPC* to *Stop* at each node (in $O(ed)$ time) results in higher cpu times, despite the savings in constraint checks.

4.3.2 maxRPC3-start

A simple way to reduce the number of constraint checks, when a value in $LastPC$ is not valid, is to keep track of the first PC-support found after preprocessing. The version of $\texttt{maxRPC3}^{rm}$ presented here, called $\texttt{maxRPC3-start}$, stores this value in a structure we call $LeftMostPC$, with $O(ed)$ size. In case of PC-support loss, instead of searching from scratch, we start from the value stored in $LeftMostPC$ that contains the first PC-support found in the *initialization* function. Thus, we omit values between the first value in a domain and the $LeftMostPC$ value to save redundant checks. For every value $a_i \in D(x_i)$ and constraint $c_{i,j}$, $LeftMostPC_{x_i,a_i,x_j}$ is initialized to $\perp$, like the $LastPC$ and $LastAC$ structures, and it is updated in the *initialization* function, exactly when $LastPC$ is updated. To obtain algorithm $\texttt{maxRPC3-start}$ from $\texttt{maxRPC3}^{rm}$, we make the following simple changes.

- We insert in line 11 of *initialization* the assignment:

$$LeftMostPC_{x_i,a_i,x_j} \leftarrow a_j;$$

  Note that while we still exploit the bidirectionality of $LastPC$, this property does not hold for $LeftMostPC$. That is, if the first PC-support for a_i in $D(x_j)$ is value a_j, this does not necessarily mean that the first PC-support for a_j in $D(x_i)$ is a_i.

- In order to start the search for a new PC-support from the first PC-support found, we replace line 1 in *checkPCsupLoss*^{rm} with:

  1:    **for each** $a_j \in D(x_j), a_j \geq LeftMostPC_{x_i,a_i,x_j}$ **do**

  This change will affect also the *checkPCwitLoss*^{rm} function which calls *checkPCsupLoss*^{rm} in line 12.

$\texttt{maxRPC3-start}$ is sound and complete as it is guaranteed than no value earlier than the corresponding $LeftMostPC$ value can be a potential PC-support for some value $a_i \in D(x_i)$. The node and branch time complexity of $\texttt{maxRPC3-start}$ is $O(en^2d^4)$, the same as $\texttt{maxRPC3}^{rm}$, as in the worst case, the $LeftMostPC$ values are the first values in each variable's domain. $\texttt{lmaxRPC3-start}$ is the light version that results from removing the corresponding *checkPCwitLoss-start* function. Its complexity is $O(end^4)$, the same as $\texttt{lmaxRPC3}^{rm}$.

Table 4.1: Time and space complexities of (l)maxRPC algorithms.

Algorithm	Time complexity	Space complexity	Maintains structures	Algorithms	Time complexity	Space complexity	Maintains structures
maxRPC1	$O(end^3)$	$O(end)$	Yes				
maxRPC2	$O(end^3)$	$O(end)$	Yes	lmaxRPC2	$O(end^3)$	$O(end)$	Yes
maxRPC3	$O(end^3)$	$O(end)$	Yes	lmaxRPC3	$O(end^3)$	$O(end)$	Yes
maxRPC^{rm}	$O(en^2d^4)$	$O(end)$	No	lmaxRPC^{rm}	$O(end^4)$	$O(ed)$	No
maxRPC3^{rm}	$O(en^2d^4)$	$O(ed)$	No	lmaxRPC3^{rm}	$O(end^4)$	$O(ed)$	No
maxRPC3-resOpt	$O(en^2d^4)$	$O(ed)$	No	lmaxRPC3-resOpt	$O(end^4)$	$O(ed)$	No
maxRPC3-start	$O(en^2d^4)$	$O(ed)$	No	lmaxRPC3-start	$O(end^4)$	$O(ed)$	No

Table 4.1 summarises the asymptotic branch time and space complexities of the available (l)maxRPC algorithms. Under the column "maintains structures" we indicate whether a given algorithm requires to incrementally maintain some data structure or not.

4.4 Heuristics for maxRPC Algorithms

Numerous heuristics for ordering constraint or variable revisions have been proposed and used within AC algorithms [107, 45, 22, 4]. Generally, many constraint solvers employ heuristics to order the application of propagators or/and the revision of variables and constraints [97]. Heuristics such as the ones used by AC algorithms can be also used within a maxRPC algorithm to efficiently select the next variable to be removed from the propagation list. In addition to this, maxRPC and lmaxRPC algorithms can benefit from the use of heuristics elsewhere in their execution. Once a variable x_j has been removed from the propagation list, heuristics can be applied in many ways in either a maxRPC or a lmaxRPC algorithm. In the following we summarize the possibilities of heuristic using algorithm (1)maxRPC3 for illustration.

H1 A heuristic can be used to select the next variable x_j to remove from the propagation list Q (line 4 of Algorithm 1). Such heuristics are successfully used within AC algorithms.

H2 After a variable x_j is removed from Q all neighboring variables x_i are revised. lmaxRPC (resp. maxRPC) will detect a failure if the condition of PC-support loss (resp. either PC-support or PC-witness loss) occurs for all values of x_i. In such situations, the sooner x_i is considered and the failure is detected, the more constraint checks will be saved. Hence, the order in which the neighboring variables of x_j are considered can be determined using a fail-first type of heuristic (line 5 of Algorithm 1).

H3 Once an AC-support $a_j \in D(x_j)$ has been found for a value $a_i \in D(x_i)$, we try to establish if it is a PC-support. If there is no PC-witness for the pair (a_i, a_j) in some variable x_k then a_j is not a PC-support. Therefore, we can again use fail-first heuristics to determine the order in which the variables forming a triangle with x_i and x_j are considered (line 1 of Function *searchPCwit*).

The above cases apply to both lmaxRPC and maxRPC algorithms. In addition, a maxRPC algorithm can employ heuristics as follows:

H4 For each value $a_i \in D(x_i)$ and each variable x_k constrained with both x_i and x_j, Function *checkPCwitLoss* checks if the pair (a_i, a_k) still has a PC-witness in $D(x_j)$. Again heuristics can be used to determine the order in which the variables constrained with x_i and x_j are considered (line 1 of *checkPCwitLoss*).

H5 In Function *checkPCwitLoss*, a new PC-support for a_i in $D(x_k)$ may be sought. The order in which variables constrained with both x_i and x_k are considered can be determined heuristically as in the case of H3 above (within the call to *searchPCwit*).

As explained, the purpose of such ordering heuristics will be to "fail-first" [48]. That is, to quickly discover potential failures (in the case of H2 above), refute values that are not PC-supports (H3 and H5) and delete values that have no PC-support (H3). Such heuristics can be applied within any coarse-grained maxRPC algorithm to decide the order in which variables are considered. Examples of heuristics that can be used are the following.

dom Consider the variables in ascending domain size. This heuristic can be applied in any of the five cases.

del_ratio Consider the variables in ascending ratio of the number of remaining values to the initial domain size. This heuristic can be applied in any of the five cases.

wdeg For H1 consider the variables in descending weighted degree. For H2 consider the variables x_i in descending weight for the constraint $c_{i,j}$. In the case of H3 consider the variables x_k in descending average weight for the constraints $c_{i,k}$ and $c_{j,k}$. Similarly for H4 and H5.

dom/wdeg Consider the variables in ascending value of dom/wdeg. This heuristic can be applied in any of the five cases.

Experiments demonstrated that applying heuristics H1 and H2 can sometimes be effective, while doing so for H3, H4, and H5 may save constraint checks but usually penalizes cpu times because of the overhead involved in computating the heuristics. Although the primal purpose of the heuristics is to save constraint checks, it is interesting to note that some of the heuristics can also divert search to different areas of the search space when a variable ordering heuristic like dom/wdeg is used, resulting in fewer node visits. For example, two different orderings of the variables in the case of H2 may result in different constraints causing a failure. As dom/wdeg increases the weight of a constraint each time it causes a failure and uses the weights to select the next variable, this may later result in different branching choices. This is explained for the case of AC in [4].

4.5   Experiments

To evaluate the various maxRPC algorithms, we experimented with several classes of structured and random binary CSPs taken from C.Lecoutre's XCSP repository. Excluding instances that were very hard for all algorithms, our evaluation was done on 200 instances in total from various problem classes (see Table 4.2). More details about these instances can be found in C.Lecoutre's homepage[5].

All algorithms used the dom/wdeg heuristic for variable ordering [23] and lexicographic value ordering. As explained in Section 2.4.2, dom/wdeg increases the weight of a constraint when this constraint causes a value removal. This process is rather straightforward when AC is used for constraint propagation, but perhaps not so when stronger local consistencies are used. For the case of maxRPC we chose to increase constraint weights in the following way. When a failure occurs, the weight of constraint $c_{i,j}$ is updated, right after line 7 and 11 of Algorithm 1 and after line 13 in the *initialization* function.

In all following tables, the results of the best algorithm, with respect to run-time, are highlighted with bold. If not explicitly mentioned, the propagation list Q was implemented as a FIFO queue and no heuristic from Section 5 was used.

Table 4.2 compares the performance of stand-alone algorithms used for preprocessing. We give average results for all the instances, grouped into specific problem classes. We include results from coarse-grained maxRPC algorithms, maxRPC2, maxRPC3, maxRPC^{rm}, maxRPC3^{rm} and from their corresponding light versions.

Regarding existing algorithms, results demonstrate that maxRPC^{rm} is particularly costly on large instances because of the penalties associated in initializing its data structures. Specifically, this algorithm timed out on some large instances of the Queens problem class, which explains the empty data entries in the table. In comparison, maxRPC2 displays a better average performance which is not surprising given its lower complexity. The new algorithm maxRPC3 is very close to maxRPC2 in run times, apart from the first and last classes where it is notably faster. The same

---

[5]http://www.cril.univ-artois.fr/~lecoutre/benchmarks.html

holds for maxRPC3^{rm} with the exception of the geometric class where it is clearly worse than the rest of the algorithms. Any gain in performance displayed by the new algorithms is due to the elimination of many redundant constraint checks as the corresponding numbers show.

Table 4.2: Mean stand-alone performance in all 200 instances grouped by problem class. Cpu times (t) in secs, removed values (rm) and constraint checks (cc) are given.

Problem class		maxRPC2	maxRPC3	maxRPC^{rm}	maxRPC3^{rm}	lmaxRPC2	lmaxRPC3	lmaxRPC^{rm}	lmaxRPC3^{rm}
RLFAP	t	1.581	1.125	5.754	1.064	0.942	**0.928**	0.929	0.931
(scen,graph)	rm	3,458	3,458	3,456	3,458	3,458	3,458	3,458	3,458
	cc	15.2M	8.9M	14.9M	8.2M	7.2M	7.1M	6.6M	7.2M
Random	t	0.149	0.153	**0.121**	0.146	0.148	0.151	0.156	0.149
(modelB,	rm	20	20	21	21	25	25	25	31
forced)	cc	0.181M	0.179M	0.181M	0.179M	0.178M	0.177M	0.178M	0.178M
Graph Coloring	t	1.076	1.001	1.146	1.009	0.981	0.987	0.988	**0.980**
	rm	255	255	255	255	255	255	255	255
	cc	17M	16.1M	16.9M	16M	15.8M	15.8M	15.8M	15.8M
Quasigroup	t	0.211	0.201	0.276	0.215	0.173	**0.166**	0.173	0.174
(qcp,qwh	rm	1,167	1,167	1,167	1,167	1,167	1,167	1,167	1,167
bqwh)	cc	0.67M	0.43M	0.62M	0.42M	0.43M	0.38M	0.41M	0.38M
Geometric	t	0.217	0.214	**0.163**	0.336	0.222	0.213	0.214	0.218
	rm	0	0	0	0	0	0	0	0
	cc	0.33M	0.33M	0.33M	0.33M	0.33M	0.33M	0.33M	0.33M
QueensKnights	t	30.705	29.724	-	29.310	27.827	28.073	27.791	**27.732**
Queens,	rm	96	96	-	96	96	96	96	96
QueenAttack	cc	426M	390M	-	389M	366M	366M	366M	366M
driver,haystacks	t	1.449	1.107	1.781	1.086	0.996	**0.931**	0.979	1.002
blackHole	rm	247	247	247	247	247	247	247	247
job-shop	cc	14.4M	10M	13.5M	9.9M	9.3M	8.9M	9.3M	8.9M

Comparing light to full maxRPC algorithms it is perhaps surprising that the light versions typically achieve the same number of value deletions as their full counterparts. This means that approximation algorithms for maxRPC are quite effective. Any differences in value deletions among maxRPC algorithms are caused by the different order of operations in which inconsistency is discovered for some instances. In classes where the constraints checks for a maxRPC and a corresponding lmaxRPC algorithm are the same or very close, there are very few, if any, value deletions.

Table 4.3 compares the performance of search algorithms that apply lmaxRPC throughout search on several problem classes including instances from RLFAPs, random, Quasigroup, geometric, and Queen problems. These instances have been selected to demonstrate cases where either the new algorithms achieve a clear improvement making the best algorithm among them outperform or compete with MAC, or cases where, despite the improvement, the maxRPC-based algorithms are still significantly inferior to MAC. Hence, we present some extreme behaviors for both situations. The algorithms compared are lmaxRPC^{rm}, lmaxRPC3^{rm}, lmaxRPC3-resOpt and lmaxRPC3-start. We do not present results from maxRPC^{rm} and maxRPC3^{rm}, since these two algorithms, and especially maxRPC^{rm}, are inferior to the light versions when used during search. To be precise, maxRPC3^{rm} is competitive on some instances but clearly worse on average. On the other hand, maxRPC^{rm} is substantially slower on all the tested instances and exceeds the time limit of two hours on the hardest among them. Algorithms (l)maxRPC2 and (l)maxRPC3 are even less competitive when used during search, because of the overheads for the copying and restoration of the *LastPC* and *LastAC* data structures. (l)maxRPC3 is typically more efficient than (l)maxRPC2.

In general, any maxRPC algorithm is clearly inferior to the corresponding light version when applied during search. The reduction in visited nodes achieved by the former is relatively small and

Table 4.3: Cpu times (t) in secs, nodes (n) and constraint checks (cc) from various instances.

Instance		$AC3^{rm}$	$lmaxRPC^{rm}$	$lmaxRPC3^{rm}$	lmaxRPC3-resOpt	lmaxRPC3-start
scen11-f7	t	**109.3**	482.6	186.6	214	159.4
	n	353,901	76,954	76,954	57,037	76,954
	cc	467M	5,184M	1,596M	1,011M	1,323M
graph9-f9	t	**8.7**	54.5	21	45.6	17.5
	n	46,705	16,839	16,839	14,838	16,839
	cc	25M	458M	184M	145M	153M
rand-2-40-11	t	14.1	17.6	11.6	**8.9**	11.5
-414-200-30	n	164,958	28,655	28,655	21,105	28,655
	cc	61M	249M	98M	70M	97M
will199GPIA-6	t	**1.6**	5.9	2.5	7.9	2.7
	n	6,996	3,316	3,316	4,300	3,316
	cc	6M	53M	21M	22M	20M
qcp150-120-5	t	22.9	29.3	**15.5**	73.8	15.7
	n	525,629	130,384	130,384	237,644	130,384
	cc	37M	265M	43M	69M	42M
qcp150-120-9	t	95.2	120.6	**57.7**	157.4	59
	n	2,437,173	627,679	627,679	617,662	627,679
	cc	157M	1,060M	163M	151M	162M
qwh20-166-1	t	15.3	21.7	**12.2**	42.7	12.8
	n	234,095	54,286	54,286	31,346	54,286
	cc	19M	156M	18M	10M	18M
qwh20-166-6	t	758.3	462.5	**245.9**	3,342.5	256.2
	n	10,691,633	984,555	984,555	2,364,104	984,555
	cc	911M	3,381M	377M	921M	372M
qwh20-166-7	t	64.5	46.2	**24.7**	319.3	26.3
	n	1,050,144	124,212	124,212	241,184	124,212
	cc	85M	342M	40M	75M	39M
geo50-20-d4-75-1	t	**54.4**	248.2	140.5	143.7	145.7
	n	260,996	122,750	122,750	124,535	122,750
	cc	6M	1,454M	377M	1,376M	375M
queenAttacking6	t	32.9	60.8	**23.9**	94	24.3
	n	234,759	18,488	18,488	137,731	18,488
	cc	104M	888M	242M	860M	238M
queensKnights	t	**3.1**	27.6	16.5	13.4	11.6
-15-5-mul	n	5,819	3,5862	3,586	2,924	3,586
	cc	23M	462M	233M	174M	183M
haystacks-05	t	4.5	2.6	2	2.8	**1.8**
	n	1,182,023	167,629	167,629	223,547	167,629
	cc	13M	13M	7M	10M	6M

does not compensate for the higher run times of enforcing maxRPC. To put the performance of the lmaxRPC algorithms in perspective, we include results from $MAC3^{rm}$ which is considered one of the most efficient versions of MAC [68, 77]. All of the algorithms used a 2-way branching scheme.

Experiments showed that `lmaxRPC`^{rm} is the most efficient among existing algorithms when applied during search, which confirms the results given in [106]. Accordingly, `lmaxRPC3`^{rm} is the most efficient among our algorithms. It is over two times faster than `lmaxRPC`^{rm} on hard instances, while algorithms `lmaxRPC3-resOpt` and `lmaxRPC3-start` are also competitive in many instances. The overhead of copying *LastPC* to *Stop* causes `lmaxRPC3-resOpt` to slow down search in many cases, despite the reduction in the number of constraint checks.

Instance qwh20-166-6 is a pathological case for `lmaxRPC3-resOpt` as this algorithm requires considerable effort compared to the other algorithms. Recall that this algorithm does not exploit the bidirectionality of support, as explained in section 4.1, meaning that variable revisions, constraint checks, and failures may occur in different orders compared to other algorithms. Through the interaction with the dom/wdeg variable ordering heuristic this may cause a different search direction (see discussion at the end of Section 5), explaining the pathological case.

lmaxRPC3-start and lmaxRPC3^{rm} have similar performance when the numbers of constraint checks are similar. More precisely, lmaxRPC3-start is better only when the PC-support found in preprocessing is lexicographically bigger from the first value in any domain. Since this case does not occur very often, there are no significant benefits when compared to lmaxRPC3^{rm} that starts searching from scratch.

Importantly, the speed-ups obtained can make a search algorithm that efficiently applies lmaxRPC competitive with MAC on many instances. For instance, in qwh20-166-6 lmaxRPC3^{rm} achieves a better run time than MAC by a factor of three while lmaxRPC^{rm} is 2 times slower compared to lmaxRPC3^{rm}.

We can see that our methods can reduce the numbers of constraint checks by as much as one order of magnitude (e.g. in quasigroup problems qcp and qwh). This is mainly due to the elimination of redundant checks inside function *searchPCwit*. Cpu times are not cut down by as much, but a speed-up of more than 2 times can be obtained (e.g. qcp150-120-9 and qwh20-166-6). However, there are still many instances where MAC remains considerably faster despite the improvements (e.g. graph9-f9, geo50-20-d4-75-1).

Table 4.4: Mean search performance in all 200 instances grouped by class.

Problem class		AC3^{rm}	lmaxRPC^{rm}	lmaxRPC3^{rm}	lmaxRPC3-resOpt	lmaxRPC3-start
RLFAP	t	**13.5**	61.7	21.7	26.7	18.8
(scen,graph)	n	42,250	8,727	8,727	7,326	8,727
	cc	56M	625M	201M	139M	166M
Random	t	**2.7**	5.8	3.6	3.9	3.6
(modelB,forced)	n	29,538	7,385	7,385	7,835	7,385
	cc	11M	82M	30M	31M	30M
Graph Coloring	t	**4.8**	61	25	45.9	29.7
	n	3,910	2,225	2,225	2,866	2,225
	cc	12M	984M	284M	303M	283M
Quasigroup	t	55.6	47.8	**22**	231.7	22.8
(qcp,qwh,bqwh)	n	866,099	117,974	117,974	204,407	117,974
	cc	70M	315M	39M	71M	38M
Geometric	t	**11.3**	50.6	29.1	30.3	30.1
	n	55,825	26,687	26,687	27,656	26,687
	cc	55M	721M	314M	314M	313M
QueensKnights,	t	**7.1**	133.6	42.7	56.3	42.5
Queens,QueenAttack	n	38,663	4,829	4,829	22,321	4,829
	cc	27M	1,583M	563M	655M	552M
driver,blackHole	t	**1.6**	14.7	5.6	15.5	5.7
haystacks,job-shop	n	115,717	28,750	28,750	34,001	28,750
	cc	3M	141M	33M	35M	32M

In Table 4.4 we summarize the results of our experiments by giving averages over different problem classes. These results demonstrate that lmaxRPC3^{rm} outperforms lmaxRPC^{rm} in all problem classes, often considerably. This was the case in all 200 instances tried. Algorithms lmaxRPC3-resOpt and especially lmaxRPC3-start display similar performance to lmaxRPC3^{rm}. lmaxRPC3-resOpt displays its worst performance in quasigroup problems where it performs twice as much constraint checks on average. Taking also into account that lmaxRPC3-resOpt copies *LastPC* to *Stop* explains the variance in the results given in Tables 4.3 and 4.4. In general, lmaxRPC3^{rm} is competitive with MAC on RLFAP and random instances and outperforms it on the Quasigroup classes. In contrast, lmaxRPC3^{rm} is clearly inferior to AC3^{rm} on Queens class and in the last category that includes instances from various other structured problem classes.

4.5.1   *d*-way branching

We have also experimented with the above search algorithms under the *d*-way branching scheme using again the dom/wdeg heuristic for variable ordering. Table 4.5 reports results from the same instances as Table 4.3, in order to directly compare our algorithms on the two different branching schemes. We exclude `lmaxRPC3-resOpt` which is the less competitive among the algorithms of Table 4.3. We can observe that `lmaxRPC3`^{rm} is faster by a factor of two on the RLFAP instance graph9-f9, while with 2-way branching `AC3`^{rm} was superior. Differences in the relative performance of AC and maxRPC occur in other problems as well (e.g. random, quasigroup and queensAttacking). For example, in qwh instances `lmaxRPC3`^{rm} has better run-time results against `AC3`^{rm} but not by as large margins as under 2-way branching. In comparison to `lmaxRPC`^{rm}, `lmaxRPC3`^{rm} remains advantageous in all instances.

Table 4.5: Cpu times (t) in secs, nodes (n) and constraint checks (cc) from various problem instances when *d*-way branching is used.

Instance		AC3^{rm}	lmaxRPC^{rm}	lmaxRPC3^{rm}	lmaxRPC3-start
scen11-f7	t	981.9	3,338	1,128	**870**
	n	3,696,154	552,907	552,907	552,907
	cc	4,287M	31,098M	9,675M	8,193M
graph9-f9	t	57.1	85.3	33.3	**30.9**
	n	273,766	26,276	26,276	26,276
	cc	158M	729M	290M	242M
rand-2-40-11	t	**11.3**	33.4	26.9	21.5
-414-200-30	n	110,091	49,100	49,100	49,100
	cc	51M	484M	189M	187M
will199GPIA-6	t	**3**	11.7	4.8	5.1
	n	13,243	4,971	4,971	4,971
	cc	13M	108M	42M	41M
qcp150-120-5	t	**15.9**	34.8	17.8	18.6
	n	233,311	100,781	100,781	100,781
	cc	27M	330M	54M	53M
qcp150-120-9	t	**66.5**	162.9	78.4	81.2
	n	2,437,173	627,679	627,679	627,679
	cc	157M	1,060M	163M	162M
qwh20-166-1	t	**14.6**	28.2	15.7	16.4
	n	234,095	54,286	54,286	54,286
	cc	19M	156M	18M	18M
qwh20-166-6	t	462.7	674.3	**346.2**	367
	n	4,651,632	919,861	919,861	919,861
	cc	633M	5,089M	566M	558M
qwh20-166-7	t	30	51.9	**27.8**	29.1
	n	263,713	76,624	76,624	76,624
	cc	42M	392M	45M	44M
geo50-20-d4-75-1	t	**38.7**	144.8	81.9	82.3
	n	181,560	79,691	79,691	79,691
	cc	192M	2,045M	880M	876M
queenAttacking6	t	**54.7**	406.8	153.9	146.6
	n	262,087	103,058	103,058	103,058
	cc	211M	6,035M	1,640M	1,623M
queensKnights	t	**18.2**	82.6	40.4	23.5
-15-5-mul	n	35,445	13,462	13,462	13,462
	cc	154M	963M	387M	282M
haystacks-05	t	0.7	0.7	0.8	0.7
	n	110,638	20,278	20,278	20,278
	cc	1.4M	1.9M	1.1M	1.0M

Table 4.6 summarizes results from the application of lmaxRPC during search using *d*-way branching. We give average results for all the tested instances, grouped into specific problem

classes, as in Table 4.4. As can be seen, $lmaxRPC3^{rm}$ and lmaxRPC3-start improve on the existing best algorithm considerably, making lmaxRPC outperform MAC on the quasigroup problem classes and be quite competitive on the RLFAP class. As expected, when comparing the same (AC or maxRPC) algorithm under the two different branching schemes, 2-way branching is typically superior.

Table 4.6: Mean search performance in all 200 instances grouped by class, when d-way branching is used.

Problem class		$AC3^{rm}$	$lmaxRPC^{rm}$	$lmaxRPC3^{rm}$	lmaxRPC3-start
RLFAP	t	124	157.3	157.3	**123.2**
(scen,graph)	n	424,128	74,083	73,083	73,083
	cc	559M	4,394M	1,387M	1,092M
Random	t	**2.2**	7.7	5.3	4.8
(modelB,forced)	n	19,809	9,270	9,270	9,270
	cc	9M	110M	40M	40M
Graph Coloring	t	**8.9**	110.3	46.9	43.4
	n	5,919	2,983	2,983	2,983
	cc	23M	1,735M	455M	454M
Quasigroup	t	35.5	57.4	**29.6**	31.2
(qcp,qwh,bqwh)	n	387,495	103,994	103,994	103,994
	cc	51M	458M	56M	55M
Geometric	t	**8.2**	29.7	17.2	17.3
	n	39,879	17,273	17,273	17.273
	cc	39M	418M	180M	179M
QueensKnights,	t	**14.7**	206.1	73.6	67.6
Queens,QueenAttack	n	67,019	24,859	24,859	24,859
	cc	73M	2,796M	839M	807M
driver,blackHole	t	**0.8**	13.2	5.2	5.3
haystacks,job-shop	n	13,075	11,349	11,349	11,349
	cc	1M	121M	25M	25M

Overall, our results demonstrate that the efficient application of a maxRPC approximation throughout search can give an algorithm that is quite competitive with MAC on some classes of binary CSPs with either of the two standard branching schemes. This confirms the conjecture of [31] about the potential of maxRPC as an alternative to AC. In addition, our results, along with ones in [106], show that approximating strong and complex local consistencies can be very beneficial.

4.5.2 Heuristics

We have also run experiments to evaluate several of the heuristics described in Section 4.4. In these experiments we have mainly used the best algorithm, $lmaxRPC3^{rm}$, under 2-way braching. Intuitively, the use of heuristics may improve the algorithm's performance as explained in Section 4.4. Since only light versions of maxRPC are practical for use during search, we have only tested heuristics H1, H2 and H3. Recall that heuristics H4 and H5 are not applicable for light maxRPC algorithms.

With respect to the specific strategy for ordering variables under the different heuristics, we have tried all the "fail-first" methods analyzed in Section 4.4 (i.e. dom, del_ratio, wdeg, dom/wdeg). dom and wdeg were not as efficient as the other methods and are thus ommitted from Table 4.7. The algorithm used is $lmaxRPC3^{rm}$, except from the last column where we report results from lmaxRPC3-start. Apart from column $H1 + H2(del\_ratio)$, where the heuristic is mentioned explicitly, in the rest of the columns we use dom/wdeg.

Considering the results in Table 4.7 compared to results in Table 4.4 it seems that the application

Table 4.7: Mean search performance in all 200 instances grouped by class, when different heuristics are used.

Problem class		$AC3^{rm}$	$lmaxRPC3^{rm}$	H1	H2	H1+H2	H1+H2+H3	H1+H2(del_ratio)	lmaxRPC3-start+H1+H2
RLFAP	t	**13.5**	21.7	18.8	18.5	18	22.6	22.5	**13.9**
(scen,graph)	n	42,250	8,727	7,993	9,059	7,940	7,940	8,624	7,940
	cc	56M	201M	157M	143M	152M	163M	200M	130M
Random	t	**2.7**	3.6	3.3	7.1	5.4	9.7	5.1	5.4
(modelB,forced)	n	29,538	7,385	7,508	15,431	11,452	11,452	10,369	11,452
	cc	11M	30M	25M	55M	38M	37M	39M	38M
Graph Coloring	t	**4.8**	25	24.7	25.9	28.5	259.9	25	27.7
	n	3,910	2,225	2,163	2,175	2,043	2,043	2,079	2,043
	cc	12M	284M	248M	254M	236M	236M	218M	258M
Quasigroup	t	55.6	22	**20.6**	37.2	34.9	101.1	26.8	35.9
(qcp,qwh,bqwh)	n	866,099	117,974	109,945	159,440	143,206	143,206	122,291	143,206
	cc	70M	39M	35M	54M	47M	47M	38M	46M
Geometric	t	**11.3**	29.1	21.8	18.2	17.5	30.9	31.1	17.5
	n	55,825	26,687	24,938	17,184	18,295	18,295	26,580	18,295
	cc	55M	314M	224M	178M	164M	159M	310M	164M
QueensKnights,	t	**7.1**	42.7	50.7	46.8	53.1	154.3	44.1	51
Queens,QueenAttack	n	38,663	4,829	13,452	8,469	10,034	10,034	4,849	10,034
	cc	27M	563M	624M	588M	649M	640M	563M	616M
driver,blackHole	t	**1.6**	5.6	6.7	7	6.4	27.3	7.3	5.9
haystacks,job-shop	n	115,717	28,750	51,511	53,685	56,148	56,148	29,761	56,148
	cc	3M	33M	30M	31M	31M	32M	33M	31M

of heuristics does not offer any benefits as the algorithm's performance is marginally improved, if at all. In some problem classes using no heuristic at all is the best choice.

The most promising is the application of both H1 and H2 (H1+H2), where x_j extracted from Q and x_i, which is the neighbouring variable of x_j, are ordered in ascending order of the dom/wdeg value. The less efficient combination is the H1+H2+H3 because of the run-time overhead caused by the often computation of all three heuristics. Comparing del_ratio and dom/wdeg on H1+H2 we conclude that the former is preferable on Quasigroup and Queen problems while the latter is better on RLFAP and Geometric problems. On the rest of the problem classes they display similar performance.

4.5.3 Interleaving AC and maxRPC

Since there are problem classes where either an algorithm that maintains AC or one that maintains lmaxRPC is preferable, we have experimented with hybrid propagation schemes that interleave `lmaxRPC3`^{rm} and `AC3`^{rm}. Specifically, we have considered the following simple ways to interleave the two algorithms under 2-way branching: At any left branch we run `lmaxRPC3`^{rm} (respectively `AC3`^{rm}) after a value assigment, while at any right branch we run `AC3`^{rm} (respectively `lmaxRPC3`^{rm}) after a value removal. Table 4.8 summarizes the results of our experiments with these methods.

Given the results in Table 4.8, the first observation we can make is that none of the two hybrid propagation schemes is substantially worse than both `lmaxRPC3`^{rm} and `AC3`^{rm} on any problem class. In contrast, there are problem classes where the hybrids outperform either maxRPC (e.g. geometric) or AC (quasigroups) by substantial margins. This means that, as expected, the hybrid methods achieve a compromise between maxRPC and AC, which is evident by looking at both cpu times and node visits. Applying maxRPC at left branches results in performance closer to maintaining maxRPC, while when AC is applied at left branches the performance is closer to MAC. This is not surprising since the effects of constraint propagation are stronger after variable assignments compared to value removals. Therefore, the local consistency applied at left branches is the "dominant" one that determines the behaviour of the algorithm. As a result, the former hybrid method is better on quasigroup problems but worse on graph coloring and queens instances, while the two are close on the rest of the problem classes.

Table 4.8: Mean hybrid search performance in all 200 instances grouped by class.

Problem class		$AC3^{rm}$	$lmaxRPC3^{rm}$	$(x = a) \wedge (x \neq a)$ $lmaxRPC3^{rm} \wedge AC3^{rm}$	$(x = a) \wedge (x \neq a)$ $AC3^{rm} \wedge lmaxRPC3^{rm}$
RLFAP	t	**13.5**	21.7	21.9	19.5
(scen,graph)	n	42,250	8,727	17,231	25,748
	cc	56M	201M	193M	103M
Random	t	**2.7**	3.6	3.2	4.1
(modelB,forced)	n	29,538	7,385	11,488	16,668
	cc	11M	30M	24M	30M
Graph Coloring	t	**4.8**	25	21.6	5.9
	n	3,910	2,225	2,745	2,654
	cc	12M	284M	240M	58M
Quasigroup	t	55.6	**22**	30.2	40.9
(qcp,qwh,bqwh)	n	866,099	117,974	233,919	324,373
	cc	70M	39M	43M	60M
Geometric	t	**11.3**	29.1	16.6	15.3
	n	55,825	26,687	25,042	28,785
	cc	55M	314M	164M	140M
QueensKnights,	t	**7.1**	42.7	42.2	9.9
Queens,QueenAttack	n	38,663	4,829	9,645	11,648
	cc	27M	563M	535M	211M
driver,blackHole	t	**1.6**	5.6	2.1	**1.8**
haystacks,job-shop	n	115,717	28,750	64,891	86,446
	cc	3M	33M	30M	31M

The preliminary results presented here give a strong indication that interleaving AC and stronger local consistencies, such as maxRPC, during search can be quite beneficial. Further research is certainly required to develop more informed and efficient ways of interleaving different local consistencies.

4.6 Conclusion

Although maxRPC has been identified as a promising strong local consistency for binary constraints, it has received rather narrow attention since it was introduced. Only two new algortihms have been proposed since the introduction of maxRPC1, the first algorithm for maxRPC, and they have only been evaluated on random problems, if at all.

In this chapter we have identified sources of redundancies in the existing maxRPC algortihms which largely contribute to the high cost of maintaining maxRPC during search. Based on this, we presented new algorithms for maxRPC, and their light versions that approximate maxRPC. These algorithms build on and improve existing maxRPC algorithms, achieving the elimination of many redundant constraint checks. We also investigated heuristics that can be used to order certain operations within maxRPC algorithms.

Experimental results from various problem classes demonstrate that our best method, $lmaxRPC3^{rm}$, constantly outperforms existing algorithms, often by large margins. Significantly, the speed-ups obtained allow $\texttt{lmaxRPC3}^{rm}$ to compete with and outperform MAC on some problems, justifying the conjecture of [31] about the potential of maxRPC as an alternative to AC.

Strong Local Consistencies for Non-Binary (Table) Constraints

In this chapter, we are concerned with strong local consistencies for non-binary and especially table constaints. Many strong local consistencies have been proposed in the literature (Section 3.2). Among domain filtering consistencies, maxRWPC displays promising performance. Based on maxRPWC and two state-of-the-art GAC algorithms for table constraints (Section 3.3), we develop new efficient domain, as well as, relation filtering algorithms that achieve stronger pruning than GAC.

Scecifically, we propose new filtering algorithms for positive table constraints that achieve stronger local consistency properties than GAC by exploiting intersections between constraints. The first algorithm, called maxRPWC+, is a domain filtering algorithm that is based on the local consistency maxRPWC and extends the GAC algorithm of [72]. The second algorithm extends the state-of-the-art STR-based GAC algorithms to stronger relation filtering consistencies, i.e., consistencies that can remove tuples from constraints' relations. Experimental results from benchmark problems demonstrate that the proposed algorithms are more robust than the algorithm of [72] in classes of problems with intersecting table constraints, being orders of magnitude faster in some cases. Also, the most competitive among the proposed algorithms can outperform STR2 by significant margins in some classes, but it can also be drastically outperformed in other classes.

5.1 Introduction

Table constraints are ubiquitous in constraint programming (CP). First, they naturally arise in many real applications from areas such as configuration and databases. And second, they are a useful modeling tool that can be called upon to, for instance, easily capture preferences [56]. Given their importance in CP, it is not surprising that table constraints are among the most widely studied constraints and as a result numerous specialized algorithms that achieve GAC (i.e., domain consistency) on them have been proposed.

Since GAC is a property defined on individual constraints, algorithms for GAC operate on one constraint at a time trying to filter infeasible values from the variables of the constraint. Recently, many algorithms have been proposed that achieve GAC and are specialized for table constraints [72, 63, 69]. A different line of research has investigated stronger consistencies and algorithms to enforce them. Some of them are domain filtering, meaning that they only prune values from the domains of variables, e.g. see [31, 19], whereas a few other ones are higher-order (see Section 3.2.4). In contrast to GAC algorithms, the proposed algorithms to enforce these stronger consistencies are able to consider several constraints simultaneously. For example, pairwise consistency (PWC) [53] considers intersections between pairs of constraints.

As we discussed in Section 3.2, one of the most promising such consistencies is Max Restricted Pairwise Consistency (maxRPWC) [19] which is the domain filtering counterpart of pairwise consistency. In practice, strong consistencies are mainly applicable on constraints that are extensionally defined since intentionally defined constraints usually have specific semantics and are provided with efficient specialized filtering algorithms. However, a significant shortcoming of existing works on maxRPWC and other strong local consistencies is that the proposed algorithms for them are generic. That is, they are designed to operate on intensional and extensional constraints indistinguishably, failing to recognize that strong consistencies are predominantly applicable on extensional constraints and should thus be specialized for such constraints.

Despite the wealth of research on strong consistencies, they have not been widely adopted by CP solvers. State-of-the art solvers such as Gecode, ILOG, Choco, Minion, etc. predominantly apply GAC, and lesser forms of consistency such as bounds consistency, when propagating constraints. Regarding table constraints, CP solvers typically offer one or more of the above mentioned GAC methods for propagation.

In this chapter, we propose specialized filtering algorithms for table constraints that achieve stronger consistency properties than GAC. We contribute to both directions of domain and relation filtering methods by extending existing GAC algorithms for table constraints. The proposed methods are a step towards the efficient handling of intersecting table constraints and also provide specialization of strong local consistencies that can be useful in practice.

The first algorithm, called maxRPWC+, extends the GAC algorithm for table constraints given in [72] and specializes the generic maxRWPC algorithm maxRPWC1. The proposed domain filtering algorithm incorporates several techniques that help alleviate redundancies (i.e., redundant constraint checks and other operations on data structures) displayed by existing maxRPWC algorithms. We also describe a variant of maxRPWC+ which is more efficient when applied during search due to the lighter use of data structures.

The second algorithm, called HOSTR*, extends the state-of-the-art GAC algorithm STR to a higher-order local consistency that can delete tuples from constraint relations as well as values from domains. HOSTR* is actually a family of algorithms that combines the operation of STR (or a refinement of STR such as STR2) when establishing GAC on individual constraints and the operation of maxRPWC+ when trying to extend GAC supports to intersecting constraints. We describe several instantiations of HOSTR* which differ in their implementation details.

We theoretically study the pruning power of the proposed algorithms and place them in a partial hierarchy which includes GAC, maxRPWC, and FPWC (namely PWC+GAC). We show that the level of local consistency achieved by HOSTR* is incomparable to that achieved by maxRPWC+ and to maxRPWC, but weaker than FPWC. Interestingly, a simple variant of HOSTR* ahieves FPWC, albeit with a high cost. maxRPWC+ achieves a consistency that is incomparable to maxRPWC but still stronger than GAC.

Experimental results from benchmark problems used in the evaluation of filtering algorithms for table constraints demonstrate that the best among the proposed algorithms are clearly more robust than the GAC algorithm of [72], namely, their performance is stable over different problem classes and when they are less efficient than GAC they are never exponentially worse. Significantly, in some classes of problems with intersecting table constraints, our methods can be orders of magnitude faster. In addition, our specialized algorithms are considerably faster than generic maxRPWC algorithms, showing that specialized algorithms for strong consistencies can be useful in practice. Finally, the best among the proposed algorithms outperforms the state-of-the-art GAC algorithm STR2 on some problem classes, sometimes by large margins. However, it is also outperformed by

STR2 on other problem classes with the differences being quite large in some cases.

The rest of this chapter is structured as follows. Section 5.2 presents algorithm maxRPWC+ and a variant of this algorithm that is more efficient when used during search. Section 5.3 extends STR-based algorithms to achieve stronger consistencies than GAC. In Section 5.4 we give experimental results. Finally, in Section 5.7 we conclude.

5.2 Algorithm maxRPWC+

In this section we will first describe a specialized algorithm for table constraints that is based on maxRPWC and then present an efficient variant of it that makes a lighter use of its data structures. The presented algorithm, called maxRPWC+, builds upon the generic maxRPWC algorithm maxRPWC1 and the specialized GAC algorithm of [72] (called GAC-va hereafter). maxRPWC+ not only specializes maxRPWC to table constraints but also introduces several techniques that help eliminate redundancies displayed by existing algorithms, such as unnecessary constraint checks and other operations on data structures. As in GAC-va, the main idea behind maxRPWC+ is to interleave support and validity checks.

The approach of GAC-va involves visiting both lists of valid and allowed tuples in an alternating fashion when looking for a support (i.e., a tuple that is both allowed and valid). Its principle is to avoid considering irrelevant tuples by jumping over sequences of valid tuples containing no allowed tuple and over sequences of allowed tuples containing no valid tuple. This is made possible because of the lexicographic ordering of tuples. The core operation of GAC-va, that is also exploited by our algorithm, is the construction of a valid tuple that is verified for being a GAC-support by searching for it in the list of allowed tuples using binary search. If it is not found, then the smallest allowed tuple that is greater than the aforementioned valid one is considered and its validity is checked. If it is not valid, then next valid tuple is constructed and so on.

Algorithm maxRPWC+ uses the following data structures:

- For each variable-value pair (x_i, a_i) and each constraint c involving x_i, $allowed(c, x_i, a_i)$ is the list of allowed tuples in c that include the assignment (x_i, a_i).

- For each constraint c and each value $a_i \in D(x_i)$, where $x_i \in scp(c)$, $Last_{c,x_i,a_i}$ gives the most recently discovered (and thus lexicographically smallest) maxRPWC-support of a_i in c. The same data structure is used by maxRPWC1 but it is exploited in a less sophisticated way as will be explained.

Before going into the details of the algorithm we describe a simple modification that can be incorporated into any maxRPWC algorithm to boost its performance.

Restricted maxRPWC From the definition of maxRPWC we can see that the value deletions from some $D(x_i)$ may trigger the deletion of a value $b \in D(x_j)$ in two cases:

1. b may no longer be maxRPWC because its current maxRPWC-support in some constraint c is no longer valid and it was the last such support in c. We call this case *maxRPWC-support loss*.

2. The last maxRPWC-support of b in some constraint c may have lost its last PW-support in another constraint c' intersecting with c. We call this case *PW-support loss*.

Although detecting PW-support loss is necessary for an algorithm to achieve maxRPWC, our experiments have shown that the pruning it achieves rarely justifies its cost. Hence, `maxRPWC+` applies maxRPWC in a restricted way by only detecting maxRPWC-support loss. However, the resulting method is still strictly stronger than GAC. This is clear if we consider that the "stronger" relationship is immediately derived by the definitions. Now consider a problem with constraints $alldiff(x_1, x_2, x_3)$ and $x_1 = x_2$, and domains $\{0, 1, 2\}$ for all variables. This problem is GAC but the application of restricted maxRPWC will detect its inconsistency. Although a restricted version of maxRPWC is stronger than GAC, it obviously is only achieves an approximation of maxRPWC. A similar approximation of the related binary local consistency maxRPC has also been shown to be efficient compared to full maxRPC (see [106] and Chapter 3.4).

5.2.1 Algorithm description

Given a table constraint c_i, we now describe how algorithm `maxRPWC+` can be used to filter the domain of any variable $x_j \in scp(c_i)$. We assume that the domain of some variable in $scp(c_i)$ (different than x_j) has been modified and as a result the propagation engine will revise all other variables in $scp(c_i)$. Initially, Function 11 is called.

Function 11 *revisePW+* (c_i, x_j)

1: **for each** $a_j \in D(x_j)$ **do**
2:     $\tau \leftarrow seekSupport\text{-}va(c_i, x_j, a_j)$;
3:     **while** $\tau \neq \top$ **do**
4:         **if** $isPWconsistent+(c_i, \tau)$ **then break**;
5:         $\tau \leftarrow seekSupport\text{-}va(c_i, x_j, a_j)$;
6:     **if** $\tau = \top$ **then** remove a_j from $D(x_j)$;

For each value $a_j \in D(x_j)$ Function 11 first searches for a GAC-support. This is done by calling function *seekSupport-va* which is an adaptation of Algorithm 12 of `GAC-va` in [72]. This function makes an additional first check to verify if $Last_{c_i,x_j,a_j}$, which is the most recently found maxRPWC-support, and thus also GAC-support, is still valid. Note that as in [72] the search starts from the first valid tuple. If $Last_{c_i,x_j,a_j}$ is valid, $\tau = Last_{c_i,x_j,a_j}$ is returned, else the valid and allowed tuples of c_i are visited in an alternating fashion. This is done by applying a dichotomic search in the list $allowed(c_i, x_j, a_j)$ to locate the lexicographically smallest valid and allowed tuple τ of c_i, such that $\tau > Last_{c_i,x_j,a_j}$ and $\tau[x_j] = a_j$. More precisely, τ can be either a valid tuple found in the list of allowed tuples of c_i or $\top$, in case of validity or support check failure. If such a tuple τ is found, we then check it for PW consistency through Function *isPWconsistent+* (Function 12). If a_j does not have a GAC-support (i.e., *seekSupport-va* returns $\top$) or none of its GAC-supports is a PW-support, then it will be removed from $D(x_j)$.

The process of checking if a tuple τ of a constraint c_i is PW consistent involves iterating over each constraint c_k that intersects with c_i on at least two variables and searching for a PW-support for τ (Function 12 line 1). For each such constraint c_k `maxRPWC+` first tries to quickly verify if a PW-support for τ exists by exploiting the $Last$ data structure as we now explain.

Fast check for PW-support

For each variable x_k belonging to the intersection of c_i and c_k, we check if $\tau' = Last_{c_k,x_k,\tau[x_k]}$ is valid and if it includes the same values for the rest of the variables in the intersection as τ (line 6

Function 12 *isPWconsistent+* (c_i, τ): **boolean**

1: **for each** $c_k \neq c_i$ s.t. $|scp(c_k) \cap scp(c_i)| > 1$ **do**
2:     PW=FALSE;
3:     max_$\tau' \leftarrow \perp$;
4:     **for each** $x_k \in scp(c_k) \cap scp(c_i)$ **do**
5:         $\tau' \leftarrow Last_{c_k, x_k, \tau[x_k]}$;
6:         **if** *isValid*(c_k, τ') AND $\tau'[scp(c_k) \cap scp(c_i)] = \tau[scp(c_k) \cap scp(c_i)]$ **then**
7:             PW=TRUE; **break**;
8:         **if** $\tau' >$ max_τ' **then** max_$\tau' \leftarrow \tau'$;
9:     **if** $\neg$PW **then**
10:        **if** *seekPWSupport*$(c_i, \tau, c_k, max\_\tau') = \top$ **then**
11:           **return** FALSE;
12: **return** TRUE;

---

in Function 12). Function *isValid* simply checks if all values in the tuple are still in the domains of the corresponding variables. If these conditions hold for some variable x_k in the intersection then τ is PW-supported by τ'. Hence, we move on to the next constraint intersecting c_i.

Else, we find max_τ' the lexicographically greatest $Last_{c_k, x_k, \tau[x_k]}$ among the variables that belong to the intersection of c_i and c_k and we search for a new PW-support in Function *seekP-WSupport* (line 10). In case *seekPWSupport* returns $\top$ for some c_k then *isPWconsistent+* returns FALSE and a new GAC-support must be found and checked for PW consistency.

Fast check for lack of PW-support

Function 13 seeks a PW-support for τ in $rel[c_k]$. Before commencing with this search, it performs a fast check aiming at detecting a possible inconsistency (and thus avoiding the search). In a few words, this check can sometimes establish that there cannnot exist a PW-support for τ. This is accomplished by exploiting the lexicographical ordering of the tuples in the constraints' relations.

Function 13 *seekPWsupport* $(c_i, \tau, c_k, max\_\tau')$

1: **if** $\neg$ *isValid*(c_k, max_τ') **then** $max\_\tau' \leftarrow setNextTuple(c_i, \tau, c_k, max\_\tau')$;
2: **if** $max\_\tau' \neq \top$ **then** $\tau' \leftarrow checkPWtuple(c_i, \tau, c_k, max\_\tau')$;
3: **else return** $\top$;
4: $x_{ch} \leftarrow$ select a variable $\in scp(c_i) \cap scp(c_k)$
5: **while** $\tau' \neq \top$ **do**
6:     $\tau'' \leftarrow binarySearch(allowed(c_k, x_{ch}, \tau'[x_{ch}]), \tau')$;
7:     **if** $\tau'' = \tau'$ OR *isValid*(c_k, τ'') **then return** τ'';
8:     **if** $\tau'' = \top$ **then return** $\top$;
9:     $\tau' \leftarrow setNextTuple(c_i, \tau, c_k, \tau'')$;
10: **return** $\top$;

In detail, the validity of max_τ' is first checked in line 1. If *isValid* returns FALSE, then function *setNextTuple* is called to find the lexicographically smallest valid tuple in c_k that is greater than max_τ' and is such that $max\_\tau'[scp(c_k) \cap scp(c_i)] = \tau[scp(c_k) \cap scp(c_i)]$. If no such tuple exists, *setNextTuple* returns $\top$, and the search terminates since no PW-support for τ exists in c_k. If a tuple max_τ' is located then Function *checkPWtuple* is called to essentially perform a lexicographical comparison between max_τ' and τ taking into account the intersection of the two constraints (line 2). According to the result we may conclude that there can be no PW-support of τ in c_k and thus Function 13 will return $\top$. Consequently, lines 2-3 of Function 13 perform the fast check for lack of PW-support.

The addition of this simple check enables `maxRPWC+` to perform extra pruning compared to a typical maxRPWC algorithm. Before explaining how *checkPWtuple* works, we demonstrate this with an example.

Example 1 Consider a problem with two constraints c_1 and c_2 where $scp(c_1) = \{x_1, x_2, x_3, x_4\}$ and $scp(c_2) = \{x_3, x_4, x_5, x_6\}$. Assume that the GAC-support $\tau = (0, 2, 2, 1)$ has been located for value 0 of x_1 and that there exists a valid PW-support for τ in c_2 (e.g., $\{2, 1, 2, 2\}$). Also, assume that $Last_{c_2, x_3, 2}$ and $Last_{c_2, x_4, 1}$ are tuples $\tau' = (2, 2, 0, 1)$ and $\tau'' = (1, 1, 2, 3)$, meaning that $max\_\tau' = \tau'$. Since τ has a PW-support, a maxRPWC algorithm will discover this and will continue to check the next constraint intersecting c_1. However, since $\tau'[x_4]$ is greater than $\tau[x_4]$, it is clear that there is no PW consistent tuple in c_2 that includes values 2 and 1 for x_3 and x_4 respectively. If we assume that τ is the last GAC-support of $(x_1, 0)$ then `maxRPWC+` will detect this and will delete 0 from $D(x_1)$, while a maxRPWC algorithm will not.

Function 14 *checkPWtuple* $(c_i, \tau, c_k, max\_\tau')$

1: **for each** $x_k \in scp(c_k)$ **do**
2:    **if** $x_k \notin scp(c_k) \cap scp(c_i)$ **then**
3:       **if** $max\_\tau'[x_k]$ is last value in $D(x_k)$ **then continue**;
4:       **else break**;
5:    **else**
6:       **if** $max\_\tau'[x_k] < \tau[x_k]$ **then break**;
7:       **if** $max\_\tau'[x_k] > \tau[x_k]$ **then return** $\top$;
8: **return** max_τ';

Function *checkPWtuple* (Function 14) checks if there can exist a tuple greater or equal to max_τ' that has the same values for the variables of the intersection as τ. Crucially, this check is done in linear time as follows: Assuming $max\_\tau' =< (x_1, a_1), ..., (x_m, a_m) >$ then this tuple is scanned from left to right. If the currently examined variable x_k belongs to $scp(c_k) \cap scp(c_i)$ and $a_k > \tau[x_k]$, where a_k is the value of x_k in max_τ', then we conclude that there can be no PW-support for τ in c_k (line 7). If x_k does not belong to $scp(c_k) \cap scp(c_i)$ then if the value it takes in max_τ' is the last value in its domain, we continue scanning (line 3). Otherwise, the scan is stopped because there may exist a tuple larger or equal to max_τ' that potentially is a PW-support of τ. However, max_τ' can still be used to avoid searching for a PW-support from scratch. Hence it is returned to *seekPWsupport*.

The soundness of the described process is guaranteed by the assumption that tuples in relations are stored in lexicographical order, which is typically the case. Given this assumption, it is certain that if a tuple τ which we try to extend to a PW-support is lexicographically smaller than max_τ', with respect to the values of the shared variables, then there can be no PW-support for τ. Otherwise, the lexicographical order would be violated.

Searching for PW-support

In case no inconsistency is detected through the fast check, then the search for a PW-support for τ begins, starting with the tuple τ' returned from *checkPWtuple*. We first check if τ' is an allowed tuple using binary search in a similar way to GAC-va. However, since there are more than one variables in the intersection of c_i and c_k, the question is which list of allowed tuples to consider when searching. Let us assume that the search will be performed on the list $allowed(c_k, x_{ch}, \tau'[x_{ch}])$ of variable x_{ch}. After describing the process, we will discuss possible criteria for choosing this variable.

Binary search will either return τ' if it is indeed allowed, or the lexicographically smallest allowed tuple τ'' that is greater than τ', or $\top$ if no such tuple exists. In the first case a PW-support for τ has been located and it is returned. In the third case, no PW-support exists. In the second case, we check if τ'' is valid, by using function *isValid* and if so, then it constitutes a PW-support for τ. Otherwise, function *setNextTuple* is called taking τ'' and returning the smallest valid tuple for $scp(c_k)$ that is lexicographically greater than τ'', such that $\tau'[scp(c_k) \cap scp(c_i)] = \tau[scp(c_k) \cap scp(c_i)]$ (line 9). If *setNextTuple* returns $\top$ the search terminates, otherwise, we continue to check if the returned tuple is allowed as explained above, and so on.

Selecting the list of allowed tuples

Since there are $|scp(c_k) \cap scp(c_i)|$ variables in the intersection of c_i and c_k, there is the same number of choices for the list of allowed tuples to be searched. Obviously, the size of the lists is a factor that needs to be taken into account. The selection of x_{ch} (line 4 of Function 13) can be based on any of the following (and possibly other) criteria:

1. Select the variable x_{ch} having minimum size of $allowed(c_k, x_{ch}, \tau'[x_{ch}])$.

2. Select the variable x_{ch} having the minimum number of tuples in $allowed(c_k, x_{ch}, \tau'[x_{ch}])$ between τ' and $\top$.

3. Select the leftmost variable in $scp(c_k) \cap scp(c_i)$.

4. Select the rightmost variable in $scp(c_k) \cap scp(c_i)$.

The first heuristic considers a static measure of the size of the lists. The second considers a more dynamic and accurate measure. In the experiments, presented below, we have used the fourth selection criterion. Although this seems simplistic, as Example 2 demonstrates, there are potentially significant benefits in choosing the rightmost variable.

Example 2 Consider a constraint c_k on variables $x_1, \ldots, x_4$ with domains $D(x_1) = D(x_4) = \{0, \ldots, 9\}$ and $D(x_2) = D(x_3) = \{0, 1\}$. Assume that we are seeking a PW-support for tuple τ of constraint c_i in c_k. Also, $scp(c_k) \cap scp(c_i) = \{x_1, x_4\}$, $\tau[x_1] = 1$, $\tau[x_4] = 0$, and $|allowed(c_k, x_1, 1)| = |allowed(c_k, x_4, 0)|$. Figure 5.11 (partly) shows the lists $allowed(c_k, x_1, 1)$ and $allowed(c_k, x_4, 0)$. If we choose to search for a PW-support in $allowed(c_k, x_1, 1)$ then in the worst case binary search will traverse the whole list since tuples with value 0 for x_4 are scattered throughout the list. In contrast, if we choose $allowed(c_k, x_4, 0)$ then search can focus in the highlighted part of the list since tuples with value 1 for x_1 are grouped together.

x1	x2	x3	x4
1	0	0	0
••••	•••	•••	•••
1	0	0	9
1	1	0	0
••••	•••	•••	•••
1	1	0	9
••••	•••	•••	•••
1	1	1	9

x1	x2	x3	x4
0	0	0	0
••••	•••	•••	•••
0	1	1	0
1	0	0	0
••••	•••	•••	•••
1	1	1	0
••••	•••	•••	•••
9	1	1	0

Figure 5.11: $allowed(c_k, x_1, 1)$ and $allowed(c_k, x_4, 0)$.

5.2.2 Theoretical Results

We now analyze the worst-case complexity of the *revisePW+* function of `maxRPWC+`. The symbols M, N, S are explained in the proof.

Proposition 5 The worst-case time complexity of *revisePW+*(c_i, x_j) is $O(d.e.N.M(d + r.log(S)))$.

   Proof: Let us first consider the complexities of the individual functions called by *seekPWsupport*. The cost of *setNextTuple* to construct a valid tuple for the variables that do not belong to the intersection is $O(d + (r - f_{min}))$. The cost of *checkPWtuple* is linear, since it requires at most $O(r)$ checks to determine if any of $x_k \in c_k$ is inconsistent with $\tau[x_k]$. The worst-case time complexity of *binarySearch* is $O(r.log(S))$ with $S = |allowed(c_k, x_{ch}, \tau'[x_{ch}])|$. The worst-case time complexity for one execution of the loop body is then $O(d + (r - f_{min}) + r.log(S)) = O(d + r.log(S))$. Let us assume that M is the number of sequences of valid tuples that contain no allowed tuple, and for each tuple τ'' belonging to such a sequence $\tau''[scp(c_k) \cap scp(c_i)] = \tau[scp(c_k) \cap scp(c_i)]$. Then M bounds the number of iterations of the while loop in *seekPWsupport*. Therefore the worst time complexity of *seekPWsupport* is $O(M(d + r.log(S)))$.

   The cost of *isPWconsistent+* is $O(e.M(d + r.log(S)))$, since in the worst case *seekPWsupport* is called once for each of the at most e intersecting constraints. The maximun number of iterations for the while loop in *revisePW+* is N, where N is the number of sequences of valid tuples in c_i containing no allowed tuple. The cost of one call to *seekSupport-va* is $O(d + r.log(S))$ [72]. Therefore, for d values the complexity of *revisePW+* is $O(d.N(e.M(d + r.log(S)) + (d + r.log(S)))) = O(d.e.N.M(d + r.log(S)))$. ■

   Note that M and N are at most $t_{c_k} + 1$ and $t_{c_i} + 1$ respectively, since in the worst case there is a sequence of valid tuples in between every pair of consecutive allowed tuples in a constraint's relation.

   The complexity given by Proposition 5 concerns one call to *revisePW+* for one constraint. If *revisePW+* is embedded within an AC3-like algorithm (as `maxRPWC1` is) to achieve the propagation of all constraints in the problem then the worst-case time complexity of `maxRPWC+` will be $O(e^2.r.d^2.N.M(d + r.log(S)))$ since there are e constraints and each one is enqueued dr times in the worst case (i.e. once for each value deletion from a variable in its scope). Assuming the implementation of [72], the space complexity of `maxRPWC+` is $O(e.r.|allowed(c, x, a)| + e.r.d)$, where $|allowed(c, x, a)|$ is the maximum size of any constraint's relation and ekd is the space required for the *Last* structure.

Regarding the pruning power of maxRPWC+, it is easy to show that it is strictly stronger than GAC (the arguments in the discussion on the pruning power of restricted maxRPWC are directlty applicable). Also, the local consistency achieved by maxRPWC+ is incomparable to maxRPWC. This is because a maxRPWC algorithm may achieve stronger pruning than maxRPWC+ due to the detection of PW-support loss in addition to maxRPWC-support loss. On the other hand, the fast check for lack of PW-support enables maxRPWC+ to prune extra values compared to maxRPWC.

Proposition 6 maxRPWC+ achieves a local consistency that is incomparable to maxRPWC.

Proof: For an example where maxRPWC+ achieves more puning than maxRPWC consider Example 1. For the opposite consider a problem with 0-1 domains that includes two constraints c_1 and c_2 with $scp(c_1) = \{x_1, x_2, x_3\}$ and $scp(c_2) = \{x_2, x_3, x_4\}$ having the allowed tuples $\{(0,0,0), (1,0,1), (1,1,0)\}$ and $\{(0,0,0), (0,1,1), (1,0,1)\}$ respectively. Now assume that value 0 is deleted from $D(x_4)$ which means that tuple $(0,0,0)$ of c_2 will be invalidated. maxRPWC+ will revise all other variables involved in c_2 and only check for maxRPWC-support loss. Both values for x_2 and x_3 have maxRPWC-supports on c_2 so no deletion will be made. On the other hand, maxRPWC will also check for PW-support loss by looking at constraint c_1. It will discover that value 0 of x_1 is no longer maxRPWC (its GAC-support has no PW-support on c_2) and will therefore delete it. ∎

5.2.3 A lighter version of maxRPWC+

Although maxRPWC+ removes many redundancies that are inherent to generic algorithms through the exploitation of the *Last* data structure, it suffers from an important drawback: the overhead required for the restoration of *Last* after a failed instantiation. One way around this problem is to use *Last* as a *residue*. That is, as a list of supports that have been most recently discovered but are not maintained/restored during search. The resulting algorithm does not remove all the redundancies that maxRPWC+ does, but it is much cheaper to apply during search. This is similar to the relation between the optimal AC algorithm AC2001/3.1 [18] and the residue-based AC3^{rm} [68], as well as, the optimal maxRPC algorithm maxRPC3 and its corresponding residue-based version maxRPC3^{rm} (Chapter 3.4).

The residue-based version of maxRPWC+, which hereafter is called maxRPWC+r, is an algorithm that exploits backtrack-stable data structures inspired from AC3^{rm} and maxRPC3^{rm} (rm stands for multidirectional residues). The *Last* structure is not maintained incrementally as by maxRPWC+, but it is only used to store residues. As explained, a residue is a support which has been located and stored during the execution of the procedure that proves that a given tuple is maxRPWC. The algorithm stores the most recently discovered support, but does not guarantee that any lexicographically smaller value is not a maxRPWC-support. Consequently, when we search for a new maxRPWC-support in a table, we always start from scratch. *Last* need not be restored after a failure; it can remain unchanged, hence a minimal overhead on the management of data.

To obtain the residue-based maxRPWC+r algorithm, we need to make the following simple modifications. In Function 12 we omit line 8, since $Last_{c_k, x_k, \tau[x_k]}$ may not be the lexicographically smallest tuple in c_k and thus, we cannot locate the max_τ' tuple. Subsequently, in Function 13 max_τ' is set to *setNextTuple*$(c_i, \tau, c_k, \bot)$ (namely the search for a PW-support in c_k starts from scratch). Additionally, the fast check for lack of PW-support, handled in *checkPWtuple* (line 2) is not feasible. Lines 1-3 of Function 13 are replaced with the following two:

1: $max\_\tau' \leftarrow$ *setNextTuple*$(c_i, \tau, c_k, \bot)$;
2: **if** $max\_\tau' = \top$ **then return** $\top$;

Regarding the time complexity of maxRPWC+r, the cost of calling Function *revisePW+* once is the same as in maxRPWC+. However, if we consider that repeated calls may be required due to the effects of constraint propagation then the complexity of maxRPWC+r for the whole problem is $O(e^2.r.d^3.N.M(d + r.log(S))))$.

Finally, regarding the pruning power of maxRPWC+r it is easy to see that this algorithm achieves a local consistency that is stronger than GAC (again the arguments in the discussion on the pruning power of restricted maxRPWC are directlty applicable). Also, it achieves a local consistency weaker than maxRPWC+ since the two algorithms are essentially the same, minus the fast check for lack of PW-support.

5.3   Extending STR to a higher-order consistency

Algorithms based on STR, especially STR2 and STR3, have been shown to be the most efficient GAC algorithms for table constraints, along with the MDD approach of [25]. The idea of STR algorithms is to dynamically maintain the tables of supports while enforcing GAC, based on an optimization of simple tabular reduction (STR), a technique proposed by J. Ullmann [103].

5.3.1   The HOSTR* algorithm

In this section we present ways to extent STR algorithms in order to achieve more pruning than GAC. From now on we call these algorithms HOSTR*, which is derived from *higher-order* STR. The '*' stands for a particular STR algorithm (i.e., when extending STR2 we name the algorithm HOSTR2).

Algorithm 15 presents the main framework for HOSTR by extending the basic STR algorithm, as proposed in [103], to achieve a stronger consistency. We choose to present an extension of STR as opposed to STR2 and STR3 because of STR's simplicity. STR2 and STR3 can be extended in a very similar way.

We now present the data structures used by STR and HOSTR.

- $rel[c]$: is the set of allowed tuples associated with a positive table constraint c. This set is represented by an array of tuples indexed from 1 to $rel[c].length$ which denotes the size of the table (i.e., the number of allowed tuples).

- $position[c]$: is an array of size $rel[c].length$ that provides indirect access to the tuples of c. At any given time the values in $position[c]$ are a permutation of $\{1, 2, \ldots, t_c\}$. The ith tuple of c is $rel[c][position[c][i]]$. The use of this data structures enables restoration of deleted tuples in constant time.

- $currentLimit[c]$: is the position of the last current tuple in $rel[c]$. The current table of c is composed of exactly $currentLimit[c]$ tuples. The values in $position[c]$ at indices ranging from 1 to $currentLimit[c]$ are positions of the current tuples of c.

- $pwValues[x]$: is a set for each variable x, that contains all values in $D(x)$ which are proved to have a PW-support when HOSTR is applied on a constraint c. STR uses a similar data structure to store the values that are GAC-supported.

- X_{evt} is a set of variables. After HOSTR has finished processing a constraint c, X_{evt} will contain each variable $x \in scp(c)$ s.t. at least one value was removed from $D(x)$.

Structures $position[c]$ and $currentLimit[c]$, which basically implement the structure called sparse set [24], allow restoration of deleted tuples in constant time (during backtrack search); for more information, see [103].

Propagation in STR based algorithms can be implemented by means of a queue that handles constraints. Once a constraint is removed from the queue, STR iterates over the valid tuples in the constraint until $currentLimit[c]$ is reached. STR removes any tuple that has become invalid through the deletion of one of its values (justi like the **while** loop in Algorithm 15). Importantly, when a tuple is removed it still remains in $rel[c]$; it's index is swaped in $position[c]$ with the index pointed by $currentLimit[c]$ (i.e., the index of the last valid tuple of $rel[c]$) in constant time. Additionally, the only information that is restored upon backtracking is $currentLimit[c]$ instead of the removed tuples. Thus, after finishing the **while** loop iteration, only valid and allowed tuples are kept in tables. Any values that are no longer supported, are deleted (the **for** loop in Algorithm 15).

HOSTR is identical to STR, except for the extra PW-check it applies when a tuple is verified as valid. To be precise, if an allowed tuple τ is proved valid by function *isValid* then HOSTR checks if it is also PW-consistent. This is done by calling the *isPWConsistent-STR* function (line 7).

We omit the detailed desction of functions *isValid* and *removeTuple*, which can be found in [63]. Briefly, *isValid* takes a tuple τ and returns true iff none of the values in τ has been removed from the domain of the corresponding variable. *removeTuple* again takes a tuple τ and removes it in constant time by replacing $position[c][i]$, where i is the position of τ in $rel[c]$, with $position[c][currentLimit[c]]$ (namely by swaping indexes and not tuples) and then decrementing $currentLimit[c]$ by one. As a result this procedure violates the lexicographic ordering of the remaing tuples in $position[c]$.

Once a tuple τ of constraint c has been verified as valid, Function *isPWconsistent-STR* of HOSTR is called. This function iterates over each constraint c_k that intersects with c on at least two variables and searches for a PW-support for τ. If τ has no PW-support on some c_k then it will be removed in line 13 of Algorithm 15.

Once the traversal of the valid tuples has terminated, HOSTR (and STR) updates the X_{evt} set to include any variable that belongs to $scp(c)$ and has had its domain reduced (lines 14-21). Thereafter, all constraints that involve at least one variable in X_{evt} will be added to the propagation queue.

Concerning the implementation of *isPWconsistent-STR*, there are several options, with each one resulting in a different variant of HOSTR. The following variants differ in the way search for a PW-support is implemented.

1. **Linear:** For each constraint c_k *isPWconsistent-STR^l* iterates in a linear fashion over each τ' that currently belongs to $rel[c_k]$ to locate a valid tuple such that $\tau'[scp(c_k) \cap scp(c)] = \tau[scp(c_k) \cap scp(c)]$, until $currentLimit[c_k]$ is reached. This version does not require the use of any additional data structures.

2. **Binary:** For each constraint c_k *isPWconsistent-STR^b* locates a τ' by applying a binary search on the initial $rel[c_k]$. Then it checks its validity and whether it satisfies the condition $\tau'[scp(c_k) \cap scp(c)] = \tau[scp(c_k) \cap scp(c)]$. A requirement of this version is that the original table is stored. Note that binary search on the current tables as they are stored by STR is not possible since the lexicographic ordering of the tuples is violated.

3. **STR/maxRPWC+ Hybrid:** In addition to the data strucutes of STR, this version keeps the $allowed(c, x, a)$ lists of maxRPWC+ (see Section 5.2). Then, following maxRPWC+, for each

---

Algorithm 15 $HOSTR\star$ (c: constraint): set of variables

1: **for each** unassigned variable $x \in scp(c)$ **do**
2:     $pwValues[x] \leftarrow \emptyset$;
3: $i \leftarrow 1$;
4: **while** i $\leq$ currentLimit[c] **do**
5:     index $\leftarrow$ position[c][i];
6:     $\tau \leftarrow$ rel[c][index];
7:     **if** $isValid(c, \tau)$ AND $isPWconsistent\text{-}STR(c,\tau)$ **then**
8:         **for each** unassigned variable $x \in scp(c)$ **do**
9:             **if** $\tau[x] \notin$ pwValues[x] **then**
10:                pwValues[x] $\leftarrow$ pwValues[x] $\cup \{\tau[x]\}$;
11:            i $\leftarrow$ i + 1;
12:    **else**
13:        $removeTuple(c, i)$; // currentLimit[c] decremented
    // domains are now updated and Xevt computed
14: $X_{evt} \leftarrow \emptyset$;
15: **for each** unassigned variable $x \in scp(c)$ **do**
16:    **if** pwValues[x] $\subset D(x)$ **then**
17:        $D(x) \leftarrow$ pwValues[x];
18:        **if** $D(x) = \emptyset$ **then**
19:            **throw** INCONSISTENCY;
20:        $X_{evt} \leftarrow X_{evt} \cup \{x\}$;
21: **return** X_{evt};

---

constraint c_k *isPWconsistent-STR^h* visits the lists of valid and allowed tuples in an alternating fashion, using binary search, to locate a valid tuple τ' such that $\tau'[scp(c_k) \cap scp(c)] = \tau[scp(c_k) \cap scp(c)]$.

In practice, the STR/maxRPWC+ hybrid approach is by far the most efficient among the above methods. *isPWconsistent-STR^h* which implements this method closely follows the operation of maxRPWC+ when looking for a PW-support, minus the usage of the *Last* structure. This is displayed in Function 16. For each c_k *isPWconsistent-STR^h* calls function *setNextTuple* to find the lexicographically smallest valid tuple in c_k, such that $\tau'[scp(c_k) \cap scp(c)] = \tau[scp(c_k) \cap scp(c)]$. The search in c_k (line 2) starts from scratch (i.e., $\perp$), since HOSTR does not store information about recently found maxRPWC-supports. If no such tuple exists, *setNextTuple* returns $\top$, and the search terminates since no PW-support for τ exists in c_k. Else, we check if τ' is an allowed tuple using binary search as explained in Function 13.

5.3.2 Theoretical Results

For a given constraint c, the worst-case time complexity of STR is $O(r'd + rt')$, where r' denotes the number of uninstantiated variables in $scp(c)$ and t' denotes the size of the current table of c [63]. The worst-case space complexity of STR is $O(ert)$. We now give the worst-case time complexity of HOSTR when implemented using the STR/maxRPWC+ Hybrid approach.

Proposition 7 The worst-case time complexity of HOSTR for the processing of one constraint is $O(r'.d + r.t'(e.M(d + r.log(S))))$.

Function 16 *isPWconsistent-STR^h*(c, τ): **boolean**

1: **for each** $c_k \neq c$ s.t. $|scp(c_k) \cap scp(c)| > 1$ **do**
2:     $\tau' \leftarrow setNextTuple(c, \tau, c_k, \bot)$;
3:     $x_{ch} \leftarrow$ select a variable $\in scp(c) \cap scp(c_k)$;
4:     **while** $\tau' \neq \top$ **do**
5:        $\tau'' \leftarrow binarySearch(allowed(c_k, x_{ch}, \tau'[x_{ch}]), \tau')$;
6:        **if** $\tau'' = \tau'$ OR $isValid(c_k, \tau'')$ **then return** TRUE;
7:        **if** $\tau'' = \top$ **then return** FALSE;
8:        $\tau' \leftarrow setNextTuple(c, \tau, c_k, \tau'')$;
9: **return** TRUE;

Proof: HOSTR is identical to STR with the addition of the call to functions *isPWconsistent-STR^h* each time a valid tuple is verified. The time complexity of Function *isPWconsistent-STR^h* is $O(e.M(d + k.log(S)))$ (see the proof of Proposition 5 for details). Thefefore, the worst-case time complexity of HOSTR is $O(r'.d + r.t'(e.M(d + r.log(S))))$. ■

If HOSTR is embedded within an AC-3 like algorithm to propagate all constraints then the time complexity will be $O(e.d.r.(r'.d + r.t'(e.M(d + r.log(S)))))$ since there are e constraints and each one is enqueued dr times in the worst case (i.e. once for each value deletion from a variable in its scope). The space complexity of HOSTR is $O(e(rt + r.|allowed(c, x, a)|))$ since in addition to the original tables we need the $allowed(c, x, a)$ lists.

Now we prove that HOSTR, implemented in any of the above ways, is incomparable to maxRPWC+ and maxRPWC, in terms of pruning, and weaker than FPWC.

Proposition 8 *The local consistency achieved by* HOSTR *is incomparable to that achieved by* maxRPWC+.

Proof: First, consider the problem in Example 1. Since max_τ' is lexicographically greater than the PW-support of τ on c_2 (let us assume that this is the only PW-support for τ), this tuple must be PW inconsistent. This means that when HOSTR processes c_2 it will delete this tuple. If, however, this does not cause any value deletions then it will not be propagated any further and c_1 will not be processed. Hence, HOSTR will not be able to delete 0 from $D(x_1)$. As explained in Example 1, maxRPWC+ will be able to make this deletion.

To show that HOSTR can delete values that maxRPWC+ cannot delete, consider the problem depicted in Figure 5.12. There are five variables $x1, \ldots, x5$ with $\{0, 1\}$ domains and one variable ($x6$) with domain 0. There are three table constraints with their allowed tuples shown in Figure 5.12. Value 0 of $x1$ has tuple (0,0,0) as GAC-support in $rel[c_1]$. This tuple has the PW-support (0,0,0,0) in $rel[c_2]$, and therefore if maxRPWC+ is applied it will not delete it (as it will not delete any other value). Now assume that HOSTR processes $c2$ first. Tuple (0,0,0,0) does not have a PW-support in $c3$, and therefore it will be removed. When $c1$ is processed, HOSTR will determine that tuple (0,0,0) has no PW-support in $c2$, since (0,0,0,0) has been deleted, and will therefore be removed. As a result, value 0 of $x1$ will loose its only GAC-support in $c1$ and will be deleted. ■

The extra pruning achieved by HOSTR compared to maxRPWC+ in the above example is a direct consequence of the fact that HOSTR, like STR, removes tuples from constraint relations. Now note that if constraint $c1$ is processed first in the example then no value deletion will be made. This is because when $c1$ is processed tuple (0,0,0) in $rel[c_1]$ will have the PW-support (0,0,0,0) in $rel[c_2]$ and therefore value 0 of $x1$ will not be deleted. When $c2$ is later processed, tuple (0,0,0,0)

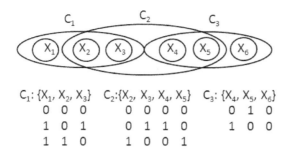

Figure 5.12: HOSTR vs. maxRPWC+.

will indeed be removed but no value from any of the variables in $scp(c2)$ will be deleted. This means that X_{evt} will be empty and as a result no constraint will be added to the propagation queue. Therefore, $c1$ will not be processed again. Hence, the pruning power of HOSTR cannot be characterized precisely because it depends on the ordering of the propagation queue.

Proposition 9 The local consistency achieved by HOSTR is incomparable to maxRPWC.

Proof: First, consider the example of Figure 5.12. If maxRPWC is applied on this problem it will achieve no pruning. But as explained in the proof of Proposition 8, HOSTR will delete value 0 of $x1$ if c_2 is processed before c_1. Therefore, HOSTR can achieve stronger pruning than maxRPWC.

Now consider the example in the proof of Proposition 6. After the deletion of value 0 from $D(x_4)$, HOSTR will add x_4 to X_{evt} and enqueue c_2. When c_2 is then processed no value deletion will be made and therefore propagation will stop. On the other hand, as explained, maxRPWC will delete value 0 from $D(x_1)$. ∎

Proposition 10 HOSTR achieves a local consistency that is strictly weaker than FPWC.

Proof: We first show that any deletion made by HOSTR will also be made by FPWC. HOSTR will delete a tuple $\tau \in rel[c]$ if τ is invalid or if Function *isPWconsistent-STR^h* cannot find a PW-support for τ on some constraint c'. By definition, PWC deletes any value that is invalid or not PWC. Hence, it will also delete τ. Correspondingly, HOSTR will delete a value $a \in D(x)$ if it does not participate in any valid and PW consistent tuple on some constraint c that involves x. Considering an algorithm that applies FPWC, PWC will delete all invalid and PW inconsistent tuples from $rel[c]$. Hence, the application of GAC that follows will delete a.

Finally, consider the example in Figure 5.12. As explained, if c_1 is processed before c_2, HOSTR will achieve no pruning. In contrast, and independent of the order in which constraints are processed, PWC will remove tuple (0,0,0,0) from $rel[c_2]$ and because of this tuple (0,0,0) will be removed from $rel[c_1]$. Then when GAC is applied value 0 will be removed from $D(x_1)$ because it will have no support in c_1. Hence, FPWC is strictly stronger than HOSTR. ∎

A stronger version of HOSTR Motivated by the inability to precisely characterize the pruning power of HOSTR due to its dependance on the propagation order, we propose a simple modification to HOSTR which achieves a stronger consistency property that can be precisely characterized. This algorithm, which we call full HOSTR (fHOSTR) differs from HOSTR in the following: If after traversing the tuples of a constraint c, at least one tuple has been removed then all variables that belong to $scp(c)$ are added to X_{evt}. This means that all constraints that involve any of these variables will be then added to the propagation queue. Recall that HOSTR adds a variable to X_{evt} only if a value has been deleted from the domain of this variable.

It is easy to see that in the example in Figure 5.12 fHOSTR will make the same value and tuple deletions as FPWC. Generalizing this, we now prove that fHOSTR achieves the same pruning as FPWC.

Proposition 11 Algorithm fHOSTR achieves FPWC.

Proof: We show that any deletion made by FPWC will also be made by fHOSTR. Consider any value a that is removed from a domain after FPWC is applied. This is because all supports for this value on some constraint c have been deleted. These tuples were deleted because they are not valid or not PWC. In the former case, since fHOSTR fully includes the operation of STR, it will delete any invalid tuple when processing constraint c and therefore will also delete value a. In the latter case, consider the deletion of any tuple τ because it is not PWC. This means that all of τ's PW-supports on some constraint c' have been deleted. When processing c', once the last PW-support of τ is deleted, fHOSTR will enqueues all constraints that intersect with c', including c. Then when c is processed, fHOSTR will not be able to find a PW-support for τ on c' and will thus delete it. Hence, all support of a will be deleted and as a result a will be deleted. ∎

To complete the theoretical analysis of the algorithms' pruning power, we now show that fHOSTR is strictly stronger than maxRPWC+.

Proposition 12 The local consistency achieved by fHOSTR is strictly stronger than that achieved by maxRPWC+.

Proof: First we show that any deletion made by maxRPWC+ will be also made by fHOSTR. Consider a value a that is removed from $D(x)$ after maxRPWC+ is applied. This is because either:

1. a is not GAC,

2. no GAC-support of a on a constraint c has a PW-support on some constraint c_k,

3. the deletion is triggered by the "fast check for lack of PW-support".

In the first case, the STR step of fHOSTR will obviously discover that a is not GAC. In the second case, the lack of PW-support for a tuple τ that includes a on some constraint c_k means that no potential PW-support for τ is valid. When fHOSTR processes tuple τ of c it will try to extend it to a PW-support in all intersecting constraints. Hence, it will consider c_k and recognize that τ has no valid PW-support in c_k. The same argument holds for all the GAC-supports of a in c.

Finally, if a is deleted by the "fast check for lack of PW-support" then the following must hold for each PW-consistent GAC-support τ for a in some constraint c. Any PW-support τ' of τ in some c_k is lexicographically smaller than $Last_{c_k,x_i,b}$, where $x_i \in scp(c_k)$ is a variable that belongs to the intersection of c and c_k and b is its value in τ'. maxRPWC+ must have moved the pointer $Last_{c_k,x_i,b}$ to some tuple τ'' beyond the PW-supports of τ because when trying to find a PW consistent GAC-support for b in c_k, all tuples lexicographically smaller than τ'', including all the PW-supports of τ, were determined as PW inconsistent. Now when fHOSTR processes c_k it will determine that all the PW-supports of τ are not themselves PW consistent and will thus delete them. Therefore, all constraints that involve variables in $scp(c_k)$, including c, will be enqueued. When c is later processed, no PW-support for τ (or any of a's GAC-supports in general) will be found, and thus a will be deleted.

For an example where fHOSTR achieves stronger pruning than maxRPWC+ consider the second example in the proof of Proposition 8. ∎

Algorithm fHOSTR achieves a stronger local consistency than HOSTR and maxRPWC+ but has a serious drawback: Its time complexity, when embedded within an AC-3 like algorithm to propagate all constraints, is $O(e^2.t.(r'.d + r.t'(e.M(d + r.log(S)))))$ since there are e constraints and each constraint c is enqueued $O(et)$ times in the worst case (i.e. once for each tuple deletion from a constraint intersecting c). This complexity is prohibitive for large table constraints.

Figure 5.13 summarizes the relationships between the local consistencies discussed throughout this chapter with respect to their pruning power.

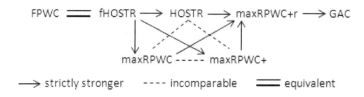

Figure 5.13: Summary of the relationships between consistencies.

5.4 Experiments

We ran experiments on benchmark non-binary problems with table constraints from the CSP Solver Competition[6]. The arities of the constraints in these problems range from 3 to 18. We tried the following classes: *forced random problems*, *random problems*, *positive table constraints*, *BDD*, *Dubois*, and *Aim*. These classes represent a large spectrum of instances with positive table constraints that are very commonly used for the evaluation of GAC algorithms and additionally, non-trivial intersections exist between their constraints. The first two classes only include constraints of arity 3, while the others include constraints of large arity (up to 18). Note that there exist classes of problems with table constraints where maxRPWC and similar methods do not offer any advantage compared to GAC because of the structure of the constraints. For example, on crossword puzzles constraints intersect on at most one variable. Our algorithms cannot achieve extra filtering compared to GAC in such problems.

In more detail, the 150 tried instances belong to classes that have the following attributes:

- The first two series *Random-fcd* and *Random* involve 20 variables and 60 ternary relations of almost 3,000 tuples each.

- The series *BDD* involves 21 Boolean variables and 133 constraints generated from binary decision diagrams of arity 18 that include 58,000 tuples.

- The two series *Positive table-8* and *Positive table-10* contain istances that involve 20 variables. Each instance of the series *Positive table-8* (resp.,*Positive table-10*) involves domains containing 5 (resp. 10) values and 18 (resp. 5) constraints of arity 8 (resp. 10). The constraint tables contain about 78,000 and 10,000 tuples, respectively.

- The *Dubois* class contains instances involving 80 boolean variables and quaternary constraints.

[6]http://www.cril.univ-artois.fr/CPAI08/

- The *Aim-100* and *Aim-200* series involve 100 and 200 Boolean variables respectively, with constraints of small arities (mainly ternary and a few binary).

The algorithms were implemented within a CP solver, written in Java, and tested on an Intel Core i5 of 2.40GHz processor and 4GB RAM. A CPU time limit of 6 hours was set for all algorithms and all instances. Search used the *dom/ddeg* heuristic for variable ordering and lexicographical value ordering. We have chosen *dom/ddeg* [15] as opposed to the generally more efficient *dom/wdeg* [23] because the decisions made by the latter are influenced by the ordering of the propagation queue making it harder to objectively compare the pruning efficiency of the algorithms [4]. Having said this, experiments with *dom/wdeg* did not give significantly different results compared to *dom/ddeg* as far as the relative efficiency of the algorithms is concerned.

We present results from STR2, GAC-va and maxRPWC1 compared to the proposed algorithms, HOSTR2^h, maxRPWC+ and maxRPWC+r. We include maxRPWC1 in the comparison since this is the most efficient domain filtering maxRPWC algorithm. For GAC-va and maxRPWC1 we used their residual versions, in order to avoid the maintainance of the *LastGAC* structure during search. This resulted in faster run times.

5.4.1 Preprocessing

Table 5.9 shows the mean CPU times (in miliseconds) obtained by the tested algorithms on each problem class for the initialization (i) and the preprocessing (p) phase. During initialization, the data structures of a specific algorithm are initialized, while preprocessing includes one run of a specific filtering algorithm before the search commences. Therefore, initialization time is the time required for each algorithm to construct all its structures, while preprocessing time is the time for a stand alone use of a specific algorithm.

Table 5.9: Mean CPU times of the initialization (i) and the preprocessing (p) phase in miliseconds from various problem classes.

Problem Class		STR2	GAC-va	maxRPWC1	HOSTR2^h	maxRPWC+r	maxRPWC+
Random-fcd	i	**31**	208	115	345	202	263
	p	111	**44**	696	399	154	250
Random	i	19	216	**10**	249	249	272
	p	87	**54**	738	291	186	247
Positive table-8	i	83	1,357	**5**	1,305	1,510	1,628
	p	271	**26**	2,891	36,621	343	359
Positive table-10	i	2	156	**0**	236	263	304
	p	47	**9**	4,997,817	363,000	620,210	772,193
BDD	i	237	7,065	**123**	10,017	8,530	8,334
	p	1,415	**270**	477,497	2,218	6,159	16,875
Dubois	i	10	**4**	12	13	10	12
	p	0	0	5	0	2	2
Aim-100	i	108	**40**	126	244	111	195
	p	**2**	14	160	19	19	38
Aim-200	i	397	**56**	303	465	270	280
	p	**4**	27	174	30	53	97

Algorithms that obtain GAC are routinely faster in both phases in all tested classes. As expected, strong local consistencies, spend extra time to record the intersections of the constraints during the initialization, while they are more expensive when they are applied stand-alone (i.e., during preprocessing). Interestingly, maxRPWC1 has low initialization times, since it does not use the *allowed* data structure that all proposed strong local consistencies use. On the contrary, maxRPWC1 is by far inferior compared to all other algorithms during preprocessing. Particularly, on *Positive table-8* and *Positive table-10* it is more than two orders of magnitude worse than all proposed algorithms. STR2 uses lighter data structures compared to GAC-va, resulting in being faster during initialization in the majority of the classes. On the other hand, GAC-va is usually faster during preprocessing, since STR2 traverses the whole table of tuples for each constraint.

Regarding the initialization times of the three strong consistency algorithms, maxRPWC+r appears to be the fastest. HOSTR2^h needs more time for the initialization since it uses the structures of both STR2 and maxRPWC+. Concerning the preprocessing, results are more varied since there are classes where maxRPWC+r dominates HOSTR2^h and vice versa. This is due to the different approaches of STR-like and GAC-va-like algorithms, as the former iterate over tuples and the latter over values and tuples, thus it is not clear which one is preferable for stand-alone use. On the other hand, it is clear that maxRPWC+r, being lighter, is faster than maxRPWC+.

Finally, the high preprocessing times for all proposed methods on the *Positive table-10* class are due to the high memory consumption on these large instances. However, as we show below, preprocessing by these algortithms is able to determine the unsatisfiability of the instances without requiring search. This makes them much more efficient than GAC-va, albeit STR2, which has a lower memory consumption, solves the instances in under one second on average. However, on *Positive table-8* both maxRPWC+ and maxRPWC+r are very close to STR2 and two (resp. one) orders of magnitude faster compared to HOSTR2^h (resp. maxRPWC1) preprocessing times.

5.4.2   Search

In Table 5.10 we present selected results from search algorithms that apply the tested filtering algorithms throughout search, while in Table 5.11 we give the average performance of the search algorithms in each problem class[7]. Note that results from class *Aim-200* were obtained using the *dom/wdeg* variable ordering heuristic. This is because none of the algorithms was able to solve these problems within the time limit using *dom/ddeg*.

Among the three proposed algorithms, maxRPWC+r is the most efficient with HOSTR2^h being a close second. maxRPWC+r is faster than HOSTR2^h on *Random, Random-fcd* and especially on *Positive table-8* (e.g., on the rand-8-20-5-18-800-12 instance it is over 6 times faster), while it is slower on *Positive table-10*. On the rest of the classes HOSTR2^h is better than maxRPWC+r, but without considerable differences. maxRPWC+r is also constantly faster compared to maxRPWC+, with the differences being considerable in the *Dubois* and *Aim* classes.

Comparing our algorithms against maxRPWC1 we observe that they are particularly more efficient on instances of large arities. These are the instances of *Positive Table* and *BDD* classes, whose arities vary from 8 to 18. Both maxRPWC+r and maxRPWC+ are notably faster, especially on *Positive table-10* and *BDD* they are superior by over one order of magnitude. There are also cases (i.e., *Positive table-8*), where maxRPWC1 was not able to solve the majority of the instances within the cutoff limit.

Now comparing GAC to strong local consistencies, all of the proposed algorithms typically outperform GAC-va, even by orders of magnitude in some cases. maxRPWC+r outperforms GAC-va on all tested classes, achieving significant differences in some cases (i.e., *Positive table-10, BDD, Aim*). Specifically, GAC-va reached the cutoff limit on all instances of *Positive table-10* class and could not detect unsatisfiability (neither could STR2). Importantly, as shown in Table 5.10, there are instances where maxRPWC+r significantly outperforms the state-of-the-art STR2 (e.g., the *Aim* instances), albeit it is also significantly outperformed on other instances.

---

[7]These results include initialization and preprocessing times.

Table 5.10: CPU times (t) in secs and nodes (n) from various representative problem instances.

Instance		STR2	GAC-va	maxRPWC1	HOSTR2^h	maxRPWC+r	maxRPWC+
rand-3-20-20 60-632-fcd-5	t	242	408	308	291	237	**195**
	n	160,852	160,852	66,335	66,601	66,469	66,585
rand-3-20-20 60-632-fcd-7	t	90	132	174	131	**78**	82
	n	73,536	73,536	19,680	19,791	19,988	18,668
rand-3-20-20-60-632-5	t	**472**	1,061	867	879	567	564
	n	501,583	501,583	152,712	152,763	153,138	152,892
rand-3-20-20-60-632-14	t	**16**	33	32	38	18	17
	n	19,996	19,996	3,976	3,986	4,002	3,898
rand-8-20-5-18-800-7	t	**17**	1,145	1,616	1,860	494	754
	n	17,257	17,257	3,424	3,444	3,447	3,430
rand-8-20-5-18-800-12	t	**19**	10,914	-	12,625	2,823	3,654
	n	105,521	105,521	-	28,830	28,752	28,662
rand-10-20-10-5-10000-1	t	**0.4**	-	3,811	174	203	208
	n	1,110	-	0	0	0	0
rand-10-20-10-5-10000-4	t	**0.3**	-	6,438	1,283	1,212	1,298
	n	1,110	-	0	0	0	0
bdd-21-133-18-78-6	t	30	7,653	2.4	**0.6**	1.5	2
	n	20,582	20,582	0	0	0	0
bdd-21-133-18-78-11	t	39	8,310	1,714	**1.2**	11.6	16.8
	n	19,364	19,364	21	21	21	21
dubois-21	t	110	109	56	**40**	53	314
	n	58,447,186	58,447,186	19,704,488	23,237,970	23,237,970	23,237,970
dubois-26	t	4,044	3,456	3,427	**1,463**	1,830	12,174
	n	1,823,036,754	1,823,036,754	808,626,856	744,052,050	744,052,050	744,052,050
aim-100-1-6-sat-2	t	6,423	232	0.4	**0.15**	0.18	0.25
	n	29,181,742	29,181,742	100	100	100	100
aim-100-2-0-sat-3	t	2,448	1,812		**0.23**	0.39	0.4
	n	177,832,989	177,832,989	100	100	111	111
aim-200-2-0-sat-1	t	57	19	0.5	**0.4**	0.5	0.6
	n	2,272,993	1,326,708	257	2,210	2,210	1,782
aim-200-2-0-sat-4	t	30	21	0.7	0.8	**0.4**	0.7
	n	987,160	1,196,073	611	2,887	1,965	1,965

All of tried algorithms completed all instances within the cutoff limit except from maxRPWC1, which did not solve 13 instances out of 20 from the *Positive table-8* class. Also, GAC-va reached the cutoff limit on all instances of the *Positive table-10* class.

Looking at the average performances in Table 5.11, maxRPWC+r (and HOSTR2^h) is faster than STR2 in the *BDD*, *Dubois* and *Aim* classes with the differences being considerable in the two *Aim* classes. On the other hand, STR2 dominates in the *Random* and *Positive table* classes, with the differences being very significant in the latter.

Regarding the pruning power of the strong local consistency algorithms, which is to some extent reflected on node visits, it is worth noticing that the differences are negligible in the majority of the classes. Though in both *Aim* classes the pruning of maxRPWC1 results in competitive CPU times. Spcciffically, on *Aim*, maxRPWC1 visits significantly less nodes compared to our domain filtering algorithms. Additionally, on *Aim-200* maxRPWC1 benefits from the *dom/wdeg* variable ordering heuristic and along with the different queue handling of HOSTR2^h (i.e., queue of constraints), results in significant node differences. Note that both variable ordering heuristics used are dynamic and may result in different variable orderings and thus, in a different search trees. This is why node visits relfect the pruning power of propagation only to some extent.

The dominance of STR2 in the *Positive Table* classes is due to the structure of these problems which include constraints of large arity (8 and 10) resulting in many constraint intersections with a large number of shared variables in each intersection (up to 8). In addition, the tables of the con-

Table 5.11: Mean CPU times (t) in secs and nodes (n) from various problem clases.

Problem Class		STR2	GAC-va	maxRPWC1	HOSTR2^h	maxRPWC+r	maxRPWC+
Random-fcd	t	**152**	232	310	305	176	171
	n	132,492	132,492	49,009	49,317	49,420	48,608
Random	t	**154**	382	461	504	298	288
	n	211,456	211,456	79,928	77,955	80,316	78,802
Positive table-8	t	**15**	4,152	-	5,002	1,168	1,576
	n	52,313	52,313	-	10,087	9,787	10,039
Positive table-10	t	**0.3**	-	4,998	363	620	773
	n	1,110	-	0	0	0	0
BDD	t	30	8,513	924	**3**	18	24
	n	19,139	19,139	11	11	11	11
Dubois	t	2,026	1,956	1,413	**807**	1,005	6,751
	n	1,008,184,658	1,008,184,658	419,586,728	401,069,394	401,069,394	401,069,394
Aim-100	t	6,390	7,156	**748**	1,019	863	3,899
	n	643,784,411	643,784,411	10,095,756	34,062,528	34,062,529	34,062,529
Aim-200	t	13	6	**3**	4	**3**	15
	n	479,073	432,930	14,937	97,529	104,748	88,541

straints are quite large. Consequently, in *Positive table-8* the benefits of the extra pruning achieved by a stronger consistency do not reflect on CPU times because of the extra cost incurred. And as discussed previously, all algorithms apart from STR2 suffer from memory exhaustion on *Positive table-10* instances.

CPU times from all tested instances comparing maxRPWC+r to HOSTR2^h, GAC-va, STR2 and maxRPWC1 are presented in Figures 5.14, 5.15, 5.16 and 5.17 respectively, in a logarithmic scale. Different signs display instances from different problem classes and are calculated by CPU time ratios of the compared algorithms. Those signs placed above the diagonal correspond to instances that were solved faster by maxRPWC+r. In Figure 5.14 most instances are gathered around the diagonal indicating closely matched performance of the proposed algorithms. As detailed above, maxRPWC+r is superior to HOSTR2^h on *Positive table-8* and inferior on *BDD* and *Aim-100*, but without significant differences.

Comparing maxRPWC+r to GAC-va, STR2 and maxRPWC1 in Figures 5.15, 5.16 and 5.17 respectively, we can see the benefits of our approach: In Figure 5.15 only a few instances are below the diagonal indicating that maxRPWC+r is clearly superior to GAC-va. Also, there are many instances where GAC-va thrashes while maxRPWC+r does not. A similar picture is noticed in Figure 5.17, where the majority of the instances are gathered above the diagonal. Only a few instances from *BDD* and *Aim* are solved faster by maxRPWC1.

Looking at Figure 5.16 we see a much more varied picture. Although on most instances maxRPWC+r and STR2 are closely matched, there are numerous instances where one of the two methods thrashes and vice versa. This demonstrates that efficient algorithms for strong local consistencies on table constraints constitute a viable alternative to the standard GAC approach, but at the same time further research is required to develop methods that can be more robust than state-of-the-art GAC algorithms such as STR2 on a wider range of problems.

A similar pattern emerges when comparing HOSTR2^h to GAC-va and STR2. This is shown in Figures 5.18 and 5.19 respectively. Again HOSTR2^h is clearly better than GAC-va on instances of large arity (i.e., *BDD*, *Positive table-10*), while when compared to STR2 it gives mixed results. Specifically, it is superior on instances with constraints of small arity, like *Dubois* and *Aim*. On the other hand, despite that it is inferior on many instances from both *Positive table* classes, it is faster by an order of magnitude on *BDD* instances. On this class, although the arity of the constraints

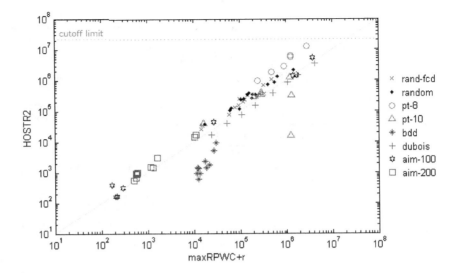

Figure 5.14: $\texttt{HOSTR2}^h$ vs. $\texttt{maxRPWC+r}$.

is very high (18) and the relation tables are large, the intersections between constraints include up to 16 variables. This allows $\texttt{HOSTR2}^h$ to quickly find a solution (or prove unsatisfiability). This is a general observation that demonstrates the practical usefulness of all strong local consistencies proposed: They can efficiently exploit constraint intersections.

5.5   maxRPWC+ for Intensional Constraints

Although $\texttt{maxRPWC+}$ is specialized for table constraints, it can be applied on intensional constraints after some modifications. This may be useful in cases of constraints without specialized filtering algorithms, or to simply explore the potential of a strong local consistency on any given constraint without having to invent specialized algorithms.

Function *seekSupport-v* for intensional constraints is similar to the corresponding function (*seekSupport*) for extensional ones. The difference is that the search for GAC-support is a linear scan of the tuples after $Last_{c_i,x_j,a_j}$ in lexicographical order. That is, only the list of valid tuples is traversed.

Function 17 *seekPWsupport-v* $(c_i, \tau, c_k, max\_\tau')$

1: **if** $\neg\ isValid(c_k, max\_\tau')$ **then** $max\_\tau' \leftarrow setNextTuple(c_i, \tau, c_k, max\_\tau')$;
2: **if** $max\_\tau' \neq \top$ **then** $\tau' \leftarrow checkPWtuple(c_i, \tau, c_k, max\_\tau')$;
3: **else return** $\top$;
4: **while** $\tau' \neq \top$ **do**
5:    **if** $isConsistent(c_k, \tau')$ **then return** τ';
6:    $\tau' \leftarrow setNextTuple(c_i, \tau, c_k, \tau')$;
7: **return** $\top$;

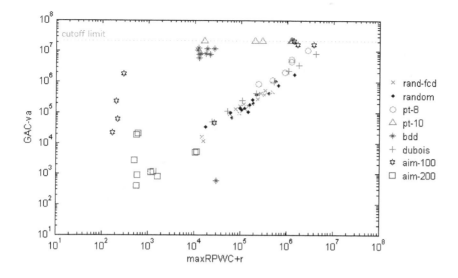

Figure 5.15: $\texttt{GAC-va}$ vs. $\texttt{maxRPWC+r}$.

The corresponding function that searches for a PW-support is Function *seekPWsupport-v* (Function 17). Lines 5-6 show the different approach we use on intensional constraints. Instead of interchangeably visiting valid and allowed tuples, we just check if the valid tuple τ' satisfies the constraint c_k by calling function *isConsistent*. If τ' is inconsistent then a new tuple τ' is constructed by *setNextTuple* (line 6), such that $\tau'[scp(c_k) \cap scp(c_i)] = \tau[scp(c_k) \cap scp(c_i)]$. If *setNextTuple* returns $\top$ the search terminates, otherwise, we continue to check if the returned tuple is consistent as explained above, and so on.

The worst-case time complexity of $\texttt{maxRPWC+}$ for intensional constraints is $O(e^2 r^2 d^{2r - f_{min}})$, which is the same as that of $\texttt{maxRPWC1}$ if we consider that in the worst case $p = 2r - f_{min}$. The space complexity of $\texttt{maxRPWC+}$ is $O(erd)$ which is the space required for *Last* and is the same as $\texttt{maxRPWC1}$ but lower than both $\texttt{maxRPWC2}$ and $\texttt{maxRPWC3}$.

5.6   An extension of GAC2001/3.1 derived from maxRPWC+

Inspired from $\texttt{maxRPWC+}$, we propose an extension to the standard GAC algorithm $\texttt{GAC2001/3.1}$ [18] that achieves a stronger local consistency than GAC by considering intersections of constraints. Importantly, this algorithm is also applicable on intensional constraints as opposed to $\texttt{GAC-va}$, $\texttt{maxRPWC+}$ and $\texttt{HOSTR}\star$ that are applicable only on positive table constraints. The worst-case time complexity of the proposed algorithm, called $\texttt{GAC+}$, is higher than that of $\texttt{GAC2001/3.1}$ only by a factor e, where e is the number of constraints in the problem. Experimental results demonstrate that in many cases $\texttt{GAC+}$ can reduce the size of the search tree compared to GAC, resulting in improved cpu times. Also, in cases where there is no gain in search tree size, there is only a negligible overhead in cpu time.

$\texttt{GAC+}$ extends the generic GAC algorithm $\texttt{GAC2001/3.1}$ through the intelligent exploitation of simple data structure used by $\texttt{GAC2001/3.1}$. In Section 5.2 we presented $\texttt{maxRPWC+}$, an

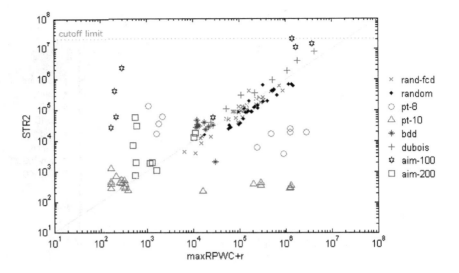

Figure 5.16: STR2 vs. maxRPWC+r.

algorithm that extends GAC-supports to intersecting constraints. As described there, for each intersecting constraint, maxRPWC+ quickly verifies the lack of PW-support by exploiting the *Last* data
structure. We adopted the fast check for the lack of PW-supports to build on GAC2001/3.1. We
incorporated this check in GAC+ to achieve extra prunning in cases where constraint intersections
exist. Significantly, the new algorithm remains generic, meaning that it is applicable on any kind
of constraints (i.e., both on extensional and intensional constraints).

Algorithm 18 Algorithm GAC+

1: **if** PREPROCESSING **then** L=L $\cup$ $\{x_i\}$, $\forall x_i \in V$;
2: **else** L={ currently assigned variable };
3: **while** L $\neq \emptyset$ **do**
4: 　　L=L$-\{x_i\}$;
5: 　　**for each** $c_k \in C$ s.t. $x_i \in scp(c_k)$ **do**
6: 　　　**for each** $x_j \in V$ s.t. $x_j \in scp(c_k)$ AND $x_j \neq x_i$ **do**
7: 　　　　**if** *revise_GAC+*$(c_k, x_j) > 0$ **then**
8: 　　　　　**if** DWO(x_j) **then return** FAILURE;
9: 　　　　　L=L $\cup$ $\{x_j\}$;
10: **return** SUCCESS;

In more detail, when GAC+ is applied it deletes all values that are not GAC and in addition
it can delete some extra values that are GAC but are not maxRPWC. To achieve this it utilizes
the *LastGAC* data structure of GAC2001/3.1. To recall the use of this data structure, for each
constraint c and each value $a_i \in D(x_i)$, where $x_i \in scp(c)$, $LastGAC_{c,x_i,a_i}$ gives (i.e. points to)
the most recently discovered support of a_i in c.

Algorithm GAC+ utilizes a list L where variables that have their domains pruned are inserted.
Once a variable x_i is extracted from L, each constraint c_k that involves x_i is examined (line 5 in

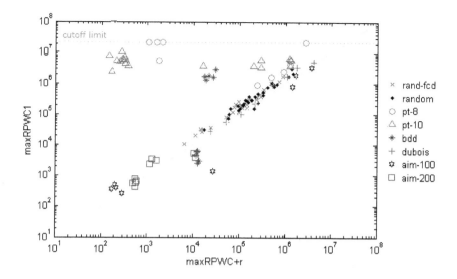

Figure 5.17: maxRPWC1 vs. maxRPWC+r.

Algorithm 18) and all the variables that appear in c_k, except x_i, are revised. This is done by calling Function *reviseGAC+*.

This function takes a constraint c_i and a variable x_j, s.t. $x_j \in scp(c_i)$, and for each value $a_j \in D(x_j)$ first checks if a_j has a support in c_i. In case $LastGAC_{c_i,x_j,a_j}$ is valid then this tuple is a support for a_j. If $LastGAC_{c_i,x_j,a_j}$ is not valid anymore, a new support is seeked. This is done by iterating through the tuples of c_i in lexicographical order starting from the one immediatelly after $LastGAC_{c_i,x_j,a_j}$ (line 5 in Function 19). In case a tuple τ that is valid and consistent is located, then a support for a_j has been established and $LastGAC_{c_i,x_j,a_j}$ is set to τ. Up to this point GAC+ operates just like a typical GAC algorithm. However, once a support τ is located, GAC+ performs an additional operation which can sometimes determine that τ has no PW-support in some intersecting constraint. Namely, the algorithm iterates over the constraints intersecting with c_i on more than one variable and for each such constraint c_k calls Function *checkPWtuple2*[8].

Function *checkPWtuple2* is similar to Function *checkPWtuple* and *Lex_Max* locates the lexicographically largest $LastGAC_{c_k,x_k,\tau[x_k]}$ for all variables x_k that belong to the intersection of c_i and c_k (lines 1-4). Then it checks if there can exist a tuple greater or equal to this one that has the same values for the variables of the intersection as τ. Crucially, this check is done in linear time as explained in 5.2.

As implied by its description, *checkPWtuple2* can verify the lack of PW-support mainly in cases where the variables in the intersection appear consecutively at the start of constraint's c_k scope. Hence, this function performs a limited, and cheap, check for PW consistency. That is, it can sometimes determine that a verified support τ is not PW consistent (i.e. it has no PW-support on some constraint). In such a case, the search for a support for a_j is resumed in *reviseGAC+*.

The following example illustrates the basic idea behind GAC+, which is also exploited by maxRPWC+. Therefore, we rephrase Example 1 by replacing *Last* structure with *LastGAC* in

---

[8]Constraints that intersect on exactly one variable are not considered because after making the problem GAC they cannot possibly contribute to any extra pruning [ ].

Function 19 reviseGAC+(c_i, x_j)

1: removedValues = 0;
2: **for each** $a_j \in D(x_j)$ **do**
3:    SUPPORT_FOUND=FALSE;
4:    **if** $\neg isValid(LastGAC_{c_i, x_j, a_j})$ **then**
5:       **for each** τ of $c_i > LastGAC_{c_i, x_j, a_j}$, s.t. $\tau[x_j] = a_j$ **do**
6:          **if** $isValid(\tau)$ AND $isConsistent(c_i, \tau)$ **then**
7:             $LastGAC_{c_i, x_j, a_j} = \tau$;
8:             PW_CONSISTENCY=TRUE;
9:             **for each** $c_k \neq c_i$ s.t. $|scp(c_k) \cap scp(c_i)| > 1$ **do**
10:                **if** $checkPWtuple2(c_i, \tau, c_k)$ **then**
11:                   PW_CONSISTENCY=FALSE; **break**;
12:             **if** PW_CONSISTENCY **then**
13:                SUPPORT_FOUND=TRUE; **break**;
14:    **if** $\neg$ SUPPORT_FOUND **then**
15:       remove a_j from $D(x_j)$;
16:       removedValues = removedValues + 1;
17: **return** removedValues;

Function 20 checkPWtuple2(c_i, τ, c_k)

1: Lex_Max=NULL;
2: **for each** $x_k \in scp(c_k) \cap scp(c_i)$ **do**
3:    **if** $\tau' = LastGAC_{c_k, x_k, \tau[x_k]} > Lex\_Max$ **then**
4:       Lex_Max=τ';
5: **for each** $x_k \in scp(c_k)$ **do**
6:    **if** $x_k \notin scp(c_k) \cap scp(c_i)$ **then**
7:       **if** $Lex\_Max[x_k]$ is last value in $D(x_k)$ **then continue**;
8:       **else break**;
9:    **else**
10:       **if** $Lex\_Max[x_k] < \tau[x_k]$ **then break**;
11:       **if** $Lex\_Max[x_k] > \tau[x_k]$ **then return** FALSE;
12: **return** TRUE;

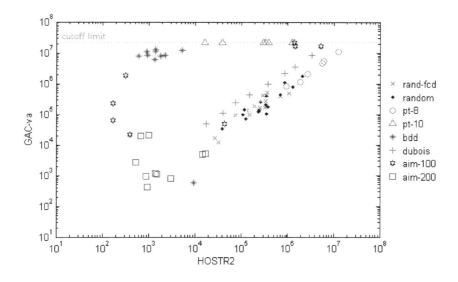

Figure 5.18: GAC-va vs. HOSTR2[h].

order to show the extra prunnig offered by GAC+.

Example 3 *Consider two constraints c_1 and c_2 with $scp(c_1) = \{x_1, x_2, x_3, x_4\}$ and $scp(c_2) = \{x_3, x_4, x_5, x_6\}$. Assume that the support $\tau = \{0, 2, 2, 1\}$ has been located for value 0 of x_1, and that $LastGAC_{c_2, x_3, 2}$ is tuple $\tau' = \{2, 2, 0, 1\}$. Since $\tau'[x_4]$ is greater than $\tau[x_4]$, it is clear that there is no valid and consistent tuple in c_2 that includes values 2 and 1 for x_3 and x_4 respectively. That is, no PW-support for τ exists in c_2 and hence value 0 of x_1 is not maxRPWC. If we assume that τ is the last support of $(x_1, 0)$ in c_1 then GAC+ will determine (simply by comparing τ to τ') that 0 should be deleted from $D(x_1)$. In contrast, a GAC algorithm cannot infer this since it does not consider constraint intersections at all.*

The following proposition is a direct consequence of the limited check for PW consistency that GAC+ performs.

Proposition 13 GAC+ achieves a level of local consistency that is strictly stronger than GAC and strictly weaker than maxRPWC.

Proof: We first show that any deletion made by a GAC algorithm will also be made by GAC+. The proof is straightforward if we consider that GAC+ is identical to GAC2001/3.1 plus the calls to Function *checkPWtuple2*, which can only result in extra pruning. Then, we need to show that there exist values that are pruned by GAC+ and not by a GAC algorithm. Example 3 displays a case where value 0 of x_1 is GAC but GAC+ detects that it is not PW consistent and thus, removes it. Hence, GAC+ is strictly stronger than GAC.

Every value that is pruned by GAC+ is also pruned by a maxRPWC algorithm. Both algorithms delete values that are not GAC. Now, consider the case of the extra prunning described in the example 3. maxRPWC will find that τ is a GAC support of value 0 of x_1 and then will search for its PW-support in c_2. It will detect that there is no tuple in c_2 that includes values 2 and 1 for x_3 and x_4 respectively. Since τ is the last support of $(x_1, 0)$ in c_1 maxRPWC will also delete it from

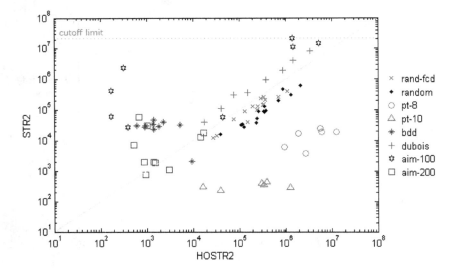

Figure 5.19: STR2 vs. HOSTR2[h].

$D(x_1)$. Now, assume the case where $\tau'[x_4]$ is not greater than $\tau[x_4]$, i.e., $\tau' = \{2, 0, 0, 1\}$, which means that GAC+ will not make any pruning. Also, assume that the lexicographically greater tuple in c_2 is the $\{2, 2, 0, 1\}$ tuple. maxRPWC will detect that $\tau = \{0, 2, 2, 1\}$ has no PW-support and thus, will delete 0 from $D(x_1)$. Hence, GAC+ is strictly weaker than maxRPWC. ■

As mentioned, the ability of GAC+ to delete extra values compared to a GAC algorithm depends on the ordering of the variables in the scope of the constraints. For instance, if the scope of constraint c_2 in Example 3 is $scp(c_2) = \{x_3, x_5, x_4, x_6\}$ with $LastGAC_{c_2,x_3,2}$ being $\tau' = \{2, 0, 2, 1\}$ then we cannot deduce that no PW-support for τ exists in c_2 unless 0 is the last value in $D(x_5)$. This is because a tuple that is lexicographically greater than τ', e.g. $\{2, 1, 1, 1\}$ may be a PW-support of τ. However, the ordering of the constraints' scope can be altered if necessary. For example, if a subset of the variables in a constraint appears in many intersections with other constraints then these variables can be moved to the front of the constraint's scope to facilitate pruning by GAC+. This can be done for all constraints in a preprocessing step.

Finally, we discuss the worst-case complexity of GAC+. Since GAC+ uses the same $LastGAC$ data structure as GAC2001/3.1, it has the same O(erd) space complexity.

Proposition 14 The worst-case time complexity of GAC+ is $O(e^2 r^2 d^r)$.

Proof: GAC+ is identical to GAC2001/3.1 with the addition of lines 8-13 to *reviseGAC+*. In *reviseGAC+*, for each variable x_j and each of its d values, d^{r-1} tuples are first checked for GAC consistency with O(r) cost for each check. Then, for each tuple and each constraint c_k interecting c_i *checkPWtuple2* is called.

Let us now consider the cost of *checkPWtuple2*. Finding the lexicographically largest $LastGAC$ among the at most f_{max} variables in $scp(c_k) \cap scp(c_i)$ costs O(f_{max}), assuming that the lexicographic comparison of two tuples is implemented efficiently. The **for** loop of line 5 costs O(r) since in the worst case all values in the tuple must be examined. Hence, the cost of *checkPWtuple2* is O($f_{max} + r$)=O(r).

Hence, *reviseGAC+* costs $O(dd^{r-1}(r + er)) = O(erd^r)$. This function can be called at most rd times for each constraint c_i and variable $x_j \in scp(c_i)$. However, the cost of *reviseGAC+* for each x_j and each c_i is amortized over all the kd calls because of the use of $LastGAC$ (see [18] for details). Since there are at most e constraints and r variables per constraint, the worst-case time complexity of GAC+ is $O(e^2 r^2 d^r)$. ∎

5.6.1 Comparing GAC+ to GAC2001/3.1

We ran experiments to show the potential of GAC+, with benchmark non-binary problems taken from C. Lecoutre's repository and used in the CSP Solver Competitions. We tried the following classes: *Golomb rulers, random problems, forced random problems, chessboard coloration, Schurr's lemma, modified Renault, positive table constraints* and *BDD*. The first five classes only include constraints of arity up to 4, while the other three include constraints of large arity (up to 18).

The algorithms were implemented within a CP solver written in Java from scratch. Search used a binary branching scheme, the *dom/wdeg* heuristic for variable ordering [23], and lexicographical value ordering. The searches for GAC on extensional constraints of large arity were performed using the efficient algorithm of [72]. The ordering of variables in the constraint scopes was not altered to facilitate propagation for GAC+, although this is an interesting direction for future work.

In Table 5.12 we present indicative results from search algorithms that maintain a certain local consistency throughout search. We compare GAC+ to GAC (implemented using algorithm GAC2001/3.1). The results demonstrate that, on the majority of instances, GAC+ improves upon the performance of GAC2001/3.1.

Specifically, GAC+ is clearly better than GAC2001/3.1 on *Golomb rulers* instances as well as *random* and *forced random* problems. Often there are large margins between the performances of the two algorithms. For example on *rand-3-20-20-60-632-fcd-15* GAC+ is 3 times faster than GAC2001/3.1. These results are due to the stronger pruning achieved by GAC+ which results in significant reduction in the number of nodes.

GAC+ does not achieve notable additional pruning on *positive table constraints*. Albeit, it is still faster than GAC2001/3.1. Results are somewhat mixed on the *modified Renault* and *BDD* classes. However, GAC+ is faster than GAC2001/3.1 in the majority of the instances.

GAC+ is not successful, in terms of pruning, on the *chessboard coloration* and *Schurr's lemma* classes. This is due to the structure of the instances in these classes. In *chessboard coloration* constraints have relatively small arity (4) and they are very loose (disjunctions of $\neq$ constraints). This minimizes the extra pruning that can be achieved by GAC+. Note that in some cases GAC+ results in more node visits than GAC2001/3.1, meaning that its few extra value deletions actually mislead the variable ordering heuristic. In *Schurr's lemma* problems there are only a few constraint intersections on more than one variable. As a result, our method cannot exploit the problems' structure for additional pruning. However, despite the lack of additional pruning in these two classes, the overheads of GAC+ do not slow down search notably compared to GAC2001/3.1.

To sum up, we presented GAC+, an extension to the standard GAC algorithm that achieves a stronger local consistency level than GAC. This is accomplished through the exploitation of two things: the data structure already used by GAC2001/3.1 (i.e., $LastGAC$) and the technique for fast check for PW-support of maxRPWC+. The worst-case time complexity of GAC+ is very close to that of GAC algorithms, which is also reflected on the practical performance of the algorithm as it does not slow down search in a significant way even in cases where no additional pruning compared to GAC is achieved. On the other hand, there exist cases where the additional pruning of

Table 5.12: Search tree nodes and cpu times in secs from various representative problem instances.

Instance	Node visits		CPU time	
	GAC2001/3.1	GAC+	GAC2001/3.1	GAC+
renault-mod-5	1,070	1,038	**326**	332
renault-mod-10	1,532	1,514	48	**47**
renault-mod-24	753	674	217	**206**
renault-mod-25	1,273	545	510	**365**
renault-mod-31	863	796	76	**69**
bdd-21-133-18-78-6	41,199	39,002	3,521	**2,777**
bdd-21-133-18-78-7	36,383	31,713	**4,312**	4,462
ruler-25-8-a4	2,697	2,316	96	**67**
ruler-34-9-a4	8,495	9,430	1,264	**934**
rand-3-20-20-60-632-fcd-4	223,155	113,814	275	**154**
rand-3-20-20-60-632-fcd-8	136,912	110,585	171	**145**
rand-3-20-20-60-632-fcd-15	85,940	25,858	109	**35**
rand-3-20-20-60-632-4	124,450	37,612	165	**51**
rand-3-20-20-60-632-7	114,375	112,592	**150**	155
rand-3-20-20-60-632-9	73,408	48,956	102	**67**
pt-8-20-5-18-800-4	37,466	37,416	1,301	**1,181**
pt-8-20-5-18-800-7	15,845	15,757	505	**464**
cc-8-8-2	13,278	13,762	**7.2**	7.8
cc-9-9-2	12,945	12,828	**12**	13
lemma-20-9	370,992	370,992	**101**	102
lemma-30-9	367,664	367,664	**249**	253

GAC+ results in important cpu time gains.

5.7 Conclusion

In this chapter, we presented specialized algorithms for table constraints that achieve local consistencies stronger than the standard GAC. These algorithms build on and extend existing algorithms for GAC and maxRWPC and contribute to both directions of domain and relation filtering local consistencies. Experimental results demonstrated the usefulness of the proposed algorithms in the presence of intersecting table constraints, showing that the best among them are clearly more robust than a standard GAC algorithm for table constraints (GAC-va), and can be competitive with a state-of-the art GAC algorithm (STR2).

Such ideas can be exploited and adopted by other even generic algorithms, like GAC2001/3.1, to further improve their performance. We believe that the presented work can pave the way for the design and implementation of even more efficient strong consistency methods for table constraints. Also, it can perhaps help initiate a wider study on specialized strong consistency algorithms for specialized (global) constraints.

Higher-order Consistencies for Table Constraints using Counters

Among the most successful GAC algorithms for table constraints we discussed in Section 3.3, we find variants of simple tabular reduction (STR), like STR2 and STR3. In this chapter, we propose an extension of STR-based algorithms that achieves Full PairWise Consistency (FPWC), a consistency stronger than GAC and max Restricted PairWise Consistency (maxRPWC). This approach involves counting the number of occurrences of specific combinations of values in constraint intersections. Importantly, the worst-case time complexity of one call to the basic filtering procedure at the heart of this algorithm is quite close to that of STR algorithms. Experiments demonstrate that methods of this chapter can outperform STR2 in many classes of problems, being significantly faster in some cases. Also, it is clearly superior to maxRPWC+ and HOSTR*, algorithms that have been proposed in Chapter 4.6 and achieve a strong local consistency on table constraints.

6.1   Introduction

GAC algorithms for table constraints have attracted considerable interest, dating back to GAC-Schema [16]. Classical algorithms iterate over lists of tuples in different ways; e.g., see [16, 75, 72]. Recent developments, however, suggested maintaining dynamically the list of supports in constraint tables: these are the variants of simple tabular reduction (STR) [103, 63, 69]. Alternatively, specially-constructed intermediate structures such as tries [44] or multi-valued decision diagrams (MDDs) [25] have been proposed. Among these algorithms and those of Section 3.3, STR2 along with the MDD approach are considered to be the most efficient ones (especially, for large arity constraints).

The majority of the algorithms prosed for higher-order local consistencies (Section 3.2.4) are generic, since they are applicable on constraints of any type, which typically results in a high computation cost. Specialized algorithms for table constraints that achieves a consistency stronger than GAC were proposed in Chapter 4.6. These algorithms, called maxRPWC+ and HOSTR*, extend the GAC algorithms of [72] and [63] respectively. They approximate a domain-filtering restriction of PWC, called max restricted pairwise consistency (maxRPWC) [19]. Interestingly, they achieve good performance compared to state-of-the-art GAC algorithms on several classes of problems, that include intersecting table constraints.

In this chapter, we propose a new higher-order consistency algorithm for table constraints, called FPWC-STR, based on STR. Actually, we show that all STR-based algorithms can be easily extended to achieve stronger pruning by introducing a set of counters for each intersection between any two constraints c_i and c_j. At any time each counter in this set holds the number of valid tuples in c_i's table that include a specific combination of values for the set of variables that are common to both c_i and c_j. We show that FPWC-STR enforces full pairwise consistency, i.e., both PWC and GAC, and we prove that it also guarantees maxRPWC. Importantly, the worst-case time complexity of one call to the basic filtering procedure at the heart of FPWC-STR is quite close to that of STR algorithms. Our experiments demonstrate that FPWC-STR can outperform STR2 on many classes of problems with intersecting table constraints (being significantly faster in some cases), and is also typically considerably faster than maxRPWC+ and HOSTR2, often by very large margins.

6.2   Extending STR

In this section, we present a simple way to filter domains and constraints by using the technique of simple tabular reduction (STR), together with a few additional data structures related to (sub)tuple counting. We explain how the update/restoration and the exploitation of introduced counters is interleaved with STR in a seamless way to obtain specialized and efficient higher-order consistency algorithms for table constraints. The new algorithms we propose will be called eSTR$\star$, derived from *extended* STR. The '$\star$' stands for a particular STR algorithm (e.g., when extending STR2 we name the algorithm eSTR2).

The central idea of eSTR$\star$ is to store the number of times that each subtuple appears in the intersection of any two constraints. Specifically, for each constraint c_i, we introduce a set of counters for each (non trivial) intersection between c_i and another constraint c_j. Assuming that Y is the set of variables that are common to both c_i and c_j, at any time each counter in this set holds the number of valid tuples in c_i's table that include a specific combination of values for Y. In this way, once a tuple $\tau \in rel[c_j]$ has been verified as valid, we can check if it has a PW-support in $rel[c_i]$ simply by observing the value of the corresponding counter (i.e., the counter for subtuple $\tau[scp(c_j) \cap scp(c_i)]$). If this counter is greater than 0 then τ has a PW-support in $rel[c_i]$. Importantly, this check is done in **constant time**.

Note that this approach is related to that in [93], where arc consistency is enforced on the dual representation of non-binary problems using counters that record information about constraint intersections. However, for any two constraints that intersect, the space complexity of that approach is exponential in the size of the subset of variables belonging to the intersection. Counters have also been exploited in algorithms AC4/GAC4 [85, 86]. Finally, there exist some connections with both the MDD-based propagation approach [50], because invalid tuples are aimed at being removed, and the intersection encoding of sliding constraints [14].

Algorithm 21 presents the main framework for eSTR$\star$ by extending the basic STR algorithm, as proposed in [103]. We choose to present an extension of STR, simply called eSTR, because of its simplicity compared to STR2 and STR3, which can be extended in a very similar way. Here, we consider a constraint-based vision[9] of STR, meaning that the propagation queue, denoted by Q, handles constraints, because it is quite adapted to our filtering operations. The level of local consistency achieved by means of the process of propagation will be discussed in the next section. Whenever a constraint is removed from the queue, STR iterates over the valid tuples in the constraint and removes any tuple that has become invalid through the deletion of one of its values (the **while** loop in Algorithm 21 ; see lines 4–14). Thus, only valid tuples are kept in tables. After finishing the iteration, all values that are no longer supported are deleted (the **for** loop in Algorithm 21 ; see lines 15–21) and for each variable x whose domain has been reduced, all constraints

---

[9]Constraint-based and variable-based propagation schemes are those that are classically implemented in constraint solvers.

involving x are added to the propagation queue Q, excluding the currently processed constraint (lines 20-21).

For each (positive table) constraint c of the CN, we have the STR data structures, described in Section 5.3.

We now describe, for each non trivial intersection of a constraint c with a constraint c_i, the additional structures used in eSTR:

- $ctr[c][c_i]$ is an array that stores the counters associated with the intersection of c with c_i. For each subtuple for variables in $scp(c) \cap scp(c_i)$ that appears in at least one tuple of $rel[c]$, there is a counter $ctr[c][c_i][j]$ that holds the number of valid tuples in $rel[c]$ that include that subtuple. The value of the index j can be found from any tuple in $rel[c]$ using the next structure.

- $ctrIndexes[c][c_i]$ is a set of indexes for the tuples of $rel[c]$. For each tuple τ, this data structure holds the index of the counter in $ctr[c][c_i]$ that is associated with the subtuple $\tau[scp(c) \cap scp(c_i)]$. $ctrIndexes[c][c_i]$ is implemented as an array of size $rel[c].length$.

- $ctrLink[c][c_i]$ is an array of size $ctr[c][c_i].length$ that links $ctr[c][c_i]$ with $ctr[c_i][c]$. For each counter $ctr[c][c_i][j]$ corresponding to a subtuple for variables in $scp(c) \cap scp(c_i)$, $ctrLink[c][c_i][j]$ holds the index of the counter in $ctr[c_i][c]$ that is associated with that subtuple. If the subtuple is not included in any tuple of $rel[c_i]$ then $ctrLink[c][c_i][j]$ is set to NULL.

Figure 6.20 illustrates eSTR's data structures. There are two constraints c_1 and c_2 intersecting on variables x_2 and x_3. Three different subtuples for variables x_2 and x_3 of the intersection are present in $rel[c_1]$: $(0,0)$, $(0,1)$ and $(1,0)$. Hence, there are three counters in $ctr[c_1][c_2]$. Each counts the number of times a specific subtuple appears in $rel[c_1]$. For each tuple in $rel[c_1]$, the corresponding entry in $ctrIndexes[c_1][c_2]$ gives the index of the counter in $ctr[c_1][c_2]$ associated with the underlying subtuple. For each counter in $ctr[c_1][c_2]$, the corresponding entry in $ctrLink[c_1][c_2]$ gives the index of the counter in $ctr[c_2][c_1]$ associated with the same subtuple. Since subtuple $(0,1)$ does not appear in $rel[c_2]$, the entry in $ctrLink[c_1][c_2]$ for this subtuple is NULL.

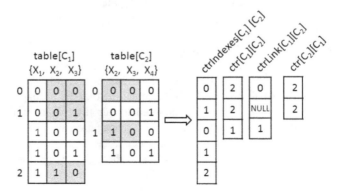

Figure 6.20: eSTR structures for the intersection of c_1 with c_2 on variables x_2 and x_3. The highlighted values show the first occurrence of the different subtuples for $scp(c_1) \cap scp(c_2)$.

The behaviour of eSTR is identical to that of STR, except: 1) it applies an extra check for PWC when a tuple is verified as valid, and 2) it decrements (resp. increments) the corresponding counters when a tuple is removed (resp. restored). Also, eSTR needs to build its data structures in an initialization step. This is done by traversing each $rel[c]$ exactly once. At the end of this step all counters are set to their proper values.

We omit the detailed description of functions *isValidTuple* and *removeTuple*, which can be found in [63]. Briefly, we describe the auxiliary functions used by the main algorithm, with a special emphasis on those that are specific to eSTR. Function isValidTuple takes a tuple τ and returns true iff τ is valid. Function removeTuple takes a tuple τ and removes it in constant time by replacing $position[c][i]$, where i is the position of τ in $rel[c]$, with $position[c][currentLimit[c]]$ (namely by swapping indexes and not tuples) and then decrementing $currentLimit[c]$ by one. As a result this procedure violates the lexicographic ordering of the remaing tuples in $position[c]$. Function 22, isPWconsistent, specific to eSTR is called at line 7 of Algorithm 21 whenever a tuple $\tau \in rel[c]$ has been verified as valid.

Algorithm 21 eSTR(c: constraint)

1: **for each** unassigned variable $x \in scp(c)$ **do**
2:    pwValues$[x] \leftarrow \emptyset$
3: $i \leftarrow 1$
4: **while** $i \leq$ currentLimit$[c]$ **do**
5:    index $\leftarrow$ position$[c][i]$
6:    $\tau \leftarrow$ table$[c][$index$]$
7:    **if** isValidTuple(c, τ) AND isPWconsistent(c, index) **then**
8:       **for each** unassigned variable $x \in scp(c)$ **do**
9:          **if** $\tau[x] \notin$ pwValues$[x]$ **then**
10:             pwValues$[x] \leftarrow$ pwValues$[x] \cup \{\tau[x]\}$
11:       $i \leftarrow i + 1$
12:    **else**
13:       removeTuple(c, i) // currentLimit$[c]$ decremented
14:       updateCtr(c, index) // Counters in ctr$[c]$ decremented
   // domains are updated and constraints are enqueued
15: **for each** unassigned variable $x \in scp(c)$ **do**
16:    **if** pwValues$[x] \subset D(x)$ **then**
17:       $D(x) \leftarrow$ pwValues$[x]$
18:       **if** $D(x) = \emptyset$ **then**
19:          **return** FAIL
20:       **for each** constraint c' such that $c' \neq c \wedge x \in scp(c')$ **do**
21:          add c' to Q
22: **return** SUCCESS

This function iterates over each constraint c_i that intersects with c and verifies if τ has a PW-support in $rel[c_i]$ or not. This is done through a look-up in the appropriate counter in constant time. Specifically, using structures $ctrIndexes[c][c_i]$ and $ctrLink[c][c_i]$ we locate the appropriate counter in $ctr[c_i][c]$ and check its value. If it is neither NULL nor 0, then τ is PW-supported. Otherwise, FALSE is returned in order to get τ removed.

Function 23, updateCtr, specific to eSTR is called at line 14 of Algorithm 21 in order to update some counters just after a tuple has been removed. For each constraint c_i that intersects with

---

Function 22 isPWconsistent(c, index): **Boolean**

1: **for each** $c_i \neq c$ s.t. $|scp(c_i) \cap scp(c)| > 1$ **do**
2:     $j \leftarrow$ ctrIndexes$[c][c_i]$[index]
3:     $k \leftarrow$ ctrLink$[c][c_i][j]$
4:     **if** $k =$ NULL OR ctr$[c_i][c][k] = 0$ **then**
5:        **return** FALSE
6: **return** TRUE

---

c, $j \leftarrow$ ctrIndexes$[c][c_i]$[index] is located. The variable j represents the index for the subtuple of the removed tuple τ in the array of counters concerning the intersection of c with c_i. Then the corresponding counter in $ctr[c][c_i]$ can be decremented. If the value of this counter becomes 0 then this means that some tuples in $rel[c_i]$ have lost their last PW-support in $rel[c]$. Since this may cause value deletions for the variables in $scp(c_i)$, constraint c_i is added to Q so that it can be processed again.

Function 23 updateCtr(c, index)

1: **for each** $c_i \neq c$ s.t. $|scp(c_i) \cap scp(c)| > 1$ **do**
2:     $j \leftarrow$ ctrIndexes$[c][c_i]$[index];
3:     ctr$[c][c_i][j] \leftarrow$ ctr$[c][c_i][j] - 1$
4:     **if** ctr$[c][c_i][j] = 0$ **then**
5:        add c_i to Q

Finally, when a failure occurs in the context of a backtrack search, certain values must be restored to domains. Consequently, tuples that were invalid may now become valid and thus must be restored. For each constraint c this is achieved in constant time by STR by just updating $currentLimit[c]$. In addition, eSTR updates all the affected counters by iterating through all tuples being restored and incrementing the corresponding counters for every c_i that intersects with c (i.e. $ctr[c][c_i]$). This costs $O(gt)$ in the worst case, where t the size of c and g the number of constraints intersecting with c. However, it is much faster in practice since usually only a few tuples are restored after each failure. Note that $currentLimit[c]$ allows us to easily locate restored tuples.

6.3 Enforcing FPWC

Assuming a CN P only involving positive table constraints, Algorithm 24, FPWC-STR, shows the full process of propagating constraints of P by calling procedure eSTR iteratively through the use of a propagation queue Q. Recall that Q may be updated when calling eSTR on a constraint c at lines 20–21 of Algorithm 21 and also at line 5 of Function 23. A weak version of FPWC-STR, denoted by FPWC-STR^w can be obtained by discarding lines 4–5 of Function 23 (i.e., the update of Q is ignored when a PW-support is lost).

Proposition 15 Algorithm FPWC-STR applied to a CN P enforces full pairwise consistency on P.

     Proof: Clearly FPWC-STR enforces GAC because each call of the form eSTR(c) guarantees that c is made GAC and everytime a value is deleted for a variable x, all constraints involving x are enqueued (and also, all constraints are enqueued initially). Now, let us consider a tuple τ, in

---

Algorithm 24 FPWC-STR($P = (\mathcal{X}, \mathcal{D}, \mathcal{C})$: CN)

1: $Q \leftarrow \mathcal{C}$
2: **while** $Q \neq \emptyset$ **do**
3:     pick and delete c from Q
4:     **if** eSTR(c) = FAIL **then**
5:         **return** FAIL
6: **return** SUCCESS

---

the table of a constraint c, which is not PWC. This means (by definition of PWC) that there exists a constraint c_i non trivially intersecting c such that no PW-support of τ in $rel[c_i]$ exists. Because everytime a tuple is deleted, the counters of underlying subtuples corresponding to constraint intersections are updated (decremented), and also considering the way these counters are initialized, during the execution of the algorithm FPWC-STR, we will necessarily have $\mathtt{ctr}[c_i][c][k]$ set to value NULL or 0 where k is the index for the subtuple $\tau[scp(c) \cap scp(c_i)]$ in this array of counters. Besides, the constraint c will necessarily be processed after $\mathtt{ctr}[c_i][c][k]$ reaches 0 (resp., after it is initialized to NULL) because of the execution of lines 4-5 of function updateCtr that adds c to Q (resp., because c is put in Q initially). When c is processed, the tuple τ will be deleted because isPWconsistent will return FALSE. Consequently, any tuple that is not PWC is deleted by our algorithm FPWC-STR. We can conclude that FPWC-STR enforces full pairwise consistency. ∎

It is interesting to note that FPWC guarantees maxRPWC as shown by the following proposition.

Proposition 16 PWC+GAC (or FPWC) and PWC+maxRPWC are equivalent
   Proof: On the one hand, clearly PWC+maxRPWC is stronger than PWC+GAC since maxRPWC is stronger than GAC. On the other hand, let us assume a CN P which is PWC and a value (x, a) of P which is not maxRPWC. This means (by definition) that there exists a constraint c involving x such that either (x, a) has no support on c, or (x, a) has no maxRPWC-support on c. However, because P is PWC, the reason why (x, a) is not maxRPWC is necessarily that (x, a) has no support on c. In other words, (x, a) is not GAC. We deduce that PWC+GAC is stronger than PWC+maxRPWC, and finally that PWC+GAC and PWC+maxRPWC are equivalent. ∎

We now analyze the worst-case time and space complexities of eSTR, the basic filtering procedure associated with each table constraint in FPWC-STR.

Proposition 17 The worst-case time complexity[10] of one call to eSTR is $O(rd + max(r, g)t)$ where r denotes the arity of the constraint, t the size of its table and g the number of intersecting constraints.
   Proof: Recall that the worst-case time complexity of STR is $O(rd + rt)$ [63]. The application of eSTR on a constraint c is identical to that of STR except for the calls to isPWconsistent and updateCtr in lines 7 and 14 of Algorithm 21, respectively. In both functions, the algorithm iterates over the set of g constraints intersecting with c, and for each one performs a constant time operation. Hence, the complexity of eSTR is $O(rd + max(r, g)t))$. ∎

One may be surprised by the fact that the worst-case time complexity of eSTR is close to that of STR, although a stronger filtering is achieved. However, the difference can be emphasized when we consider the maximum number of repeated calls to the function eSTR for a given constraint c.

---

[10]We omit to consider lines 20-21 because they concern propagation (and were hidden in the description of STR).

For STR, this is $O(rd)$ because after each removal of a value (for a variable in the scope of c), one call eSTR(c) is possible. For eSTR, this is $O(max(rd, t))$ because one call is possible after each value deletion but also after each loss of a PW-support for a tuple in $rel[c]$. Note that when we consider FPWC-STR^w, for eSTR we have $O(rd)$ as for STR: this is the reason why we introduce this variant. Overall, our intuition is that for many problems, the number of repeated calls to the filtering procedure of the same constraint is limited.

Proposition 18 The worst-case space complexity of eSTR is $O(n + max(r, g)t)$ per constraint.
    Proof: Recall that the worst-case space complexity of STR is $O(n + rt)$ per constraint [63]. Each additional eSTR structure is $O(t)$ per intersecting constraint, giving $O(gt)$. ∎

It is possible to reduce the memory requirements in two ways. First, by replacing the at most eg sets of counters with e sets, one for each constraint, in order to reduce the size of ctr and $ctrLink$. Second, by using a hash function to map each tuple $\tau \in rel[c]$ to its associated counters in $ctr[c]$. This would make the use of $ctrIndexes$ obsolete.

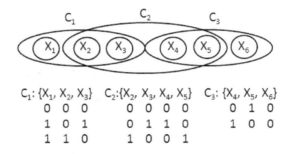

$$C_1: \{X_1, X_2, X_3\} \quad C_2: \{X_2, X_3, X_4, X_5\} \quad C_3: \{X_4, X_5, X_6\}$$

C_1			C_2				C_3		
0	0	0	0	0	0	0	0	1	0
1	0	1	0	1	1	0	1	0	0
1	1	0	1	0	0	1			

Figure 6.21: A CN that is maxRPWC but not FPWC.

To emphasize the difference between FPWC-STR and FPWC-STR^w, let us consider the CN P depicted in Figure 6.21. There are five variables $\{x_1, \ldots, x_5\}$ with domain $\{0, 1\}$, one variable x_6 with domain $\{0\}$, and three positive table constraints c_1, c_2 and c_3 (with their allowed tuples shown). One can check that P is maxRPWC. For example, the value $(x_1, 0)$ admits $(0, 0, 0)$ as support on c_1 and $(0, 0, 0, 0)$ as PW-support of $(0, 0, 0)$ in $rel[c_2]$. However P is not PWC. Indeed, the tuple $(0, 0, 0, 0)$ in $rel[c_2]$ has no PW-support in $rel[c_3]$. Consequently, FPWC-STR deletes this tuple, and $(x_1, 0)$ when c_1 is processed. Now, with FPWC-STR^w, if constraint c_1 is processed first in our example then no value deletion can be made. This is because when c_1 is processed, the tuple $(0, 0, 0)$ in $rel[c_1]$ admits $(0, 0, 0, 0)$ as PW-support in $rel[c_2]$. When c_2 is later processed, the tuple $(0, 0, 0, 0)$ is removed but no value for variables in $scp(c_2)$ can be deleted. This means that the propagation queue is left unchanged. Therefore, c_1 will not be processed again, and value $(x_1, 0)$ will not be deleted. Hence, the pruning power of FPWC-STR^w cannot be characterized precisely because it depends on the ordering of the propagation queue.

Proposition 19 The consistency level achieved by Algorithm FPWC-STR^w is incomparable to maxRPWC.
    Proof: If maxRPWC is applied on the example of Figure 6.21, it will achieve no pruning. We will show that FPWC-STR^w can delete values that maxRPWC cannot delete. Assume that FPWC-STR^w processes $c2$ first. Tuple $(0,0,0,0)$ does not have a PW-support in $c3$, and therefore

it will be removed. When $c1$ is processed, $\texttt{FPWC-STR}^w$ will determine that tuple $(0,0,0)$ has no PW-support in $c2$, since $(0,0,0,0)$ has been deleted, and will therefore be removed. As a result, value 0 of $x1$ will loose its only GAC-support in $c1$ and will be deleted. Therefore, $\texttt{FPWC-STR}^w$ can achieve stronger pruning than maxRPWC.

For the opposite, consider a problem on 0-1 domains with two constraints c_1 and c_2 where $scp(c_1) = \{x_1, x_2, x_3\}$ and $scp(c_2) = \{x_2, x_3, x_4\}$, and we have the allowed tuples $\{(0,0,0),$ $(1,0,1), (1,1,0)\}$ and $\{(0,0,0),(0,1,1),(1,0,1)\}$ respectively. Now assume that value 0 is deleted from $D(x_4)$ which means that tuple $(0,0,0)$ of c_2 will be invalidated. maxRPWC will revise all other variables involved in c_2 and only check for maxRPWC-support loss. Both values for x_2 and x_3 have maxRPWC-supports on c_2 so no deletion will be made. On the other hand, it will also check for PW-support loss by looking at constraint c_1. It will discover that value 0 of x_1 is no longer maxRPWC (its GAC-support has no PW-support on c_2) and will therefore delete it. On the other hand, $\texttt{FPWC-STR}^w$ after the deletion of value 0 from $D(x_4)$ will enqueue c_2. When c_2 is then processed no value deletion will be made and therefore propagation will stop. ∎

Proposition 20 $\texttt{FPWC-STR}^w$ achieves a local consistency that is strictly weaker than FPWC.

Proof: We first show that any deletion made by $\texttt{FPWC-STR}^w$ will also be made by FPWC. $\texttt{FPWC-STR}^w$ will delete a tuple $\tau \in rel[c]$ if τ is invalid or if Function *isPWconsistent* cannot find a PW-support for τ on some constraint c'. By definition, PWC deletes any value that is invalid or not PWC. Hence, it will also delete τ. Correspondingly, $\texttt{FPWC-STR}^w$ will delete a value $a \in D(x)$ if it does not participate in any valid and PW consistent tuple on some constraint c that involves x. Considering an algorithm that applies FPWC, PWC will delete all invalid and PW inconsistent tuples from $rel[c]$. Hence, the application of GAC that follows will delete a.

Finally, consider the example in Figure 6.21. As explained, if c_1 is processed before c_2, $\texttt{FPWC-STR}^w$ will achieve no pruning. In contrast, and independent of the order in which constraints are processed, PWC will remove tuple $(0,0,0,0)$ from $rel[c_2]$ and, because of this, tuple $(0,0,0)$ will be removed from $rel[c_1]$. Then when GAC is applied value 0 will be removed from $D(x_1)$ because it will have no support in c_1. Hence, FPWC is strictly stronger than $\texttt{FPWC-STR}^w$. ∎

6.4 Experimental Results

We ran experiments on benchmark problems from the CSP Solver Competition[11]. The arities of the constraints in these problems range from 3 to 18. We tried the following classes that include table constraints with non-trivial intersections: *random problems*, *forced random problems*, *aim-100* and *aim-200*, *Dubois*, *positive table constraints*, and *BDD*. The first four classes only include constraints of arity up to 4, while the other three include constraints of large arity (from 8 up to 18). We compared algorithms $\texttt{STR2}$, $\texttt{maxRPWC+}$, $\texttt{HOSTR2}^h$, $\texttt{FPWC-STR2}$, $\texttt{FPWC-STR2}^w$ (for abbreviation the latter two will be called $\texttt{eSTR2}$ and $\texttt{eSTR2}^w$ hereafter). All four were implemented within a CP solver written in Java and tested on an Intel Core i5 of 2.40GHz processor and 4GB RAM. A cpu time limit of 6 hours was set for all algorithms and all instances. Search used the *dom/ddeg* heuristic for variable ordering and lexicographical value ordering. We chose *dom/ddeg* as opposed to the generally more efficient *dom/wdeg* because the decisions made by the latter are influenced by the ordering of the propagation queue making it harder to objectively compare the pruning efficiency of the algorithms.

---

[11]http://www.cril.univ-artois.fr/CPAI08/

Table 6.13 shows the mean cpu times (in secs) obtained by the tested algorithms on each problem class for initialization and preprocessing. Also, it shows the mean cpu times and numbers of nodes obtained by backtracking algorithms that apply the propagation methods throughout search. During initialization, the data structures of an algorithm are initialized, while preprocessing includes one run of a propagation algorithm before search commences. In Table 6.14 we present results from selected instances focusing on the search effort. Search results from *Aim-200* were obtained using *dom/wdeg* for variable ordering because this class is hard for *dom/ddeg*.

As expected, eSTR2 and its weak version typically have much higher initialization times than STR2 and are usually slower during preprocessing. They are particularly expensive on classes of problems which include intersections on large sets of variables, as is the case with the *BDD* and *Positive-table* classes. *BDD* instances consist of constraints with arity 18 that intersect on as many as 16 variables. In addition, the constraints are very loose. As a result, eSTR2 (and eSTR2^w) exhausts all of the available memory when trying to build its data structures.

Regarding the cost of eSTR2^w and eSTR2 during initialization and preprocessing compared to maxRPWC+ and HOSTR2^h, results vary. For example, on the *Positive table* classes both maxRPWC+ and HOSTR2^h are much faster during initialization. However, both eSTR2^w and eSTR2 are many orders of magnitude faster during the preprocessing of *Positive table-10* instances which are usually proven unsatisfiable by these algorithms without search.

Comparing eSTR2 to eSTR2^w with respect to search effort, we can make two observations: First, the extra filtering of eSTR2 does pay off on some classes as node counts are significantly reduced (*Aim-100*) while on other classes it does not (*Random*). Second, the much higher time complexity bound of eSTR2 is not really visible in practice. eSTR2^w is faster than eSTR2 on average, but the differences are not very significant.

Comparing eSTR2^w and eSTR2 to STR2 it seems that there are problem classes where they can be considerably more efficient. This is definitely the case with the *Aim* classes where eSTR2^w and eSTR2 can outperform STR2 by several orders of magnitude on some instances, being one order of magnitude faster on average in the *Aim-100* class. Also, there can be significant differences in favor of eSTR2^w on instances of other classes, such as *Random, Random-forced*, and *Dubois*. On the other hand, if we consider the performance of the algorithms during both initialization and search, STR2 is better than the proposed methods on *Positive table* problems and of course *BDD*.

Now, comparing eSTR2^w and eSTR2 to the other strong local consistencies, namely, to maxRPWC+ and HOSTR2^h, it is clear that they are superior as they are faster on all the tested classes. The only cases where there are outperformed are on *BDD* and, marginally from HOSTR2^h, on *Dubois*. The differences in favor of eSTR2 and eSTR2^w can be very large. For example in the *Positive table* classes they are faster by orders of magnitude.

CPU times from all tested instances comparing eSTR2^w, which displays the best performance, to eSTR2, STR2, maxRPWC+r, HOSTR2^h, are presented in Figures 6.22, 6.23, 6.24 and 6.25 respectively, in a logarithmic scale. Different signs display instances from different problem classes and are calculated by CPU time ratios of the compared algorithms. Signs that are placed above the diagonal correspond to instances that were solved faster by eSTR2^w. We omitt presenting results from *BDD* instances where eSTR2^w axhausted the available memory.

In Figure 6.22, we compare the two new algorithms of this chapter. Most instances are gathered around the diagonal indicating closely matched performance of eSTR2^w and eSTR2. As descussed above, eSTR2^w is superior to eSTR2 on *random problems* and *forced random problems* and inferior on *Aim-100* and *Aim-200*, but the differences are marginal.

Looking at Figure 6.23 we see a much more varied picture. Evethough eSTR2^w is faster than STR2 in the majoriry of the instances, there are classes of problems where it thrashes (i.e, on

Table 6.13: Mean cpu times for initialization (i), preprocessing (p), search (s), and mean numbers of visited nodes (n).

Problem Class		STR2	maxRPWC+	eSTR2^w	eSTR2	HOSTR2^h
Random-fcd	i	**0.02**	0.3	0.67	0.69	0.35
	p	0.1	0.2	**0.09**	0.13	0.4
	s	150	182	**81**	127	305
#Inst=50	n	147,483	45,634	42,134	41,181	46,169
Random	i	**0.02**	0.3	0.63	0.62	0.31
	p	0.09	0.2	**0.08**	0.14	0.37
	s	226	327	**143**	214	568
#Inst=50	n	257,600	85,913	80,057	79,789	85,901
Positive table-8	i	**0.08**	1.8	76	85	1.5
	p	**0.3**	0.4	0.9	1.7	40
	s	**15**	1,575	47	51	5,000
#Inst=20	n	52,313	10,039	4,818	2,571	10,087
Positive table-10	i	**0.006**	0.3	12.2	16.2	0.3
	p	0.07	1,847	**0.03**	0.04	1,035
	s	0.4	1,699	**0.03**	0.04	1,035
#Inst=20	n	1,110	0	0	0	0
BDD	i	**0.24**	9.3	mem	mem	10
	p	**1.4**	6.2	-	-	2.2
	s	30	8.5	-	-	**2.5**
#Inst=10	n	19,139	11	-	-	11
Dubois	i	0.01	0.04	0.01	0.02	0.01
	p	0	0.002	0.002	0	0
	s	2,026	6,750	1,084	1,972	**807**
#Inst=8	n	1,008,184,658	401,069,394	401,069,394	419,586,728	401,069,394
Aim-100	i	**0.11**	0.29	0.20	0.21	0.24
	p	**0.002**	0.04	0.012	0.003	0.02
	s	6,390	3,899	674	**186**	1,019
#Inst=10	n	643,784,411	34,062,529	32,918,683	4,530,698	34,062,528
Aim-200	i	0.39	0.58	**0.32**	0.33	0.47
	p	**0.004**	0.1	0.01	0.02	0.03
	s	14.5	13	3.4	**1.5**	3,4
#Inst=10	n	479,073	88,541	75,209	16,034	97,529

Positive-table) while there are cases (i.e., *Aim* classes) where it is orders of magnitude faster. As also observed in Chapter 4.6, efficient algorithms for strong local consistencies on table constraints constitute a viable alternative to the standard GAC approach, but at the same time further research is required to develop methods that can be more robust than state-of-the-art GAC algorithms, such as STR2, on a wider range of problems, especially regarding large arities.

Comparing eSTR2^w to maxRPWC+r and HOSTR2^h in Figures 6.24 and 6.25 respectively, we can see the benefits of the former's approach: In Figure 6.24 only a few instances of *Aim-200* are below the diagonal indicating that eSTR2^w is clearly superior to maxRPWC+r. Also, there are many instances of *Positive-table* where maxRPWC+r thrashes while eSTR2^w does not.

A similar picture is noticed in Figure 6.25, where the majority of the instances are gathered above the diagonal. Only a few instances from *Dubois* are solved faster by HOSTR2^h but the differences are negligible. Again, eSTR2^w is clearly better than HOSTR2^h on instances of large arity (i.e., *Positive table-8*, *Positive table-10*), except from *BDD* instances. If we contrast Figure 6.24 to 6.25 we observe that in the latter the differences are more significant in favor of eSTR2^w. Finally, although the algorithms of Chapter 5.7 are faster than those of Chapter 4.6, they have lower memory requirements, meaning that in very large problems (of large arities and intersections on many variables) they are preferable, as indicated by *BDD* instances.

Table 6.14: Cpu times (t) in secs and nodes (n).

Instance		STR2	maxRPWC+	eSTR2^w	eSTR2	HOSTR2^h
rand-3-20-20 60	t	130	102	**37**	66	200
-632-fcd-8	n	128,221	33,924	27,490	27,272	34,414
rand-3-20-20 60	t	430	183	**43**	80	303
-632-fcd-26	n	534,012	38,556	26,531	26,489	38,809
rand-3-20-20-60	t	450	536	**187**	220	1,002
-632-19	n	462,920	129,618	121,199	120,795	131,051
rand-3-20-20-60	t	670	295	**74**	137	433
-632-26	n	827,513	64,665	45,268	45,426	64,857
rand-8-20-5-18	t	**17**	753	30	26	1,860
-800-7	n	17,257	3,430	1,001	626	3,444
rand-8-20-5-18	t	**19**	1,568	52	55	6,191
-800-11	n	67,803	7,920	3,299	1,279	7,876
rand-10-20-10-5	t	0.4	208	**0.02**	**0.02**	174
-10000-1	n	1,110	0	0	0	0
rand-10-20-10-5	t	0.4	1,687	**0.03**	**0.02**	334
-10000-6	n	1,110	0	0	0	0
bdd-21-133-18-78-6	t	30	1.5	-	-	**0.5**
	n	20,582	0	-	-	0
bdd-21-133-18-78-11	t	39	11.6	-	-	**1.1**
	n	19,364	21	-	-	21
dubois-22	t	315	734	96	182	**76**
	n	129,062,226	41,538,898	41,538,898	40,037,032	41,538,898
dubois-27	t	8,404	28,358	4,448	8,492	3,457
	n	4,206,712,146	1,651,070,290	1,651,070,290	1.808,444,072	1,651,070,290
aim-100-1-6-sat-2	t	423	0.16	**0.02**	**0.02**	0.05
	n	29,181,742	100	100	100	100
aim-100-2-0-sat-3	t	2,447	0.3	0.14	0.05	**0.03**
	n	177,832,989	111	111	100	100
aim-200-2-0-sat-1	t	57	0.7	0.6	**0.1**	0.2
	n	2,272,993	1,782	9,847	200	2,210
aim-200-2-0-sat-4	t	30	0.7	0.4	**0.2**	0.6
	n	987,160	1,965	4,276	499	2,887

6.5 Conclusion

In this chapter, we have introduced a new higher-order consistency algorithm for table constraints, FPWC-STR, that enforces full pairwise consistency. It is based on an original combination of two techniques that have proved their worth: simple tabular reduction and tuple counting. The basic filtering procedure of this algorithm, and its weak variant, is close to that of STR algorithms. These algorithms have been shown to be highly competitive on many problems with intersecting constraints.

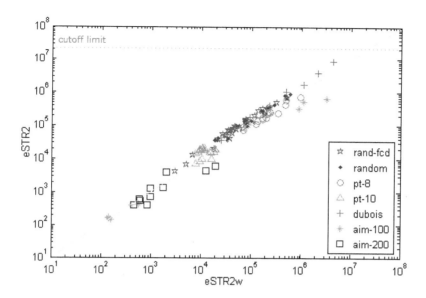

Figure 6.22: eSTR2 vs. eSTR2^w.

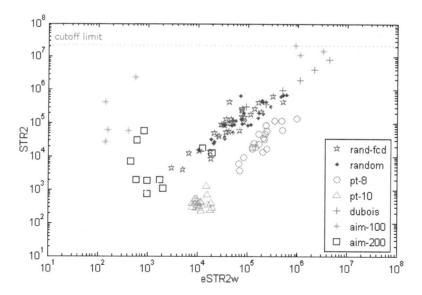

Figure 6.23: STR2 vs. eSTR2^w.

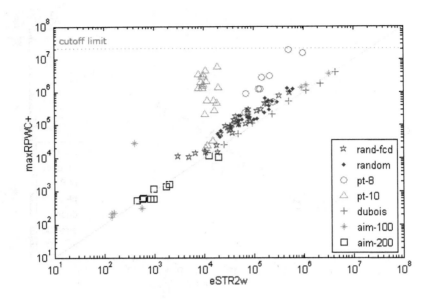

Figure 6.24: maxRPWC+r vs. eSTR2^w.

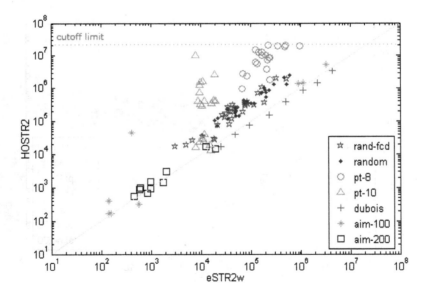

Figure 6.25: HOSTR2 vs. eSTR2^w.

Adaptive Propagation

Despite the advancements in constraint propagation methods, most CP solvers still apply fixed predetermined propagators on each constraint of the problem. However, selecting the appropriate propagator for a constraint can be a difficult task that requires expertise. Ways to overcome this include approaches that use machine learning or heuristics methods (see Section 3.4). We focus on the heuristic approach, which is uses to dynamically adapt the propagation method during search. The heuristics of this category proposed in [100] displayed promising results, but their evaluation and application suffered from two important drawbacks: They were only defined and tested on binary constraints and they required calibration of their input parameters. We follow this line of work by describing and evaluating simple, fully automated heuristics that are applicable on constraints of any arity. Experimental results from various problems show that the proposed heuristics can outperform a standard approach that applies a preselected propagator on each constraint resulting in an efficient and robust solver.

7.1   Introduction

Despite the advances in Constraint Programming (CP), there are still some important obstacles that prevent it from becoming even more widely known and applied. One significant such obstacle is the rigidness of CP solvers, in the sense that decisions about algorithms and heuristics to be used on a specific problem are taken prior to search during the modeling process and cannot change during search.

Concerning constraint propagation in particular, which is at the core of CP's strength and the focus of this chapter, the decision on which algorithm to select for the different constraints of the CP model is either predetermined or placed on the shoulders of the user/modeler. For instance, the modeler may select to propagate the alldifferent constraints in a problem using a domain consistency algorithm. However, during search it may turn out that domain consistency achieves little extra pruning compared to bounds consistency. Unfortunately, standard CP solvers do not allow to change the decisions taken prior to search "on the fly". Hence, it will not be possible to automatically switch to a bounds consistency propagator during search.

Among the various adaptive approaches in Section 3.4, heuristic methods for the automatic tuning of constraint propagation have shown interesting results [100]. Their advantage is twofold: they are inexpensive to apply, and they are perfectly suited to a dynamic application because they exploit information concerning the actual effects of propagation during search. In this chapter we are concerned with the heuristics proposed in [100] for dynamically adapting the propagation method used on the constraints of the given problem. Although this approach displayed quite promising results, it suffered by important limitations. First, the description as well as the evaluation of the heuristics was limited to binary constraints. And second, their successful application depended on user interference for careful parameter tuning. The former limits the applicability of the heuristics while the latter severely compromises their autonomicity and puts burden on the shoulders of the users.

In this chapter we confront and remedy both these problems. First, we evaluate two simple heuristics for constraints of any arity that allow to dynamically switch between two different propagators on individual constraints in a fully automated way. The first (resp. second) heuristic applies a standard propagator on a constraint (e.g. domain consistency) until the constraint causes a domain wipeout - DWO (resp. at least one value deletion). Then, in the immediately following revision of the constraint, a stronger local consistency (e.g. SAC) is applied. For the following revision we revert back to the standard propagator and this is repeated throughout search. These heuristics allow to exploit the filtering power offered by strong propagation methods without incurring severe cpu time penalties since they invoke the strong propagator very sparsely. And importantly, this is achieved without requiring any user involvement.

An experimental analysis demonstrates that a significant increase in value deletions is achieved by this limited use of a strong propagator. This is because it is more likely to obtain extra pruning after applying a strong propagator on a constraint that suffered from a DWO (or value pruning) in its last revision, as opposed to applying a strong propagator on any, say randomly selected, revision of the constraint.

We also propose and evaluate refinements of the above heuristics that, while still being fully automated, achieve better performance by targeting the use of the strong propagator on variables that are more likely to be filtered. Also, we evaluate the heuristics using different methods as the strong propagator. Overall, our experimental results demonstrate that the simple heuristics we employ outperform the rigid method that applies a standard propagator throughout search, resulting in most robust solvers.

7.2   Adaptive Propagator Selection

Modern CP solvers offer an impressive array of specialized constraint propagation algorithms that typically achieve GAC or BC on specific types of constraints. However, typically solvers follow one of the following patterns:

1. The choice of propagation algorithm for a specific constraint is made during the modeling process and cannot change during search.

2. All the available propagators for a constraint are used, in increasing order of cost, unless there is a theoretical guarantee that a propagator cannot achieve extra pruning (as discussed in [96, 95]).

A drawback of the second approach, which is more sophisticated, is that even if a propagator's cost can be accurately predicted (which is not always true), the prediction of a propagator's impact is not nearly as straightforward. Schulte and Stuckey concluded that an obvious way to further speed up constraint propagation is to consider the estimated impact for a propagator and not only its cost [97].

Exploring ways to achieve this, [100] proposed heuristics for dynamically switching between a weak (W) and a strong (S) propagator for individual constraints during search. The motivation for these heuristics was based on the observation that in structured problems propagation events

(DWOs and value deletions) caused by individual constraints are often highly clustered. That is, they occur during consecutive or very close revisions of the constraints. Hence, the intuition behind the proposed heuristics is twofold. First to target the application of the strong consistency on areas in the search space where a constraint is highly active so that domain pruning is maximized and dead-ends are encountered faster. And second, to avoid using an expensive propagation method when pruning is unlikely.

We briefly present the most successful heuristics introduced in [100], on which our heuristics are based on. The work of [100] is presented in detail in Section 3.4.

- Heuristic $H_1(l)$ monitors and counts the revisions and DWOs of the constraints in the problem. A constraint c is made S if the number of times it was revised since the last time it caused a DWO is less or equal to a (user defined) threshold l. Otherwise, it is made W.

- Heuristic $H_2(l)$ monitors revisions and value deletions. A constraint c is made S if its last revision caused at least one value deletion. Otherwise, it is made W. H_2 can be semi automated in a similar way to H_1 by allowing for a (user defined) number l of redundant revisions after the last fruitful revision. If l i-s set to 0, H_2 becomes fully automated.

As reported in [100], heuristic H_{12}^V, i.e. the disjunctive combination of H_1 and H_2, achieves particularly good performance being more robust than individual heuristics.

Some significant drawbacks of this appoach are that heuristics need the tuning of their parameters, which sometimes varies from one class of problems to another. Also, they cannot be used indepentantly to achieve their best performance (i.e., they are used in disjuction with an other heuristic) and have been only tried on binary constraints.

The following two heuristics generalize these heuristics, namely $H_1(l)$ and $H_2(l)$, to non-binary constraints in a straightforward and fully automated way.

- Heuristic H_{dwo} monitors the revisions and DWOs caused by the constraints in the problem. For any constraint c and any variable $x_i \in scp(c)$, each $v_i \in D(x_i)$ is made W unless the immediately preceding revision of c resulted in the DWO of a variable in $scp(c)$. In this case the values of $D(x_i)$ are made S.

- Heuristic H_{del} monitors revisions and value deletions. For any constraint c and any variable $x_i \in scp(c)$, each $v_i \in D(x_i)$ is made W unless the immediately preceding revision of c resulted in at least one value deletion from the domain of a variable in $scp(c)$. In this case the values of $D(x_i)$ are made S.

A significant difference between H_{dwo} and H_{del} and their corresponding versions for binary constraints, called H_1 and H_2 in [100], is that the latter required the manual setting of a parameter l to optimize their performance. For any constraint c this parameter determined the number of revisions after the latest revision of c that caused a DWO (resp. value deletion) during which S will be applied. In contrast, H_{dwo} and H_{del} do not use this parameter and as a result they are fully automated.

As reported in [100], the disjunctive combination of the two basic heuristics that applies S whenever the conditions of either of the heuristics is met, achieves particularly good performance being more robust than individual heuristics. However, given the definitions of H_{dwo} and H_{del} here, their disjunctive combination is pointless since it is equivalent to applying H_{del}. Hence, we do not consider it.

7.3 Experiments

In our experimental evaluation of the heuristics we have considered GAC as the standard propagator W, given that it is the most commonly used local consisteny. Since we are interested in non-binary problems, we have considered two strong local consistencies as the S propagators. Namely, maxR-PWC and SAC. All methods used the *dom/wdeg* heuristic for variable ordering and *lexicographic* value ordering under a binary branching scheme. The propagation queue was variable-oriented (i.e. the elements of the queue are variables) and was ordered in a FIFO manner. A cpu time limit of 6 hours was set for all instances. All the evaluated heuristic methods used the S propagator on all constraints for preprocessing.

The classes of problems we have considered include both structured and random problems, some of which are specified extensionally and others intensionally. These classes, which are taken from C.Lecoutre's XCSP repository and are commonly used in the CSP Solver Competition, are: *random* and *forced random*, *positive table*, *BDD*, *aim*, *pret*, *dubois*, *chessboard coloration*, *Schurr's lemma*, *modified Renault*.

In the case of extensionally specified constraints we have used the efficient algorithm of [72] for the implementation of GAC. This is also the basis for the implementation of SAC and maxRPWC. For the former, the implementation is straightforward. For the latter, we have used a simplified version of the algorithm presented in Section . In the case of intensionally specified constraints we have used the generic algorithms GAC2001/3.1 [18] and maxRPWC1 [19]. GAC2001/3.1 was also the basis for the implementation of SAC.

In the following, we first evaluate H_{dwo} and H_{del} using maxRPWC as the strong propagator. Then we analyze the performance of the heuristics (H_{dwo} in particular) to explain their success. Finally, we propose and evaluate refinements of the heuristics and give results from the use of SAC as the strong propagator.

7.3.1 Evaluating the heuristics

In Table 7.15 we show the mean performance of H_{dwo} and H_{del} on all tested classes, measured in cpu time and nodes explored.To put these results into perspective, we also give results from: 1) an algorithm that propagates all constraints using GAC throughout search, 2) an algorithm that propagates all constraints using maxRPWC throughout search, and 3) the H_{del} heuristic implemented as in [100], with parameter l set to 10 (i.e. maxRWPC is applied for the 10 revisions following a revision that deleted at least one value). We also report the mean percentage (%) of constraint revisions where the strong consistency (maxRPWC) was applied. Cpu times in bold demonstrate the fastest method. A dash (-) indicates that the method was unable to solve all instances within the time limit.

The results given in Table 7.15 demonstrate the efficacy of the studied fully automated heuristics. Although they do not achieve the best mean results on any class (with the exception of *BDD*), one or both of the heuristics achieve the best performance on several individual instances. But more importantly, the heuristics succeed in striking a balance between the performance of GAC and maxRPWC. Specifically, in problems where GAC thrases (*positive table-10* and *BDD*), the heuristics follow maxRPWC in solving the problems with little or no search. In problems where GAC is clearly better than maxRPWC (*chessboard coloration*, *positive table-8*, and *random*) the performance of the heuristics is closer to GAC making them clearly superior to maxRPWC. In a case where the opposite occurs, i.e. maxRWPC is better than GAC (*aim*), the heuristics follow maxRPWC making them superior to GAC. In other cases, where GAC and maxRWPC are closely matched, the performance of the heuristics typically lies in between GAC and maxRPWC.

Table 7.15: Mean cpu times (t) in secs, nodes (n), and the percentage of constraint revisions (s) carried out using maxRWPC.

Class		GAC	maxRPWC	H_{dwo}	H_{del}	H_{del} 10
Rand-fcd	t	**182**	233	229	202	195
	n	131,745	59,245	161,247	95,576	54,316
	s	0	100	1.1	24.8	73.3
Random	t	**220**	333	221	236	270
	n	151,039	79,771	154,657	105,944	72,353
	s	0	100	1.1	24.9	73
Positive table-8	t	**1,629**	3,947	2,233	1,984	3,109
	n	47,073	15,142	45,108	26,425	14,747
	s	0	100	3	26.5	77.5
Positive table-10	t	-	643	647	667	691
	n	-	0	0	0	0
	s	-	100	100	100	100
Aim	t	9.5	**2.4**	3.9	2.8	1.6
	n	1,324,118	217,459	468,262	302,870	127,723
	s	0	100	2.6	20.3	53.2
BDD	t	7,771	6.4	**3.9**	4.2	5.1
	n	36,804	10	10	10	10
	s	0	100	24.5	56.9	69.2
Chess-board	t	**4.6**	37.7	5.5	8.2	12.8
	n	57,024	43,644	66,177	65,609	59,826
	s	0	100	2.7	6	26.2
Schurr's lemma	t	63	100	**62**	73	87.2
	n	559,971	524,909	549,868	552,197	562,221
	s	0	100	1.4	17.1	59.8
Dubois	t	934	**878**	925	1,282	912
	n	175,325,461	144,632,439	161,619,009	225,836,708	163,285,042
	s	0	100	1.9	41.7	98.35
Pret	t	**46**	**46**	48	50	47
	n	37,017,710	37,017,710	37,017,710	37,017,710	37,017,710
	s	0	100	3.2	42.4	98.7
Renault	t	**118**	181	126	143	167
	n	801	334	521	413	328
	s	0	100	12	25.5	83

Comparing H_{dwo} to H_{del} we can note that there are no significant differences in their performance. This occured not only with respect to their mean performance but, largely, with respect to individual instances as well. What is interesting is that H_{dwo}, which is slightly better overall, achieves its results with only few invocations of the strong propagator as the percentages *s* show, with *positive table-10* and *BDD* being exceptions to this.

Finally, comparing H_{del} to its parameterized version with l set to 10, we can note that the fully automated version is generally preferable. It achieves better mean performance on 7 out of the 11 classes and it is not significantly outperformed in the other 4. This hints at a particular importance of the revisions that immediately follow a propagation event in terms of the likelihood of another propagation event occuring.

7.3.2 Are revisions after DWOs important?

In this section we investigate the reason for the success of H_{dwo}. In Table 7.16 we record ratios concerning value deletions to demonstrate the effects of the calls to S in revisions immediately following a revision that caused a DWO. We have picked an indicative instance from each class. D^{dwo} is the number of revisions that caused value deletions and immediately follow a revision that caused a DWO. D is the number of all revisions that caused deletions. R^{dwo} is the number of revisions that immediately follow a revision that caused a DWO. Table 7.16 gives the ratios D^{dwo}/D and D^{dwo}/R^{dwo} for GAC, maxRPWC, and H_{dwo}.

H_{dwo} has the highest percentages, compared to GAC and maxRPWC, for both ratios shown in Table 7.16. Especially on *Random*, *Random-fcd* and *Positive table* we observe that the numbers for H_{dwo} are more than two times higher, showing that **applying a strong consistency after a DWO can increase the likelihood of value pruning**. For the rest of the classes the advantage is less obvious for two reasons: either because the strong consistency cannot offer extra pruning (i.e. *pret*) or because it is applied very few times (i.e. *Chessboard coloration*). Note that no instance from the *BDD* class is included. This is because in these problems very few constraints give non-zero results for D when maxRPWC or H_{dwo} is applied (in contrast to GAC). That is, very few constraints are active during the (very short) search process with these methods.

Table 7.16: Percentages of revisions that caused value deletions after a previous DWO to all revisions that caused deletions (D^{dwo}/D) and revisions that caused value deletions after a previous DWO to all revisions executed after a previous DWO (D^{dwo}/R^{dwo}) from representative instances.

Class Instance		GAC	$maxRPWC$	H_{dwo}
Rand-fcd	D^{dwo}/D	0.55	0.59	1.01
	D^{dwo}/R^{dwo}	9.8	12.15	17.98
Random	D^{dwo}/D	0.5	0.58	1.01
	D^{dwo}/R^{dwo}	8.95	11.7	19.01
Positive table-8	D^{dwo}/D	1.48	2.95	4.92
	D^{dwo}/R^{dwo}	3.54	6.24	12.88
Aim	D^{dwo}/D	1.73	1.08	2.01
	D^{dwo}/R^{dwo}	14.61	2.27	10.24
Chessboard	D^{dwo}/D	1.37	2.49	2.75
	D^{dwo}/R^{dwo}	3.46	5.85	7.53
Schurr's lemma	D^{dwo}/D	0.02	0.92	0.01
	D^{dwo}/R^{dwo}	0.28	6.3	0.21
Dubois	D^{dwo}/D	0.22	0.62	0.11
	D^{dwo}/R^{dwo}	6.65	8.93	7.28
Pret	D^{dwo}/D	0.77	0.77	0.77
	D^{dwo}/R^{dwo}	13.58	13.58	13.58
Renault	D^{dwo}/D	2.26	2.31	2.31
	D^{dwo}/R^{dwo}	3.58	4.18	4.14

7.4 Refining the heuristics

Heuristics H_{dwo} and H_{del} apply the strong propagator S on all variables involved in a constraint if one of these variables suffered a DWO (resp. value deletion) in the previous revision of the constraint. This may incur unnecessary invocations of S that only increase the cpu time overhead without offering any filtering. The following heuristics are refinements of H_{dwo} and H_{del} that try to improve on this by targeting the use of the strong propagator on variables that are more likely to be filtered.

- Heuristic H^v_{dwo} monitors the revisions of constraints and the DWOs of the **variables' domains**. For any constraint c and any variable $x_i \in scp(c)$, each $v_i \in D(x_i)$ is made W

unless the immediately preceding revision of c resulted in the DWO of $D(x_i)$. In this case the values of $D(x_i)$ are made S.

- Heuristic H_{del}^v monitors the revisions of constraints and the value deletions from the **variables' domains**. For any constraint c and any variable $x_i \in scp(c)$, each $v_i \in D(x_i)$ is made W unless the immediately preceding revision of c resulted in at least one value deletion from $D(x_i)$. In this case the values of $D(x_i)$ are made S.

H_{dwo}^v and H_{del}^v restrict the application of the strong propagator on variables that suffered a propagation event (DWO or value deletion) in the immediately preceding constraint revision as opposed to all variables in the constraint's scope. The intuition behind this is that such variables are more likely to suffer a DWO or value deletion(s) again, especially in hard parts of the search space. The experimental results given below indicate that this is true since the effects of restricting the invocations of S on the search effort are not significant while cpu times improve.

Table 7.17 presents results from representative individual instances and from all tested classes. Columns H_{del}^v and H_{dwo}^v give results from the use of maxRPWC as the strong propagator, while column S-H_{dwo}^v gives results from the use of SAC. The last column, called Hybrid, gives results from a simple heuristic method that applies SAC and maxRPWC alternatively. Specifically, maxRPWC is selected as the S propagator when a constraint intersects with another constraint on more than one variable and SAC otherwise. Note that maxRPWC cannot achieve any extra filtering compared to GAC when constraints intersect on exactly one variable [19], while SAC can.

All *adaptive* methods significantly outperform *non-adaptive* (i.e., GAC) on many instances, while there are few cases where they are outperformed. However, in most of the latter cases the differences are negligible. On *random* and *forced random* instances H_{del}^v is usually better than GAC, namely on *rand-3-20-20-60-632-fcd-3* it is almost 10 times and on *rand-3-20-20-60-632-4* and it can be 2 times faster. Also, on *rand-3-20-20-60-632-fcd-1* and *rand-3-20-20-60-632-14* Hybrid and H_{dwo}^v respectively outperform GAC in notably less time only with 0.3% applications of maxRPWC. These results are due to the stronger pruning achieved by maxRPWC that results in significant reduction in the number of nodes, even though the percentage of its application is that low. On *positive table* problems, differences between H_{del}^v and H_{dwo}^v are marginal. Note that, both S-H_{dwo}^v and GAC reach the cutoff limit on *Positive table-10* instances.

Both H_{del}^v and H_{dwo}^v are highly successful on the *BDD* instances, where they outperform GAC by up to three orders of magnitude. Except from S-H_{dwo}^v, adaptive algorithms detect an early inconsistency on *bdd-21-133-18-78-15* and on *bdd-21-133-18-78-11* they reduce dramatically the search space and thus, find a solution in few seconds, while GAC requires few thousands of seconds. This is due to the structure of *BDD* instances which consist of large-arity constraints (up to 18) that appear in many intersections. Consequently, maxRPWC is by far superior to GAC on these problems. It is impressive that this advantage is not lost despite the very low percentage of calls to maxRPWC (less than 6%). On the *chessboard coloration, Schurr's lemma, pret* and *dubois*, they all have close performance. In these problems maxRPWC cannot exploit the problems' structure for additional pruning, as the visited nodes declare.

In addition, refined heuristics are faster than GAC on the *aim* and *modified Renault* instances and can be over ten times faster on some of them, i.e., on *aim-200-2-0-sat-4* and *renault-mod-25* and quite faster in *renault-mod-33*. In these classes, maxRPWC is more effective than GAC because there are many constraint intersections and our methods can take advantage of this. On *modified Renault* the Hybrid method is very expensive, even though it reduced the search space, while S-H_{dwo}^v again could not reach a solution in reasonable time.

Table 7.17: Cpu times (t) in secs, nodes (n) and the percentage of the strong consistency (s) from various representative problem instances.

Instance		GAC	H^v_{del}	H^v_{dwo}	$S\text{-}H^v_{dwo}$	Hybrid
rand-3-20-20-	t	521	447	435	199	**105**
60-632-fcd-3	n	395,247	218,679	369,644	42,833	89,654
	s	0	10.7	0.3	0.4	0.3
rand-3-20-20-	t	120	**15**	50	141	31
60-632-fcd-15	n	85,940	7,550	33,522	35,985	27,793
	s	0	11.1	0.3	0.3	0.2
rand-3-20-20	t	197	194	**51**	223	149
-60-632-4	n	124,450	93,568	38,062	55,978	119,677
	s	0	11.1	0.3	0.4	0.1
rand-3-20-20	t	98	**48**	69	73	53
-60-632-14	n	69,599	21,774	47,489	15,152	47,617
	s	0	10.2	0.3	0.4	0.2
pt-8-20-5-	t	1,333	**977**	1,389	1,084	1,351
18-80-4	n	37,466	18,592	36,888	28,058	36,888
	s	0	4.8	0.3	0.3	0.3
pt-8-20-5-	t	5,317	**4,594**	5,504	5,013	5,292
18-80-12	n	156,707	83,057	155,950	155,829	155,950
	s	0	4.6	0.3	0.4	0.3
pt-10-20-10-	t	-	1,767	**1,683**	-	1,802
5-10000-0	n	-	0	0	-	0
	s	-	100	100	-	100
pt-10-20-10-	t	-	1,533	**1,519**	-	1,646
5-10000-6	n	-	0	0	-	0
	s	-	100	100	-	100
bdd-21-133-	t	7,899	4.6	**3.5**	11,258	9.2
18-78-11	n	35,731	22	22	35,413	22
	s	0	5.6	2.9	4.9	5.6
bdd-21-133-	t	9,579	2.6	**1.9**	10,082	2.5
18-78-15	n	37,463	0	0	38,971	22
	s	0	100	100	0.5	100
	t	**1.4**	1.9	1.6	2.8	1.7
cc-9-9-2	n	12,945	14,652	13,256	7,556	13,256
	s	0	0.7	0.4	0.5	0.4
	t	131	148	**130**	144	133
lemma-30-9	n	367,664	357,705	367,746	313,661	358,181
	s	0	6.3	0.2	0.2	0.2
	t	292	328	**272**	338	368
dubois-23	n	233,952,261	253,527,792	223,084,005	228,337,001	261,150,057
	s	0	17.7	1.9	1.6	0.8
	t	**46**	48	48	57	53
pret-60-75	n	37,012,466	37,012,466	37,012,466	35,113,273	35,754,658
	s	0	18	1.7	1.8	0.6
aim-200-1-	t	8.4	4.8	8	6.8	**4.7**
6-unsat-3	n	1,314,067	680,737	1,282,603	745,153	563,198
	s	0	10.4	1.4	1.7	2.1
aim-200-2-	t	29	**1**	1.5	1.3	4.6
0-sat-4	n	4,180,497	51,133	320,364	168,007	481,501
	s	0	8.4	0.7	1.1	0.5
	t	521	**39**	**39**	-	607
renault-25	n	1,273	0	0	-	525
	s	0	24.3	23.6	-	0.7
	t	169	**49**	113	-	685
renault-33	n	667	8	317	-	236
	s	0	10.1	2.5	-	1.9

Table 7.18 presents mean results from all tested instances. Results from Table 7.18 are similar to those from Table 7.15 in the sense that again the heuristic methods H_{dwo}^v and H_{del}^v achieve a balance between GAC and maxRWPC. Considering these two methods, as Table 7.17 demonstrates, there are several instances where they achieve better performance than GAC. This happens not only in classes such as *BDD* where maxRPWC dominates GAC, but also in classes such as the random ones and *modified Renault* where GAC is better than maxRWPC.

On the other hand, heuristic S-H_{dwo}^v is not as successful. Although it often manages to cut down the number of node visits considerably (the two random classes and *aim*), this is not reflected to cpu times (with the exception of *aim*) meaning that singleton checks are quite expensive. In addition, there are many classes where S-H_{dwo}^v does not manage to save search effort compared to GAC. However, the performance of S-H_{dwo}^v is still close to that of GAC, being sometimes better, and it is by far superior to the performance of an algorithm that applies SAC on all variables throughout search[12].

Table 7.18: Average cpu times (t) in secs, nodes (n) and the percentage of the strong consistency (s) from all classes.

Class		GAC	H_{del}^v	H_{dwo}^v	S-H_{dwo}^v	Hybrid
Rand-fcd	t	182	179	165	192	**133**
	n	131,745	87,271	125,447	44,346	113,984
	s	0	10.7	0.3	0.4	0.2
Random	t	220	237	195	325	**176**
	n	151,039	111,768	138,985	67,690	150,706
	s	0	12	0.3	0.4	0.2
Positive table-8	t	1,629	1,609	1,746	**1,594**	1,693
	n	47,073	27,740	45,108	42,330	47,101
	s	0	4.5	0.3	0.3	0.3
Positive table-10	t	-	640	**625**	-	664
	n	-	0	0	-	0
	s	-	100	100	-	100
Aim	t	9.5	3.5	4.3	**2.2**	2.5
	n	1,324,118	391,493	547,469	186,262	250,618
	s	0	8.6	1.4	2.2	0.5
BDD	t	7,771	3.9	**3.2**	10,768	4
	n	36,804	10	10	36,896	10
	s	0	56.8	56.8	0.4	56.8
Chess-board	t	**4.6**	6.2	5.3	5.1	5.4
	n	57,024	61,374	59,390	58,491	65,640
	s	0	2.4	1.4	3.5	1.4
Schurr's lemma	t	**63**	73	**63**	67	65
	n	559,971	571,976	549,335	492,630	482,396
	s	0	8.5	0.6	0.2	0.2
Dubois	t	**934**	1,282	936	1,287	1,357
	n	175,325,461	225,836,708	172,724,047	189,160,406	215,484,904
	s	0	41.7	1.9	1.7	0.8
Pret	t	**46**	49	48	53	50
	n	37,017,710	37,017,710	37,017,710	33,190,315	34,392,941
	s	0	18.1	1.7	1.7	0.6
Renault	t	**118**	122	122	-	430
	n	801	417	544	-	580
	s	0	12.4	7.3	-	8.8

Comparing heuristics H_{dwo}^v and H_{del}^v to H_{dwo} and H_{del} on mean performance, we can note that the former are more efficient. Although they restrict the application of the strong consistency by 50% up to more than 80%, as the percentages s show, this does not incur any significant increase

---

[12]Results of this algorithm are not given because it is not competitive in cpu times in most cases.

in node visits while at the same time cpu effort is saved. In contrast, there are many cases where the number of node visits is cut down (e.g. *random* class). These results show that H_{dwo}^{v} and H_{del}^{v} achieve a better focus in the application of the strong consistency.

Finally, the Hybrid method is very competitive on all classes, except *modified Renault*, being faster than all other methods on the *random-fcd* and *random* classes. Again it is interesting that this method ahieves a good performance with very few invocations of the strong propagator.

Figure 7.26 summarizes our results by presenting pairwise comparisons on all tested instances. Figure 7.26(a) compares the cpu times of GAC to those of maxRPWC in a logarithmic scale. Points above (resp. below) the diagonal correspond to instances that were solved faster by maxRPWC (resp. GAC). This figure clearly demostrates the performance gap between GAC and maxRPWC. GAC is faster on the majority of the instances, often by large margins, but since it is a weaker consistency level, it sometimes thrashes, while the stronger maxRPWC does not. These results justify the need for a robust method that can achieve a balance between the two.

Figure 7.26(b) (resp. Figure 7.26(c)) compares the cpu times of H_{dwo}^{v} to those of GAC (resp. maxRPWC). These figures clearly demonstrate the benefits of the adaptive heuristics. Although the majority of the instances is still below the diagonal in Figure 7.26(b), they are much closer to it, indicating small differences between the two methods on those instances. These are instances where the application of maxRPWC does not offer any notable reductions in search tree size. By keeping the number of calls to the maxRPWC propagator low, the adaptive heuristic manages to avoid slowing down search considerably. On the other hand, there are still instances where GAC thrashes while H_{dwo}^{v}, following maxRPWC, does not.

In Figure 7.26(c) most instances are above the diagonal demonstrating that H_{dwo}^{v}, following GAC, is faster than maxRPWC. On the other hand, there are no instances where H_{dwo}^{v} thrashes.

7.4.1   Effects of different Queue ordering and Branching scheme

Standard solvers either use the FIFO ordering scheme for the elements of the propagation queue, or a cost-based ordering as discussed in the Introduction. Alternatively, some generic and easy to apply heuristics have been proposed for this task, and evaluated mainly on arc consistency algorithms [107, 22, 4]. Since the ordering of the queue and the adaptive propagation heuristics we evaluate are related, in the sense that they collectively determine exactly which propagators will be applied and the order of their application, we conducted experiments to assess whether different approaches to queue ordering affect the performance of the heuristics.

We conducted experiments to compare H_{dwo}^{v} against both GAC and maxRPWC while changing the conditions of the search process. That is to prove the stability of H_{dwo}^{v} when either the propagation or the look-ahead algorithm alters.

Figure 7.27 presents results from all instances when the *dom* heuristic is used to order variables in the propagation queue. This heuristic simply orders the variables in increasing domain size [107, 22]. The queue orderning, regardless of the heuristic used, results in different searching paths and thus, different node visits when a heuristic like *dom/wdeg* is used for variable ordering [4]. Despite this, H_{dwo}^{v} is still more efficient than GAC in the same problem classes as in Figure 7.26(b). The same observation can be inferred when H_{dwo}^{v} is compared to maxRPWC. Therefore, it seems that the performance of the heuristic is not affected by the way in which the queue is ordered.

Finally, Figure 7.28 presents results from all instances when *d-way* branching is applied during search. H_{dwo}^{v} is faster than GAC and maxRPWC in the same problem classes as in Figure 7.26(b) and (c) respectively. Hence, the adaptive heuristic's performace is not dependent on the branching scheme used.

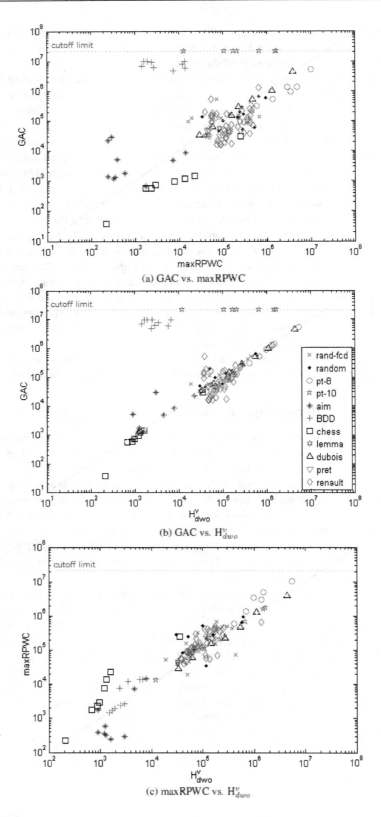

Figure 7.26: Cpu times of H_{dwo}^v compared to *GAC* and *maxRPWC*, for all evaluated instances.

7.5   Conclusion

In this chapter we described and evaluated simple heuristics for the dynamic adaptation of constraint propagation methods. These are based on the heuristics proposed in [100], but overcoming the limitations of that work, they are applicable on constraints of any arity and, importantly, they are fully automated. Experimental results show that refinements of the basic heuristics that target the use of strong propagators on variables that are more likely to be filtered achieve the best results and outperform the standard method that applies a fixed propagator throughout search, resulting in most robust solvers. We believe that this work is a step towards the efficient exploitation of the filtering power offered by strong propagators in a fully automated way.

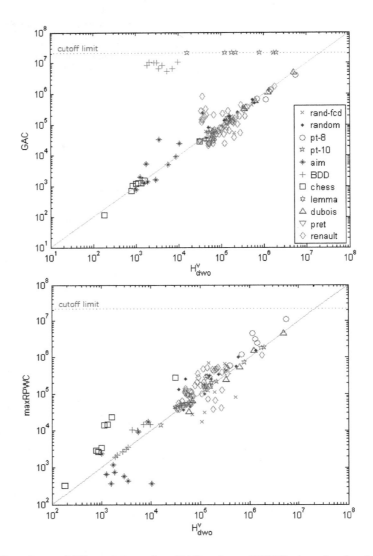

Figure 7.27: Cpu times of H^v_{dwo} compared to *GAC* and *maxRPWC* when the *dom* heuristic is used for the Queue ordering.

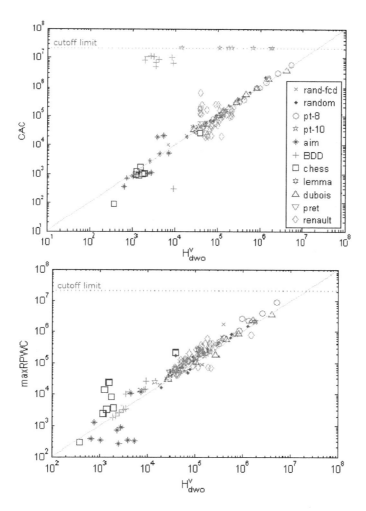

Figure 7.28: Cpu times of H_{dwo}^v compared to *GAC* and *maxRPWC* under the d-way branching scheme.

Strong Bounds Consistencies

Although many strong local consistencies that extend GAC have been proposed (see Sections 3.1 and 3.2), similar consistencies based on BC have been overlooked. In this chapter, we study Pair-Wise Bounds Consistency (PWBC), a new local consistency that extends BC by simultaneously considering combinations of constraints as opposed to single constraints. Naturally, this results in stronger filtering compared to BC. We show that some theoretical results regarding a related domain filtering consistency carry over to PWBC, while others do not. We then turn our attention to the important case of linear constraints. We describe a polynomial filtering algorithm for linear constraints that can achieve stronger pruning than BC. Interestingly, this yields a polynomial algorithm for linear inequalities which achieves stronger filtering than BC.We experiment with randomly generated problems as well as problems used for the evaluation of matchmakers in Web Services, an interesting recent application of CP. Results comparing BC propagation to PWBC reveal large differences in favour of PWBC in some cases, and thus demonstrate the potential of strong local consistencies that reason on domain bounds.

8.1   Introduction

Generalized Arc Consistency (GAC), and Bounds Consistency (BC) are the two local consistencies that are predominantly used for propagation by finite domain constraint solvers. Many stronger local consistencies based on GAC have been proposed, both for binary (see Section 3.1) and non-binary constraints (see Section 3.2). However, similar consistencies that are based on BC have been comparatively overlooked. One exception is Singleton Bounds Consistency [70] which can be seen as an adaptation of 3B Consistency [73] from numerical to finite domain CSPs.

In this chapter we introduce and study Pairwise Bounds Consistency (PWBC), a strong local consistency for non-binary constraints that extends BC. As the name suggests, PWBC is related to pairwise consistency [53], a local consistency that can filter tuples from constraint relations, and also to its domain filtering counterpart maxRPWC [19]. The application of PWBC results in the shrinking of domain bounds just like BC, but unlike BC it simultaneously considers combinations (intersections) of constraints as opposed to single constraints. Naturally, this results in stronger filtering.

We present some general theoretical results that investigate the pruning power of the new local consistency. We show that some results regarding the related domain filtering consistency maxR-PWC carry over to PWBC, while others do not. For example, BC is strictly weaker than PWBC just as GAC is strictly weaker than maxRPWC. But unlike the case of domain filtering consistencies, this result holds even when constraints intersect on one variable only[13].

---

[13] maxRPWC collapses to GAC when constraints intersect on only one variable.

We then turn our attention to the class of linear constraints. This is perhaps the most widely studied class of constraints as it has been rigorously investigated for many years by researchers in OR, discrete mathematics, logic programming, and CP. Although linear constraints are ubiquitus, it is well known that CP solvers only apply a weak form of propagation on them. For example given the constraints $x_1 + x_2 + x_3 > 5$ and $x_1 + x_2 + x_3 < 5$, and assuming that each variable has the domain $\{0, \ldots, 4\}$, a CP solver applying BC propagation will be unable to detect the inconsistency without search.

We first show that, although GAC is equivalent to BC on linear inequalities [112], PWBC remains strictly stronger than BC and strictly weaker than maxRPWC. However, it collapses to BC when constraints intersect on at most one variable. Then, and most importantly, we propose a polynomial filtering algorithm for linear constraints of inequalities. This algorithm achieves at least the same pruning as BC, and depending on characteristics of the constraints (e.g. the coefficients of the variables), it can achieve stronger pruning. For instance, it is quite suitable for linear constraints with unit coefficients. The proposed method can be easily crafted in CP solvers to enhance their pruning power on inequality constraints. For example, and in contrast to BC, it would be able to detect the inconsistency on the simple problem described above without search.

We discuss practical applications of the proposed method in areas such as constraint-based graphics [51, 81] and Quality of Service (QoS) based matchmaking for Web Services [90, 61]. The former is among the earliest applications of CP technology while the latter is a very interesting recent application.

Finally, experimental results from benchmark problems used for the evaluation of matchmaking methods in Web Services as well as from random problems reveal large differences in favour of our algorithm and thus demonstrate the potential of strong consistencies that reason on domain bounds.

8.2   PairWise Bounds Consistency

We now define a new strong bounds consistency, which is a relaxed version of maxRPWC, and theoretically compare it to BC as well as to the related domain consistencies.

Definition 17 A CSP is *Pairwise Bounds Consistent* (PWBC) iff for each $x_i \in \mathcal{X}$ and for each value $v_i \in \{min_D(x_i), max_D(x_i)\}$, for each $c_j \in \mathcal{C}$, where $x_i \in scp(c_j)$, there exists a Bound-support τ on c_j s. t. $\tau[x_i] = v_i$, and for all $c_l \in \mathcal{C}$ ($c_l \neq c_j$), s.t. $scp(c_j) \cap scp(c_l) \neq \emptyset$, there exists a Bound-support τ' on c_l s.t. $\tau[scp(c_j) \cap scp(c_l)] = \tau'[scp(c_j) \cap scp(c_l)]$.

Proposition 21 PWBC is strictly stronger than BC.
    Proof: The "stronger" relationship is straightforward from the definitions of the two consistencies. Now consider a problem with variables $x_1, \ldots, x_4$, domains $D(x_1) = D(x_2) = \{0, 1\}$, $D(x_3) = \{1, 2\}$, $D(x_4) = \{1\}$, and constraints $c_1 : x_1 + x_2 < x3$ and $c_2 : x_4 - x_1 < x_3$. The problem is BC. However, value 1 of x_3 is not PWBC since its only Bound-support $(0,0,1)$ on c_1 cannot be extended to a Bound-support on c_2. Hence, PWBC is strictly stronger than BC. ■

In contrast to the case of the corresponding domain consistencies, PWBC does not collapse to BC when constraints intersect on at most one variable.

Lemma 1 Proposition 21 holds even when constraints intersect on at most one variable.
    Proof: It suffices to find a problem where PWBC achieves more pruning than BC. Consider a problem with five variables, all having domain $\{0, \ldots, 4\}$, and two constraints: c_1 on variables

x_1, x_2, x_3, and c_2 on variables x_3, x_4, x_5. Assume that the constraints are defined in extension by their allowed tuples. Also assume that the problem is BC and that the only allowed tuple of c_1 (and therefore the only Bound-support) that includes value 0 of x_1 is tuple (0,2,2). Now assume that value 2 of x_3 is not included in any allowed tuple on c_2. PWBC will not be able to extend the Bound-support (0,2,2) to c_2 and therefore will determine that value 0 of x_1 is not PWBC. ■

Trivially, PWBC is strictly weaker than maxRPWC. For an illustration consider a problem with variables $x_1, \ldots, x_4$, domains $D(x_1) = D(x_2) = D(x_3) = D(x_4) = \{1, 3\}$, and constraints c_1 : $alldifferent(x_1, x_2, x_3)$, c_2 : $alldifferent$ (x_1, x_2, x_4). This problem is BC and PWBC but it is not GAC, and therefore it is not maxRPWC. Considering this example and the first example in the proof of Proposition 21, it is obvious that GAC is incomparable to PWBC.

8.3 Linear constraints

An important class of non-binary constraints is the class of linear arithmetic constraints. Such a constraint c with $scp(c) = \{x_1, ..., x_n\}$ is of the form

$$a_1x_1 + a_2x_2 + ... + a_nx_n \diamond b \tag{8.1}$$

$$a_i, b \in Z \quad \diamond \in \{<, >, \leq, \geq, =\}$$

Zhang and Yap proposed a polynomial BC algorithm for linear constraints [112]. They also proved that BC and GAC are equivalent on problems consisting of linear inequality constraints. There is a considerable body of work dedicated to the study of propagation methods for linear constraints, e.g. [49, 102, 2, 20]. However, and at least as far as finite domain CSPs are concerned, all these works focus almost exclusively on BC propagation. One exception is [102] where the idea of considering many linear constraints simultaneously to strengthen propagation was investigated in the context of knapsack constraints. The method proposed was based on dynamic programming and it was used as basis for one of the CSP solution counting techniques proposed in [46].

In this section we study the application of PWBC to linear constraints. After some preliminary definitions we prove theoretical results concerning linear inequalities, and we describe a new polynomial filtering algorithm for such constraints.

Essentially, the problem of enforcing n-ary consistency level is related to that of finding all solutions satisfying the given linear constraint. This may be quite expensive as observed by Zhang and Yap in [112].

8.3.1 Preliminaries

Following [112], we first introduce some basic interval arithmetic operations to simplify our presentation. Since we consider variables with integer domains, these domains can be relaxed so that they form continuous real intervals bounded by the maximum and minimum values of the corresponding domains. Based on this we assume that each variable x is associated with an interval $[l, u]$. , where $l = min_D(x_i)$ and $u = max_D(x_i)$. We use [x] to denote an interval operation on x. So we use the following notation $[x] = [l, u]$.

Given $[x] = [l_1, u_1]$ and $[y] = [l_2, u_2]$, the interval operations are defined as follows:

$$[x] + [y] = [l_1 + l_2, u_1 + u_2],$$

$$[x] - [y] = [l_1 - u_2, u_1 - l_2],$$
$$[x] - a = [l_1 - a, u_1 - a],$$
$$a[x] = \begin{cases} [al_1, au_1], & a > 0 \\ [au_1, al_1], & a < 0 \end{cases}$$
$$[x] \cap [y] = [max(l_1, l_2), min(u_1, u_2)]$$

The following example demonstrates that interval reasoning can be used to filter inconsistent values through BC but also through stronger reasoning.

Example 4 Consider a problem with variables $x_1, \ldots, x_4$, domains $D(x_1) = \{0, \ldots, 4\}$, $D(x_2) = \{0, \ldots, 3\}$, $D(x_3) = \{0, 1, 2\}$, $D(x_4) = \{-1\}$, and constraints $c_1 : x_1 \leq x_2 - x_3$ and $c_2 : x_3 - x_2 \geq x_4$. Following the interval representation of domains, we write $[x_1] = [0,4]$, $[x_2] = [0,3]$, $[x_3] = [0,2]$, $[x_4] = [-1,-1]$. Clearly, x_1 cannot take the value 4 no matter what values x_2 and x_3 take. If we enforce BC this will be detected and $[x_1]$ will become $[0,3]$. Value 4 of x_1 is the only value that will be deleted by BC. However, x_1 cannot take values 3 or 2 either. This is because due to the second constraint the difference x_3-x_2 cannot be less than -1. Consequently, x_2-x_3 cannot be more than 1. Therefore, because of the first constraint $[x_1]$ should become $[0,1]$. In other words, values 3 and 2 for x_1 have no Bound-support on c_1 that can be extended to a Bound-support on c_2. If we enforce PWBC this will be detected and values 3 and 2 of x_1 will be deleted.

Using the definitions and notation of [112], we formalize the filtering process highlighted in the above example in the following way.

Definition 18 [112] The projection π_{x_i} of a constraint c on variable $x_i \in scp(c)$ is

$$\pi_{x_i}(c) = \frac{-1}{a_i}(a_1 x_1 + \cdots + a_{i-1} x_{i-1} + a_{i+1} x_{i+1} + \cdots + a_n x_n - b)$$

Given intervals on all the variables, we can define the interval version of the projection of c on x_i as:

$$\Pi_{x_i}(c) = \frac{-1}{a_i}[a_1[x_1] + \cdots + a_{i-1}[x_{i-1}] + a_{i+1}[x_{i+1}] + \cdots + a_n[x_n] - b]$$

We call $\Pi_{x_i}(c)$ the natural interval extension of $\pi_{x_i}(c)$.

We now define the function $Proj_{x_i}(c)$ as follows:

$$Proj_{x_i}(c) = \begin{cases} \Pi_{x_i}(c), & if \diamond' is = \\ [-\infty, Ub[\Pi_{x_i}(c)]], & if \diamond' is \leq \\ [Lb[\Pi_{x_i}(c)], +\infty], & if \diamond' is \geq \end{cases}$$

where $\diamond' is \geq$ if a_i is negative and $\diamond$ is $\leq$, and $\diamond$ otherwise, and $Ub([l, u]) = u$, $Lb([l, u]) = l$.

Given a subset $\{x_i, \ldots, x_j\}$ of $scp(c)$ where $s = a_i x_i + \ldots a_j x_j$ is the part of c that involves variables $\{x_i, \ldots, x_j\}$, we can extend Definition 2 as follows:

Definition 19 The projection π_s of a constraint c on s is

$$\pi_s(c) = a_1 x_1 + \cdots + a_{i-1} x_{i-1} + a_{j+1} x_{j+1} + \cdots + a_n x_n - b$$

Given intervals on all the variables, we can define the interval version of the projection of c on s as:

$$\Pi_s(c) = [a_1[x_1] + \cdots + a_{i-1}[x_{i-1}] + a_{j+1}[x_{j+1}] + \cdots + a_n[x_n] - b]$$

The projection function $Proj_s(c)$ can be defined in a way similar to $Proj_{x_i}(c)$.

Zhang and Yap defined BC using the interval representation of domains and the projection function. For this purpose, instead of using the real interval representation of domains, it is sufficient to consider intervals with integer bounds. Given a real interval $D_i = [l, u]$, its Z-interval representation is the interval $\Box D_i = [\lceil l \rceil, \lfloor u \rfloor]$.

Definition 20 [112] A constraint c is BC with respect to $(\Box D(x_1), \dots, \Box D(x_n))$ iff $\forall x_i \in vars(c)$ $\Box D(x_1) \subseteq Proj_{x_i}(c_i)$. A linear constraint system (N, D, C) is BC with respect to $(\Box D(x_1), \dots, \Box D(x_n))$ iff every $c_i \in C$ is BC.

8.3.2 Theoretical results for linear inequalities

Trivially, PWBC is strictly stronger than GAC on linear inequalities, since GAC is equivalent to BC. But the relationship between BC and GAC does not carry over to PWBC and its corresponding domain consistency.

Proposition 22 On linear inequality constraints maxRPWC is strictly stronger than PWBC.

Proof: By definition, the "stronger" relationship holds. Now consider a problem with variables $x_1, \dots, x_4$, domains $D(x_1) = \{0, 1, 2\}$, $D(x_2) = \{0, 1, 3\}$, $D(x_3) = \{0, 2\}$, $D(x_4) = \{-2\}$, and constraints $c_1 : x_1 \leq x_2 - x_3$ and $c_2 : x_3 - x_2 \geq x_4$. The problem is BC and PWBC. For instance, value 2 of x_1 is PWBC since tuples $(2, 2, 0)$ and $(2, 3, 1)$ are Bound-supports on c_1 that include this value and can also be extended to Bound-supports on c_2 (e.g. the first one can be extended to Bound-support $(0, 2, -2)$ on c_2). On the other hand, the only support for value 2 of x_1 on c_1 (tuple $(2,3,0)$) cannot be extended to c_2. Thus, if we apply maxRPWC value 2 of x_1 will be deleted. Note that the two Bound-supports that include value 2 of x_1 mentioned above are not supports since value 2 of x_2 and value 1 of x_3 do not belong to $D(x_2)$ and $D(x_3)$ respectively. ∎

In contrast to the general case (Lemma 1), when constraints intersect on at most one variable in a problem with linear inequalities then PWBC collapses to BC.

Lemma 2 In a problem with linear inequality constraints where constraints intersect on at most one variable, PWBC is equivalent to BC.

Proof: Assume that a problem consisting of linear inequality constraints that intersect on at most one variable is BC. Consider any variable x_i and any constraint c s.t. $x_i \in scp(c)$ and $scp(c) = \{x_1, \dots, x_k\}$. Without loss of generality assume that $a_i > 0$ and that the inequality is of the form $x_i \leq \pi_{x_i}(c)$. Since the problem is BC from Definition 20 we have $[min_D(x_i), max_D(x_i)] \subseteq \Box Proj_{x_i}(c)$. This means that $min_D(x_i) \leq max_D(x_i) \leq Ub(Proj_{x_i}(c))$, where $Ub(Proj_{x_i}(c))$ is obtained by assigning each variable x_j in $scp(c)$, except x_i, to its lower or upper bound v_j depending on the interval operation on x_j in the inequality. Therefore, tuple $\tau = (v_1, \dots, max_D(x_i), \dots v_k)$ is a Bound-support on c. Now take any constraint c' intersecting with c on variable x_l. Since c' is BC, value v_l belongs to a Bound-support on c'. Hence, the Bound-support τ on c that includes value $max_D(x_i)$ can be extended to a Bound-support on c', which means that $max_D(x_i)$ is PWBC. It directly follows that $min_D(x_i)$ is also PWBC. Therefore, x_i is PWBC. ∎

8.3.3 A PWBC algorithm for linear inequality constraints

We now present a filtering algorithm for linear inequality constraints extending the BC algorithm presented in [112]. This algorithm, which we call PWBC$_l$ (from PWBC linear), achieves at least the same filtering as the algorithm of [112]. And as will be explained, depending on the problem, it can achieve stronger filtering.

As in [112] we use an AC-3 like description (see Algorithm 25), with the difference being that $PWBC_l$ is variable-based. We use a data structure Q (typically a queue) that handles variables. If $PWBC_l$ is used for preprocessing, all variables are inserted in Q and then processed. The revision process, which is explained below, may result in the shrinking of a variable's domain. In this case, the variable whose domain is filtered, is inserted in Q unless its domain is wiped out.

Algorithm 25 $PWBC_l$

1: **if** $(Preprocessing)$ **then** $Q \leftarrow V$;
2: **else** $Q \leftarrow \{$currently assigned variable$\}$;
3: **while** $Q \neq \emptyset$ **do**
4:     select and remove x_i from Q;
5:     **for each** $c_j \in C$, s.t. $x_i \in scp(c_j)$ **do**
6:         **for each** $x_k \in scp(c_j)$ s.t. $x_k \neq x_i$ **do**
7:             **if** $[x_k] \not\subseteq \Box Proj_{x_k}(c_j)$ **then**
8:                 $[x_k] \leftarrow [x_k] \cap \Box Proj_{x_k}(c_j)$;
9:             $interCheck1(x_k, c_j)$;
10:            **if** $D(x_k) = \emptyset$ **then return** FAILURE;
11:            **if** $D(x_k)$ has been filtered **then** $Q \leftarrow Q \cup \{x_k\}$;
12:        **for each** $c_l \in C$, s.t. $|scp(c_l) \cap scp(c_j)| > 1$ **do**
13:            **for each** $x_k \in scp(c_l)$ **do**
14:                $interCheck2(x_k, c_l, c_j)$;
15:                **if** $D(x_k) = \emptyset$ **then return** FAILURE;
16:                **if** $D(x_k)$ has been filtered **then** $Q \leftarrow \cup\{x_k\}$;
17: **return** SUCCESS;

procedure $interCheck1(x_k, c)$

1: **for each** c_m As.t. $c_m \neq c$ and $|scp(c_m) \cap scp(c)| > 1$ **do**
2:     $Y \leftarrow$ maximal subset of $scp(c_m) \cap scp(c)$, s.t. $|Y| > 1$ AND $x_k \notin Y$ AND the coefficients for Y in c and c_m *match*
3:     **if** $Y \neq \emptyset$ **then**
4:         **if** $[Y] \not\subseteq \Box Proj_Y(c_m)$ **then**
5:             $[Y] \leftarrow [Y] \cap \Box Proj_Y(c_m)$;
6:         **if** $[x_k] \not\subseteq \Box Proj_{x_k}(c)$ **then**
7:             $[x_k] \leftarrow [x_k] \cap \Box Proj_{x_k}(c)$;

Once a variable x_i is extracted from Q, all constraints that include x_i are processed. This involves two steps. **First,** each variable other than x_i in such a constraint c_j is revised. The revision of a variable x_k with respect to constraint c_j is done in two steps. The first one (lines 7-8) performs the basic actions of the BC algorithm of [112]. That is, it narrows the interval $[x_k]$ by intersecting it with $Proj_{x_k}(c_j)$. This operation is performed only if $[x_k]$ is not a subset of $Proj_{x_k}(c_j)$ (otherwise the intersection operation will have no effect on $[x_k]$). Independent of whether $[x_k]$ is a subset of $Proj_{x_k}(c_j)$ or not, $PWBC_l$ then tries to further narrow $[x_k]$ by considering the intersections of c_j with other constraints by calling procedure *interCheck1* with x_k and c_j as arguments.

Procedure *interCheck1* iterates over all the constraints that intersect with the processed constraint c (i.e. c_j) on more than one variable. For each such constraint c_m the algorithm seeks the maximal subset Y of $scp(c_m) \cap scp(c)$ such that it includes more than one variable, it does not include x_k, and the coefficients that the variables in this subset have in c and c_m *match* (line 2). The objective is to narrow the aggregated interval of Y through constraint c_m, if possible, and then use this to further narrow $[x_k]$ through constraint c.

Regarding the first condition in line 2 of *interCheck1*, if the subset Y contains only one variable then it cannot trigger any extra pruning on $[x_k]$ compared to BC (Lemma 2). Regarding the second condition, we require that Y does not contain x_k so that $[Y]$ is part of $\Pi_{x_k}(c_j)$ and therefore by narrowing it we can further narrow $[x_k]$. Regarding the third condition we say that two sets of coefficients $S_1 = a_1, \ldots, a_n$ and $S_2 = a'_1, \ldots, a'_n$ match if there exists a k s.t. $S_1 = k * S_2$. For instance, this occurs in the quite frequent case of unit coefficients.

If a subset Y that satisfies the conditions of line 2 is located then its interval projection on c_m and function $Proj_Y(c_m)$ are computed. If $[Y]$ is not a subset of $Proj_Y(c_m)$ then it is narrowed by intersecting it with $Proj_Y(c_m)$ (line 5). Next the interval pojection of x_k on c_j and function $Proj_{x_k}(c_j)$ are recomputed using the updated interval $[Y]$. Finally, if $[x_k]$ is not a subset of $Proj_{x_k}(c_j)$ it is further narrowed (line 7).

The **second step** in processing constraint c_j iterates over all constraints that intersect with c_j and for each variable x_k involved in such a constraint c_l, *interCheck2* is called (lines 12-14). This procedure, is very similar to *interCheck1* with the differences being that it takes 3 parameters and line 1 (the for loop) is missing. After the call, inside *interCheck2* c is set to c_l and c_m is set to c_j. The calls to *interCheck2* are necessary to achieve PWBC because by filtering x_i some Bound-supports on c_j may have been lost and as a result existing Bound-supports in c_l may no longer be extendable to c_j. Having said this, experiments have showed that a restricted version of the algorithm which does perform the second step (i.e. does not include lines 12-16) is far more competitive in cpu times. We call this algorithm restricted PWBC$_l$ (rPWBC$_l$).

We now revisit Example 4 to demonstrate the algorithm.

Example 5 The interval representation of the variables' domains is as follows: $[x_1] = [0,4]$, $[x_2] = [0,3]$, $[x_3] = [0,2]$, $[x_4] = [-1,-1]$. In the initialization phase the algorithm processes the constraints in turn and revises each variable involved in them. First the interval projection of c_1 on x_1 is computed: $\Pi_{x_1}(c_1) = [[x_2] - [x_3]] = [-2, 3]$, which means that $Proj_{x_1}(c_1) = [-\infty, 3]$. $[x_1]$ is not a subset of $Proj_{x_1}(c_1)$ and therefore it will be narrowed in line 4. The new interval will be $[x_1] = [x_1] \cap Proj_{x_1}(c_1) = [0,3]$. Now the algorithm calls procedure *interCheck1*. The for loop in line 1 will verify that constraint c_2 intersects with c_1 on more than one variable. Next a maximal subset of $scp(c_1) \cap scp(c_2)$ with matching coefficients will be sought. Such a subset exists and it is $Y = \{x_2, x_3\}$. The interval projection of c_2 on Y is: $\Pi_Y(c_2) = [x_4] = [-1, -1]$, which means that $Proj_Y(c_2) = [-1, \infty]$. $[Y]$ is $[[0,2]-[0,3]] = [-3,2]$ and it is not a subset of $Proj_Y(c_2)$. Therefore in line 5 $[Y]$ will be narrowed to $[Y] \cap Proj_Y(c_2) = [-1,2]$. The next step will be to recompute the interval of x_1 using the updated interval for Y. The interval projection of c_1 on x_1 now is: $\Pi_{x_1}(c_1) = [[x_2] - [x_3]] = [-Y] = [-2, 1]$, which means that $Proj_{x_1}(c_1) = [-\infty, 1]$. Hence, in line 7 we get $[x_1] = [x_1] \cap Proj_{x_1}(c_1) = [0,3] \cap [-\infty, 1] = [0,1]$.

The conditions in line 2 of procedure *interCheck1* need not be evaluated during the algorithm's execution. They can easily be precomputed in a preprocessing step that considers all pairs of constraints that intersect on two or more variables.

Algorithm rPWBC$_l$ only achieves an approximation of PWBC, that is still stronger than BC, and as mentioned it is faster in practice than PWBC$_l$.

Proposition 23 The worst-case time complexity of algorithm PWBC$_l$ is $O(e^2 n^3 d)$.

Proof: Each time a variable x_i is extracted from Q, all of the at most e constraints where x_i participates are processed. In the first step (lines 6-11) all of the at most $n-1$ neighbors of x_i are revised. Thus, the maximum number of revisions is O(ne). The cost of computing $Proj_{x_k}(c_j)$ in line 8 is O(n), because the maximum arity of any constraint is n. Considering the cost of *interCheck1*, each constraint c_j intersects with at most $e-1$ other constraints, meaning that the complexity of *interCheck1* is O(en). Thus the first step costs O($e^2 n^2$). In the second step (lines 12-16), *interCheck2* which has O(n) cost is called for each variable involved in a constraint intersecting with c_j. Thus we have O(en^2) cost for this step. The worst case complexity of PWBC$_l$ depends on the number of variables ever entering Q. A variable x_i enters Q every time its domain is reduced. Considering that each reduction results in at least one deletion, x_i may enter the queue at most d times. Consequently, the complexity of PWBC$_l$ is O($nd(n + e^2 n^2 + en^2)$) = O($e^2 n^3 d$). This is also the complexity of rPWBC$_l$. ■

In practice we expect the algorithm to have lower cost since usually a constraint neither includes the entire set of variables nor does it intersect with all other constraints. Also, a variable rarely belongs to all constraints.

8.4   Applications

In this section we discuss potential practical applications of the proposed method. Since linear constraints are at the core of linear and mixed integer programming, they are ubiquitous in combinatorial optimization (and not only). Here we focus on problems where CP is applicable and naturally include intersecting linear constraints that can benefit from the extra pruning achieved by our method.

8.4.1   Case Study 1: Web Services

According to W3C, Web Services (WSs) are software systems designed to support interoperable machine-to-machine interaction over a network [ ]. In the early days of WS development, the features of the services provided (i.e. the *offers*) were simply expressed as (*parameter,value*) pairs. For instance, (PRICE,100). On the other hand, user requirements (i.e. *demands*) were typically specified as Boolean expressions. For instance, (PRICE<100 AND CAPACITY>10). However, due to practical requirements, recent WS proposals exploit far richer languages to express offers and demands. Assuming that the providers advertise their offers on some repository then, once a demand is posted, the process of *matchmaking* takes place. This involves searching for a set of offers that meet the requirements of the demand.

In order to select among multiple services that appear to provide the same function, the notion of *Quality of Service* (QoS) has been proposed. QoS denotes all possible non-functional properties of a WS, related with the performance of the WS as well as with other features and characteristics of a WS that bear on its ability to satisfy stated or implied needs. A QoS offer (or demand) of a WS is a set of constraints/restrictions on some QoS attributes that restrict them to have certain values (for unary constraints) or certain combinations of values (for n-ary constraints). Hence, in addition to standard matchmaking based on the functional requirements, WS discovery algorithms can also perform QoS-based filtering (matchmaking) and ranking (selection) on WS advertisements in order to produce fewer ranked results.

Major challenges that WS technology is faced with include the following:

- Prior to avertising an offer or issuing a demand, they both should be checked for *consistency*. This is not a trivial task as offers and demands may include quite complex constraints that in some cases are contradictory.

- Checking for *conformance*, i.e. checking whether an offer meets a given demand, can be a quite challenging problem that cannot be efficiently handled by the simplistic solutions that most WS proposals offer.

- Finding the optimal offer out of a set of offers that conform to a given demand may involve solving a complex optimization problem.

To meet these challenges, [90] proposed the use of CP as a tool for the modeling of offers and demands as well as for solving the consistency, conformance, and optimal selection problems. Among the types of constraints that can be used for modeling functional and non-functional requirements, linear constraints play a key role [90, 61]. Moreover, the problems used for the experimental evluation of consistency and conformance checking in [90, 61] include numerous constraint intersections (see Section 8.5 for details).

Example 6 Assume that a WS provider offers daily excursion packages. Assume that the minimum cost of such a package for a given destination, including travel, meal, and souvenirs, is greater than 50\$. This can be captured by a constraint of the form $x_t + x_m + x_s > 50$, where variables x_t, x_m, x_s denote the cost of travel, meal, and souvenirs, and they range over $[0, 100]$. Also assume that a relevant demand is posted, describing the requirements of some family for a daily excursion. Such a demand may include the constraint $x_t + x_m + x_s < 50$ as well as other functional and non-functional constraints. The matchmaker should be able to quickly verify that the offer does not conform to the demand. Note that applying BC on these two constraints will reduce the domains to $[0..49]$ and will achieve no further pruning. On the other hand, a solver that applies PWBC will determine that the constraints are inconsistent, and therefore prove that the offer does not conform to the demand without requiring to search in a possibly large search space (given that numerous extra variables and constraints may exist).

8.4.2 Case Study 2: Constraint-based Graphics

Constraint-based interactive graphical applications (e.g. diagram editors) constitute one of the earliest applications of constraints [51]. Constraint solving allows the editor to preserve design decisions, such as alignment and distribution, and structural constraints, such as non-overlap or minimum/maximum distance between objects, during manipulation of the graphic objects. It is well-known that linear constraints play a very significant role in such applications [21]. Given the requirement for real-time user interaction, propagation methods are also important. We believe that in many cases intersecting constraints will appear in such applications, as the following example demonstrates.

Example 7 Assume that in a graphical design environment two objects need to be placed on a cartesian system, one next to the other without overlapping. Assuming that the objects are orthogonal polygons, they can be represented by the coordinates of their corners. Suppose that x_1 is the coordinate of the top right corner of the first object and x_2 is the coordinate of the top left corner of the second one. We require that the second object is placed to the right of the first one within a maximum distance of x_3 (which may be a free variable in case its specific value will be specified later). This requirement can be captured by the constraint c_1: $x_2 - x_1 \leq x_3$. Now assume that a third orthogonal polygon, with left and right coordinates y_1 and y_2 respectively, must be placed between the other two. If y denotes its length then this can be captured by constraints c_2: $y = y_2 - y_1$ and c_3: $y \leq x_2 - x_1$. Given the domains $D(x_1) = \{0, 1, 2\}$, $D(x_2) = D(y_1) = \{0, 1, 2, 3\}$, $D(y_2) = D(y) = \{1, 2, 3, 4\}$ and $D(x_3) = \{1\}$ then if BC is used for propagation value 4 of y will be the only value to be removed, while PWBC will also remove values $2, 3$ from $D(y)$.

8.5 Experiments

To evaluate the practical potential of PWBC we experimented with problems used in the evaluation of matchmakers in WSs and with randomly generated problems.

8.5.1 Web Services

The performance of the CP-based approach to matchmaking in WSs was evaluated in [90] and later in [61]. Specifically, the performance of CP solvers on the three problems of consistency, conformance, and optimal selection were evaluated using sets of linear constraints. The solvers used in the evaluation were ILOG OPL in [90] and Choco, as well as XPress-Kalis, in [61]. The results of the evaluations demonstrated that CP solvers were unable to handle certain cases, displaying an exponential increase in execution time as the number of variables or/and arity of the constraints rises.

For the purposes of this work, we reproduced the experiments of [90, 61] focusing on the consistency and conformance checking problems. In both problems domains range from 0 to 255 and constraints are of the type: $x_1 + x_2 + ... + x_k > 10$. We tested the performance of $PWBC_l$ and $rPWBC_l$ against BC on a series of instances where variables (n) ranged from 100 to 1500 and arities (k) from 3 to 20. For a given number of variables and arity (say 100 and 4 respectively) the corresponding instance includes the constraints $x_1 + x_2 + x_3 + x_4 > 10$, $x_2 + x_3 + x_4 + x_5 > 10$,..., $x_{97} + x_{98} + x_{99} + x_{100} > 10$. Hence, in any instance there are $n - k + 1$ constraints. Instances created in this way are consistent. To test the solvers in the case of inconsistency, [90, 61] added one extra constraint of the type: $x_1 + x_2 + ... + x_k < 10$. For the conformance checking problem the tested istances were very similar. Constraints are again of the type $x_1 + x_2 + ... + x_k > 10$, but in this case one constraint of the form $\neg(x_1 + x_2 + ... + x_k > 10)$ (or $\neg(x_1 + x_2 + ... + x_k < 10)$) was added (see [90] for details).

Figures 8.29 and 8.30 display the mean performance of $PWBC_l$ and $rPWBC_l$ compared to BC on the consistency problem, as n and k increase. In the left (resp. right) figures each data point gives the mean cpu time for all the tested arities (resp. variable numbers). Figure 8.29 gives results from consistent instances and Figure 8.30 from inconsistent ones.

BC is the superior method on consistent instances. $rPWBC_l$ is close to BC for small values of n and k while it progressively gets worse as n and k increase. On the other hand, the cost of $PWBC_l$ displays an exponential increase, especially as the arity rises. Note that on these problems none of the algorithms prune any values; they all find a solution without backtracking. As a consequence, $PWBC_l$ and $rPWBC_l$ suffer from many redundant calls to functions *interCheck1* and/or *interCheck2*. This is more obvious for $PWBC_l$ whose performance deteriorates significantly for large n and k.

In the case of inconsistent problems $PWBC_l$ and $rPWBC_l$ quickly find the inconsistency during preprocessing, while BC has to search in order to prove unsatisfiability. As a result, in Figure 8.30 the CPU times of both $PWBC_l$ and $rPWBC_l$ are close to zero for all instances regardless of their

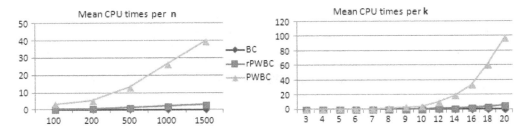

Figure 8.29: Mean CPU times (in secs) of BC, rPWBC and PWBC for the consistency case.

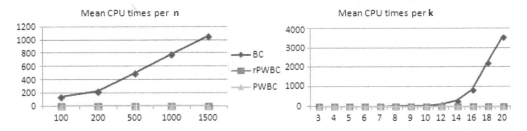

Figure 8.30: Mean CPU times (in secs) of BC, rPWBC and PWBC for the inconsistency case.

size. In contrast, BC requires more and more time as the size of the problem increases and gets exponentially worse for large n and k.

Due to space limitations, we omit the corresponding figures for the conformance checking problems since they are very similar to the ones for consistency checking. Finally, we note that our results completely agree with the results of [90] and [61] regarding the performance of BC. These results display the shortcomings of CP solvers with respect to the propagation of linear constraints. Given the results obtained, we believe that our methods, and rPWBC$_l$ in particular, constitute a step towards dealing with these shortcomings.

8.5.2 Random Problems

We also experimented with randomly generated problems. The random generator produces problems by setting the number of variables, the arity of the constraints and the density which specifies the number of constraints. The constraints are of the form $a_1x_1 + \ldots + a_nx_n \diamond b$, where $\diamond \in \{\leq, \geq\}$ and $b = 0$. The coefficients are unit and domain values range from -5 to 5. In the experiments reported below we tried 50 instances for each density. A cutoff limit of 90 minutes was imposed. We compare BC to rPWBC$_l$. We do not consider PWBC$_l$ since it is always inferior to rPWBC$_l$, as the experiments with problems from WSs demonstrated.

Results from the stand-alone use of BC and rPWBC$_l$ (e.g. for preprocessing) are presented in Figure 8.31. In these experiments the minimum domain value was randomly set to a value in the interval [-5..0] with probability 99.5%, while it was set to a value in the interval [1..5] with probability 0.5%. Consequently, some instances may be unsatisfiable. The maximum domain value was randomly set to a value in [0..5]. The generated instances have 350 variables and constraints of arity 6. The number of constraints ranges from 155 (0.01% density) to 7,761 (0.5% density).

Figure 8.31 presents results from rPWBC$_l$ and BC on problems with inequality constraints.

The left graph shows the mean cpu time and the right one the average number of removed values for various densities. What is not shown in Figure 8.31 is that rPWBC$_l$ detects more inconsistent instances than BC. Specifically, for the densities given in Figure 8.31 the % percentages of instances that were verified as inconsistent by rPWBC$_l$ were (0 2 8 42 86 96) and the corresponding numbers for BC were (0 2 8 34 72 92).

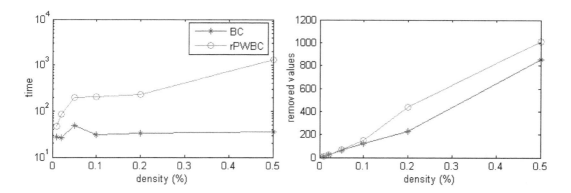

Figure 8.31: Mean cpu time (in msecs) and removed values for BC and rPWBC$_l$ during prepro-cessing.

As Figure 8.31 demonstrates, on problems that were not found to be inconsistent, rPWBC$_l$ typically removed twice or more values than BC did. The difference is more notable for densities 0.02% and 0.05%. On the other hand, rPWBC$_l$ needs more time than BC to achieve the extra pruning. This is due to the cost of functions *interCheck1* and *interCheck2*. As the number of constraints rises rPWBC$_l$ becomes costlier compared to BC. This is more evident on instances of higher density, where rPWBC$_l$ achieves little, if any, extra pruning.

In Figure 8.32 we compare search algorithms that maintain rPWBC$_l$ and BC throughout search on problems with inequalities. We used a lexicographic variable ordering to obtain a fairer comparison of the algorithms' pruning power. Recall that this heuristic selects the variable to assign a value at, in an ascending index order. Therefore, the sequence of variables visited remains the same regardless of the pruning of their domain or the degree of the constraints they participates in. The generated instances have 30 variables and constraints of arity 6. The number of constraints ranges from 296 (0.05% density) to 5,937 (1% density). We observe that rPWBC$_l$ can be orders of magnitudes faster than BC on instances of densities less than 0.5%. As the density rises, BC becomes more competitive and it outperforms rPWBC$_l$ when the density is 1%. Regarding nodes, the algorithm that maintains rPWBC$_l$ visits significantly fewer nodes than the one that maintains BC (up to three orders of magnitude fewer) for the whole range of densities considered.

Additionally, we solved larger problems using the standard dynamic variable ordering heuristic *minimum domain (dom)*. Representative results are shown in Figure 8.33. In this graph we directly compare the cpu times of rPWBC$_l$ to BC. We accumulate all instances generated with the following parameters: 63 variables and 31 constraints of arity 9 for problems with inequalities.The majority of the instaces in the gaph are above the diagonal, corresponding to instances that were solved faster by rPWBC$_l$. BC reached the cutoff limit on many instances while rPWBC$_l$ solved all of them within the limit.

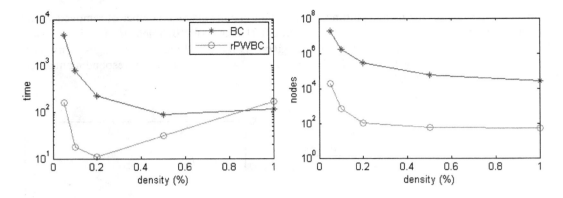

Figure 8.32: BC vs. rPWBC$_l$ using lexicographic ordering.

8.6 Conclusion

Although many strong local consistencies based on GAC have been proposed, there is gap in the literature concerning similar consistencies based on BC. We defined and studied PWBC, a new strong local consistency that extends BC taking into account combinations of constraints. We proposed a polynomial filtering algorithm for the important class of linear constraints that is based on PWBC. This algorithm can achieve stronger pruning than BC on inequalities.The proposed algorithm can be easily crafted into CP solvers to offer a viable alternative to the weak propagation of linear constraints that they currently offer. Experimental results demonstrated the potential of strong consistencies that reason on domain bounds.

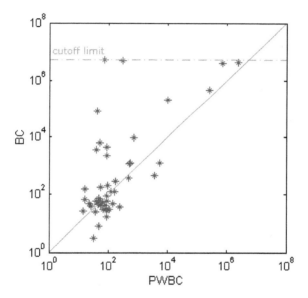

Figure 8.33: BC vs. rPWBC$_l$ using *dom* variable ordering heuristic during search. CPU times in logarithmic scale.

Conclusions and Future Work

In this chapter we summarize our main contributions and discuss perspectives for extending and exploiting the derived results in the near future.

9.1 Conclusions

The conducted doctoral research contributes to the field of Constraint Satisfaction Problems (CSPs) and Artificial Intelligence in general. Specifically, it contributes to the development of efficient constraint propagation algorithms that apply strong local consistencies on problems of binary as well as non-binary constraints. The proposed algorithms improve, theoretically and practically, existing relevant and state-of-the-art algorithms. Moreover, it presents adaptive algorithms and heuristic methods that can automatically select the appropriate propagation method during search, without requiring the user's involvement.

We now list in more detail the major contributions of this doctoral research.

- We have proposed efficient algorithms to apply strong local consistencies (i.e., maxRPC and it's approximations) on binary constraints. The proposed algorithms exploit the use of two simple data structures that exist in AC and maxRPC algorithms in order to avoid redundant iterations. On top of the variants of algorithms that achieve maxRPC and it's approximations, we have proposed heuristic techniques that can improve the algorithms' performance during search. The experimental evaluation shows that approximating strong consistencies and complex algorithms can be efficient and can thus constitute a viable alternative to AC (e.g. on certain structured problems).

- We have proposed an efficient algorithm for table constraints that extends existing ones (i.e., algorithms for GAC and maxRPWC) to achieve a stronger consistenciy. More precisely, our new algorithm, called maxRPWC+, handles intersections of table constraints, that have more than one variable in common, and builds on the GAC algorithm of [72]. We have also proposed a family of algorithms, which we call HOSTR*, that extend the state-of-the-art STR-based GAC algorithms and achieve a strong relation filtering consistency. Moreover, based on maxRPWC+, we have proposed a variant that is applicable on intensional constraints as well as a weaker algorithm, but still stronger than GAC, called GAC+. Our new algorithms, constantly outperform the maxRPWC1 algorithm [19] and are more robust than GAC-va [72] on problems with intersecting table constraints, while they are orders of magnitude faster in some cases.

- We have also proposed an efficient higher-order consistency algorithm that uses different reasoning than maxRPWC+. This algorithm makes use of counters that hold the number of occurrences of specific combinations of values in constraint intersections in order to avoid searching in tables for support tuples. Interestingly, the worst-case time complexity of one call to the basic filtering procedure of new algorithm, called eSTR, is quite close to that of STR algorithms [63]). The proposed methods, which are orders of magnitude faster in many classes of problems, pave the way for even more efficient handling of intersecting table constraints.

- We have shown that adaptive propagation schemes can efficiently exploit the advantages offered by strong propagators in a fully automated way. Specifically, we have proposed heuristic techniques for the automated selection between weak and strong propagation methods for non-binary constraints. Our experimental evaluation demonstrates that the choice of the appropriate technique for each constraint, by monitoring the internal operation and performance of the algorithms, has resulted in a robust solver and noticeable increase of performance. Namely, we have shown that adaptive methods display a stable performance and thus, are preferable than a predefined propagator.

  Aditionally, The design and implementation of adaptive and autonomous constraint solvers offer the ability to advantageously modify modeler's decisions, that typically, in mainstream CP solvers, are taken prior to search. As a result, the fully-automated heuristics of Chapter 6.5 exempt users from the need to know the internal operation of solvers or to acquire knowledge on constraint propagation algorithms.

- We have introduced and defined a new strong Bounds Consistency, which we call PWBC. Based on PWBC, we have also proposed a polynomial filtering algorithm for the important class of linear inequalities that can achieve stronger pruning than BC. The results of its application demonstrate the potential of strong consistencies that reason on bounds. We have experimentally shown that the proposed algorithm constitutes a viable alternative to the weak propagation of linear constraints that CSP solvers currently apply.

- Although many algorithms for SLCs already exist in the literature, CP solvers apply almost exclusively algorithms that achieve (G)AC and BC. This is justified since existing algorithms for SLCs are, in their majority, impractical due to their high computational cost. The presented results have shown that the new efficient propagation techniques can exploit the filtering power of SLCs by overcoming cpu penalties. Therefore, the integration of our methods into a CSP solver contributes to increasing their efficiency and robustness and thus, to the overall usability of Constraint Programming.

In conclusion, the theoretical and experimental research work, which constitutes this doctoral dissertation, features scientific originality by proposing and developing new algorithms and adaptive methods for solving CSPs. The proposed algorithms described in Chapters 3.4, 4.6, 5.7 and 7.5 proved to be very efficient for solving certain classes of Constraint Satisfaction Problems, being much faster in terms of performance than existing respective algorithms. Moreover, the exported results demonstrate the potential benefit for CP solvers when they make use of strong local consistencies instead of applind standard methods, like GAC or BC. This research has shown that weak propagation methods are is many cases of binary and non-binary problems, inefficient. Finally, the adaptive methods of Chapter 6.5, that integrate the new algorithms, constitute an important step towards building autonomous intelligent systems for solving difficult practical problems, which is the ultimate goal of Artificial Intelligence.

9.2 Future Work

Below we enumerate four major directions that we intent to focus in thenear future in order to exploit the results of this research.

1. The most straightforward direction is towards extending our study on adaptive methods, by initially incorporating all our algorithms (eSTR, PWBC) into our adaptive solver. Then, we will turn our attention to the design and development of adaptive heuristics that select the appropriate algorithm to apply when specific conditions hold for a value or tuple of a variable or a constraint respectively. In other words, the study of 'fine-grained' dynamic heuristics.

2. In the near future, we will investigate the applicability of methods, similar to those in Chapter 3.4, to efficiently achieve or approximate other local consistencies related to maxRPC, such as PIC, for binary constraints. Also, a very interesting direction is the efficient interleaved application of stronger consistencies, like maxRPC, and weaker but cheaper ones, like AC. We have presented some initial results towards this, but further research is certainly required.

3. We also intent to disseminate the practical value of the new algorithms to the CP community. A way to achieve this is by embedding them in a well-known CP solver that will allow the further use and spread of our algorithms. Such examples of established CP solvers are Minion, Gecode, Choco etc. (see Section 2.5). We believe that this research perspective will build strong foundations for the integration of Strong Local Consistencies (SLCs) into modern CP solvers, enhancing their efficacy and robustness.

4. In addition, we will carry out a wider study on specialized strong consistency algorithms for global constraints, which play a key role in the success of CP, since they encapsulate patterns that occur frequently in constraint models. In Chapter 7.5, we have presented new SLCs that extend BC, by considering combinations of constraints. We expect to further exploit these results to build specialized algorithms that achieve stronger filtering than BC for global constraints, since the research on such constraints has mailnly focused on specialized algorithms that apply GAC or BC.

5. A quite different and new research direction that we are interested to follow is the integration of our new strong propagation algorithms in parallel computing/systems. More precisely, a parallelization of our algorithms (i.e., when looking for PW-supports in tables or by splitting the search for each intersecting constraint to a different PC-unit) along with the advancements in hardware technology (i.e., by using the Graphical processing Unit (GPU) instead of the conventional Central Processing Unit (CPU)) will speed-up even more the computationally intensive steps of the algorithms.

Bibliography

[1] G. Alonso, F. Casati, H. Kuno, and V. Machiraju. *Web Services: Concepts, Architecture and Applications*. Springer-Verlag, 2004.

[2] K. Apt and P. Zoeteweij. An analysis of arithmetic constraints on integer intervals. *Constraints*, 12(4):429–468, 2007.

[3] T. Balafoutis. *Adaptive Strategies for Solving ConstraintSatisfaction Problems*. PhD thesis, University of the Aegean, 2011.

[4] T Balafoutis and K. Stergiou. Exploiting constraint weights for revision ordering in Arc Consistency Algorithms. In *ECAI-08 Workshop on Modeling and Solving Problems with Constraints*, 2008.

[5] T. Balafoutis and K. Stergiou. Evaluating and improving modern variable and revision ordering strategies in csps. *Fundamenta Informaticae*, 102(3-4):229–261, 2010.

[6] A. Balafrej, C. Bessiere, R. Coletta, and E. Bouyakhf. Adaptive parameterized consistency. In *Proceedings of CP'13*, pages 143–158, 2013.

[7] R. Bartak and R. Erben. A new algorithm for Singleton Arc Consistency. In *Proceedings of FLAIRS Conference-2004*, 2004.

[8] P. Berlandier. Improving Domain Filtering Using Restricted Path Consistency. In *Proceedings of IEEE CAIA'95*, pages 32–37, 1995.

[9] C. Bessiere. Arc-Consistency and Arc-Consistency Again. *Artificial Intelligence*, 65:179Ű–190, 1994.

[10] C. Bessiere. Chapter 3 Constraint Propagation. In Peter van Beek Francesca Rossi and Toby Walsh, editors, *Handbook of Constraint Programming*, volume 2 of *Foundations of Artificial Intelligence*, pages 29 – 83. Elsevier, 2006.

[11] C. Bessiere and R. Debruyne. Optimal and suboptimal Singleton Arc Consistency Algorithms. In *Proceedings of IJCAI-2005*, pages 54–59, 2005.

[12] C. Bessiere, E.C. Freuder, and J.C. Régin. Using Inference to Reduce Arc Consistency Computation. In *Proceedings of IJCAI'95*, pages 592–599, 1995.

[13] C. Bessiere, E.C. Freuder, and J.C. Régin. Using constraint metaknowledge to reduce arc consistency computation. *Artificial Intelligence*, 107:125–148, 1999.

[14] C. Bessiere, E. Hebrard, B. Hnich, Z. Kiziltan, and T. Walsh. SLIDE: A useful special case of the CARDPATH constraint. In *Proceedings of ECAI'08*, pages 475–479, 2008.

[15] C. Bessiere and J.C. Régin. MAC and combined heuristics: two reasons to forsake FC (and CBJ?) on hard problems. In *Proceedings of CP-1996*, pages 61–75, Cambridge MA, 1996.

[16] C. Bessiere and J.C. Régin. Arc Consistency for General Constraint Networks: Preliminary Results. In *Proceedings of IJCAI'97*, pages 398–404, 1997.

[17] C. Bessiere and J.C. Régin. Refining the basic constraint propagation algorithm. In *Proceedings of IJCAI-2001*, pages 309–315, 2001.

[18] C. Bessiere, J.C. Régin, R. Yap, and Y. Zhang. An Optimal Coarse-grained Arc Consistency Algorithm. *Artificial Intelligence*, 165(2):165–185, 2005.

[19] C. Bessiere, K. Stergiou, and T. Walsh. Domain filtering consistencies for non-binary constraints. *Artificial Intelligence*, 172(6-7):800–822, 2008.

[20] L. Bordeaux, G. Katsirelos, N. Narodytska, and M. Vardi. The Ccomplexity of Integer Bound Propagation. *JAIR*, 40:657–676, 2011.

[21] A. Borning, K. Marriott, P. Stuckey, and Y. Xiao. Solving linear arithmetic constraints for user interface applications. In *Proceedings of the of the 10th annual ACM symposium on User Interface Software and Technology*, pages 87–96, 1997.

[22] F. Boussemart, F. Hemery, and C. Lecoutre. Revision ordering heuristics for the Constraint Satisfaction Problem. In *CP-2004 Workshop on Constraint Propagation and Implementation*, Toronto, Canada, 2004.

[23] F. Boussemart, F. Hemery, C. Lecoutre, and L. Sais. Boosting systematic search by weighting constraints. In *Proceedings of ECAI-2004*, pages 482–486, Valencia, Spain, 2004.

[24] P. Briggs and L. Torczon. An efficient representation for sparse sets. *ACM Letters on Programming Languages and Systems*, 2(1-4):59–69, 1993.

[25] K. Cheng and R. Yap. An MDD-based generalized arc consistency algorithm for positive and negative table constraints and some global constraints. *Constraints*, 15(2):265–304, 2010.

[26] A. Chmeiss and L. Sais. Constraint Satisfaction Problems: Backtrack Search Revisited. In *Proceedings of ICTAI'04*, pages 252–257, 2004.

[27] C.W. Choi, W. Harvey, J.H.M. Lee, and P. Stuckey. Finite Domain Bounds Consistency Revisited. In *Proceedings of the Australian Conference on AI*, pages 49–58, 2006.

[28] R. Debruyne. A strong local consistency for constraint satisfaction. In *Proceedings of ICTAI'99*, pages 202–209, 1999.

[29] R. Debruyne and C. Bessiere. From restricted path consistency to max-restricted path consistency. In *Proceedings of CP'97*, pages 312–326, 1997.

[30] R. Debruyne and C. Bessiere. Some practical filtering techniques for the constraint satisfaction problem. In *Proceedings of IJCAI-1997*, pages 412–417, 1997.

[31] R. Debruyne and C. Bessiere. Domain Filtering Consistencies. *Journal of Artificial Intelligence Research*, 14:205–230, 2001.

[32] R. Dechter and I. Meiri. Experimental evaluation of preprocessing techniques in constraint satisfaction problems. In *Proceedings of IJCAI'89*, pages 271–277, 1989.

[33] W. Dincbas, P. Van Hentenryck, H. Simonis, A. Aggoun, T. Graf, and A. Berthier. The constraint logic programming language chip. In *Proceedings of FGCS'88*, pages 693–702, 2013.

[34] H. El Sakkout, M. Wallace, and B. Richards. An Instance of Adaptive Constraint Propagation. In *Proceedings of CP'96*, pages 164–178, 1996.

[35] S. Epstein, E. Freuder, R. Wallace, and X. Li. Learning propagation policies. In *Proceedings of the 2nd International Workshop on Constraint Propagation and Implementation*, pages 1Ű–15, 2005.

[36] S. Epstein and S. Petrovic. Learning to Solve Constraint Problems. In *ICAPS-07 Workshop on Planning and Learning*, 2007.

[37] E. Freuder and C. Elfe. Neighborhood Inverse Consistency Preprocessing. In *Proceedings of AAAI'96*, pages 202–208, 1996.

[38] E. Freuder and R.J. Wallace. Selective relaxation for constraint satisfaction problems. In *Proceedings of ICTAI'96*, 1996.

[39] E.C. Freuder. A sufficient condition for backtrack-free search. *Journal of the ACM*, 29(1):24–32, 1982.

[40] D. Frost and R. Dechter. Look-ahead value ordering for constraint satisfaction problems. In *Proceedings of IJCAI'95*, pages 572–578, 1995.

[41] P. A. Geelen. Dual viewpoint heuristics for binary constraint satisfaction problems. In *Proceedings of ECAI-92*, pages 31–35, 1992.

[42] I. P. Gent, C. Jefferson, L. Kotthoff, I. Miguel, N. C. A. Moore, P. Nightingale, and K. E. Petrie. Learning when to use lazy learning in constraint solving. In *Proceedings of ECAI-2010*, pages 873–878, 2010.

[43] I. P. Gent, C. Jefferson, and I. Miguel. Minion: A fast, scalable constraint solver. In *Proceedings of ECAI'06*, pages 98–102, 2006.

[44] I. P. Gent, C. Jefferson, I. Miguel, and Nightingale P. Data structures for generalised arc consistency for extensional constraints. In *Proceedings of AAAI'07*, pages 191–197, 2007.

[45] I.P. Gent, E. MacIntyre, P. Prosser, P. Shaw, and T. Walsh. The constraindedness of arc consistency. In *Proceedings of CP-97*, pages 327–340, 1997.

[46] C. Gomes, J. van Hoeve, A. Sabharwal, and B. Selman. Counting CSP Solutions Using Generalized XOR Constraints. In *AAAI*, pages 204–209, 2007.

[47] F. Grandoni and G. Italiano. Improved Algorithms for Max-Restricted Path Consistency. In *Proceedings of CP'03*, pages 858–862, 2003.

[48] R.M. Haralick and Elliott. Increasing tree search efficiency for constraint satisfaction problems. *Artificial Intelligence*, 14:263–314, 1980.

[49] W. Harvey and P. Stuckey. Improving linear constraint propagation by changing constraint representation. *Constraints*, 8(2):173–207, 2003.

[50] S. Hoda, W. van Hoeve, and J.N. Hooker. A systematic approach to MDD-based constraint programming. In *Proceedings of CP'10*, pages 266–280, 2010.

[51] W. Hower and W.H. Graf. A bibliographical survey of constraint-based approaches to cad, graphics, layout, visualization, and related topics. *Knowledge-Based Systems*, 9:449Ŭ–464, 1996.

[52] S.A. ILOG. Ilog solver 6.0 user's manual, 2003.

[53] P. Janssen, P. Jégou, B. Nouguier, and M.C. Vilarem. A filtering process for general constraint satisfaction problems: Achieving pairwise consistency using an associated binary representation. In *Proceedings of IEEE Workshop on Tools for Artificial Intelligence*, pages 420–427, 1989.

[54] P. Jégou. On the Consistency of General Constraint Satisfaction Problems. In *Proceedings of AAAI'93*, pages 114–119, 1993.

[55] P. Jégou and C. Terrioux. A new filtering based on decomposition of constraint sub-networks. In *Tools with Artificial Intelligence (ICTAI), 2010 22nd IEEE International Conference on*, volume 1, pages 263–270, 2010.

[56] U. Junker. Preference-Based Problem Solving for Constraint Programming. In *CSCLP*, pages 109–126, 2007.

[57] S. Karakashian, R. Woodward, C. Reeson, B. Choueiry, and C. Bessiere. A first practical algorithm for high levels of relational consistency. In *Proceedings of AAAI'10*, pages 101–107, 2010.

[58] G. Katsirelos and T. Walsh. A compression algorithm for large arity extensional constraints. In *Proceedings of CP'07*, pages 379–393. Springer-Verlag, 2007.

[59] A. R. KhudaBukhsh, L. Xu, H. H. Hoos, and K. Leyton-Brown. SATenstein: Automatically building local search SAT solvers from components. In *Proceedings of IJCAI-2009*, pages 517–524, 2009.

[60] L. Kotthoff, I. Miguel, and P. Nightingale. Ensemble Classification for Constraint Solver Configuration. In *Proceedings of CP'2010*, pages 321–329, 2010.

[61] K. Kritikos and D. Plexousakis. Mixed-Integer Programming for QoS-Based Web Service Matchmaking. *IEEE T. Services Computing*, 2(2):122–139, 2009.

[62] F. Laburthe and N. Jussien. Choco constraint programming system. *Available at http://choco.sourceforge.net*, 2003–2011.

[63] C. Lecoutre. Str2: optimized simple tabular reduction for table constraints. *Constraints*, 16(4):341–371, 2011.

[64] C. Lecoutre, F. Boussemart, and F. Hemery. Exploiting multidirectionality in coarse-grained arc consistency algorithms. In *Proceedings of the 9th International Conference on Principles and Practice of Constraint Programming (CP-2003)*, pages 480–494, 2003.

[65] C. Lecoutre and S. Cardon. A greedy approach to establish Singleton Arc Consistency. In *Proceedings of IJCAI-2005*, pages 199–204, 2005.

[66] C. Lecoutre, S. Cardon, and J. Vion. Conservative Dual Consistency. In *Proceedings of AAAI'07*, pages 237–242, 2007.

[67] C. Lecoutre, S. Cardon, and J. Vion. Second-order consistencies. *J. Artif. Int. Res.*, 40(1):175–219, 2011.

[68] C. Lecoutre and F. Hemery. A study of residual supports in arc consistency. In *Proceedings of IJCAI-2007*, pages 125–130, 2007.

[69] C. Lecoutre, C. Likitvivatanavong, and R. H. C. Yap. A path-optimal gac algorithm for table constraints. In *ECAI*, pages 510–515, 2012.

[70] C. Lecoutre and P. Prosser. Maintaining Singleton Arc Consistency. In *3rd International Workshop on Constraint Propagation And Implementation (CPAI'06)*, pages 47–61, 2006.

[71] C. Lecoutre, L. Sais, S. Tabary, and V. Vidal. Nogood recording from restarts. In *Proceedings of IJCAI'07*, pages 131–136, 2007.

[72] C. Lecoutre and R. Szymanek. Generalized arc consistency for positive table constraints. In *Proceedings of CP'06*, pages 284–298, 2006.

[73] O. Lhomme. Consistency techniques for numeric csps. In *Proceedings of IJCAI-93*, pages 232–238, 1993.

[74] O. Lhomme. Arc-consistency filtering algorithms for logical combinations of constraints. In *Proceedings of CPAIOR'04*, pages 209–224, 2004.

[75] O. Lhomme and J.C. Régin. A fast arc consistency algorithm for n-ary constraints. In *Proceedings of AAAI'05*, pages 405–410, 2005.

[76] C. Likitvivatanavong, Y. Zhang, J. Bowen, and Freuder E.C. Arc consistency in mac: A new perspective. In *Proceedings of CPAIŠ04*, pages 93–107, 2004.

[77] C. Likitvivatanavong, Y. Zhang, J. Bowen, S. Shannon, and E. Freuder. Arc Consistency during Search. In *Proceedings of IJCAI-2007*, pages 137–142, 2007.

[78] A. Mackworth. Consistency in Networks of Relations. *Artificial Intelligence*, pages 99–118, 1977.

[79] A.K. Mackworth. On reading sketch maps. In *Proceedings IJCAI'77*, pages 598–606, 1977.

[80] J.B. Mairy, P. Hentenryck, and Y. Deville. An Optimal Filtering Algorithm for Table Constraints. In *CP*, pages 496–511, 2012.

[81] K. Marriott and S.S. Chok. Qoca: A constraint solving toolkit for interactive graphical applications. *Constraints*, 7(3-4):229–254, 2002.

[82] D. Mehta and M.R.C. van Dongen. Probabilistic Consistency Boosts MAC and SAC. In *Proceedings of IJCAI'07*, pages 143–148, 2007.

[83] S. Minton. Automatically Configuring Constraint Satisfaction Programs: A Case Study. *Constraints*, 1(1/2):7–43, 1996.

[84] R. Mohr and T.C. Henderson. Arc and path consistency revisited. *Artificial Intelligence*, 28:225–233, 1986.

[85] R. Mohr and T.C. Henderson. Arc and path consistency revisited. *Artificial Intelligence*, 28:225–233, 1986.

[86] R. Mohr and G. Masini. Good Old Discrete Relaxation. In *Proceedings of ECAI'88*, pages 651–656, 1988.

[87] U. Montanari. Network of constraints: Fundamental properties and applications to picture processing. *Information Science*, 7:95–132, 1974.

[88] P. Prosser, K. Stergiou, and T. Walsh. Singleton consistencies. In *Proceedings of CP'00*, pages 353–368, 2000.

[89] P. Refalo. Impact-based search strategies for constraint programming. In *Proceedings of CP 2004*, pages 556–571, 2004.

[90] A. Ruiz Cortés, O. Martín-Díaz, A. Durán, and M. Toro. Improving the Automatic Procurement of Web Services Using Constraint Programming. *International Journal of Cooperative Information Systems*, 14(4):439–468, 2005.

[91] D. Sabin and E.C. Freuder. Contradicting conventional wisdom in constraint satisfaction. In *Proceedings of CP '94*, pages 10–20, 1994.

[92] D. Sabin and E.C. Freuder. Understanding and Improving the MAC Algorithm. In *Proceedings of CP-1997*, pages 167–181, 1997.

[93] N. Samaras and K. Stergiou. Binary Encodings of Non-binary CSPs: Algorithms and Experimental Results. *JAIR*, 24:641–684, 2005.

[94] C. Schulte, M. Lagerkvist, and G. Tack. Gecode solver. *Available at http://www.gecode.org*, 2011.

[95] C. Schulte and P. Stuckey. Dynamic analysis of bounds versus domain propagation. In *Proceedings of ICLP '08*, pages 332–346, 2008.

[96] C. Schulte and P. J. Stuckey. When do bounds and domain propagation lead to the same search space? *ACM Trans. Program. Lang. Syst.*, 27(3):388–425, 2005.

[97] C. Schulte and P.J. Stuckey. Efficient Constraint Propagation Engines. *ACM Trans. Program. Lang. Syst.*, 31(1):1–43, 2008.

[98] B.M. Smith. The brelaz heuristic and optimal static orderings. In *Proceedings of CP'99*, pages 405–418, 1999.

[99] K. Stergiou. Strong inverse Consistencies for Non-Binary CSPs. In *Proceedings of IC-TAI'07*, pages 215–222, 2007.

[100] K. Stergiou. Heuristics for Dynamically Adapting Propagation. In *Proceedings of ECAI'08*, pages 485–489, 2008.

[101] K. Stergiou and T. Walsh. Inverse Consistencies for Non-Binary Constraints. In *Proceedings of ECAI'06*, pages 153–157, 2006.

[102] M. Trick. A Dynamic Programming Approach for Consistency and Propagation for Knapsack Constraints. *Anals OR*, 118:73–84, 2003.

[103] J. R. Ullmann. Partition search for non-binary constraint satisfaction. *Inf. Sci.*, 177(18):3639–3678, 2007.

[104] P. van Beek. Backtracking Search Algorithms. In F. Rossi, P. van Beek, and T. Walsh, editors, *Handbook of Constraint Programming*, chapter 4. Elsevier, 2006.

[105] P. van Beek and R. Dechter. On the Minimality and Global Consistency of Row-convex Constraint Networks. *JACM*, 42(3):543–561, 1995.

[106] J. Vion and R. Debruyne. Light Algorithms for Maintaining Max-RPC During Search. In *Proceedings of SARA-2009*, 2009.

[107] R. Wallace and E. Freuder. Ordering heuristics for arc consistency algorithms. In *AI/GI/VI*, pages 163–169, Vancouver, British Columbia, Canada, 1992.

[108] R. J. Woodward, S. Karakashian, B. Y. Choueiry, and C. Bessiere. Solving difficult csps with relational neighborhood inverse consistency. In *AAAI*, pages 112–119, 2011.

[109] Y. Xu, D. Stern, and H. Samulowitz. Learning Adaptation to solve Constraint Satisfaction Problems. In *Proceedings of Learning and Intelligent Optimization (LION)*, 2009.

[110] R. Zabih. Some applications of graph bandwith to constraint satisfaction problems. In *Proceedings of AAAI'90*, pages 46–51, 1990.

[111] Y. Zhang and R. Yap. Making AC-3 an optimal algorithm. In *Proceedings of IJCAI-2001*, pages 316–321, 2001.

[112] Y. Zhang and R. H. C. Yap. Arc consistency on n-ary monotonic and linear constraints. In *Proceedings of CP'00*, pages 470–483, 2000.

[113] Z. Zhang and S. L. Epstein. Learned Value-Ordering Heuristics for Constraint Satisfaction. In *Proceedings of STAIR-08 Workshop at AAAI-2008*, 2008.

www.ingramcontent.com/pod-product-compliance
Lightning Source LLC
Chambersburg PA
CBHW080417060326
40689CB00019B/4282